The Talking Cure

The Talking Cure

Wittgenstein's Therapeutic Method for Psychotherapy

John M. Heaton

palgrave
macmillan

First published 2010 by
PALGRAVE MACMILLAN

Palgrave Macmillan in the UK is an imprint of Macmillan Publishers Limited, registered in England, company number 785998, of Houndmills, Basingstoke, Hampshire RG21 6XS.

Palgrave Macmillan in the US is a division of St Martin's Press LLC, 175 Fifth Avenue, New York, NY 10010.

Palgrave Macmillan is the global academic imprint of the above companies and has companies and representatives throughout the world.

Palgrave® and Macmillan® are registered trademarks in the United States, the United Kingdom, Europe and other countries.

ISBN-13: 978–0–230–23761–2 hardback

This book is printed on paper suitable for recycling and made from fully managed and sustained forest sources. Logging, pulping and manufacturing processes are expected to conform to the environmental regulations of the country of origin.

A catalogue record for this book is available from the British Library.

Library of Congress Cataloging-in-Publication Data
Heaton, John M., 1925–
   The talking cure : Wittgenstein's therapeutic method for psychotherapy / John M. Heaton.
      p. ; cm.
   Includes bibliographical references and index.
   ISBN 978–0–230–23761–2 (hardback : alk. paper)
   1. Psychotherapy—Philosophy.   2. Wittgenstein, Ludwig, 1889–1951.
   I. Title
   [DNLM: 1. Wittgenstein, Ludwig, 1889–1951.   2. Psychoanalytic Therapy—methods.   3. Language.   4. Psycholinguistics.
   WM 460.5.L2 H442t 2010]
   RC437.5.H434 2010
   616.89′14—dc22   2009048513

10   9   8   7   6   5   4   3   2   1
19   18   17   16   15   14   13   12   11   10

Printed and bound in Great Britain by
CPI Antony Rowe, Chippenham and Eastbourne

For Barbara

If the doors of perception were cleansed everything would appear to man as it is, infinite. For man has closed himself up, till he sees all things thro' narrow chinks of his cavern.

William Blake

Contents

Preface   viii

Acknowledgements   x

Abbreviations   xi

1   The Problem   1

2   Fearless Speech   15

3   Talking versus Writing   33

4   The Critical Method   51

5   Reasons and Causes   64

6   Elucidation   95

7   Back to the Rough Ground   135

8   The Self and Images   178

9   A Non-Foundational Therapy   200

References   215

Index   222

Preface

Talking cures of various kinds seem to help people who are confused and suffering. I will use Wittgenstein's work to clarify what may be going on in such cures. Psychotherapy is usually conceived as involving a search for causes; their discovery is believed to lead to the cure. This search, in the manner of modern empirical medicine, is based on various doctrines, and theories about the mind, its development, human relationships and the causes of disturbances in them. However, the fact is that psychotherapists have not been able to reach much agreement as to what is basic.

Wittgenstein does not offer an alternative theory but a different way of looking at therapy. He thought that the aim of philosophy and therapy was radically different from empirical science. They were practices that should not be based on doctrines, theses and theories. There should be no hierarchies of more or less fundamental concepts. Dogmatism was to be avoided. He sought to show how philosophical problems require therapy as they arise because we are easily bewitched by language. Our form of language becomes unclear and produces false appearances that we imagine show things as they really are. Philosophy must uncover one or another piece of plain nonsense that we have got into by running our head against the limits of language. It is through careful attention to our use of language that we dissolve the problems that confuse us. This enables us to give up futile quests for cures and answers that interpose themselves as screens, making us imagine that we and the world *must* be a certain way. When the aspects of things that are important to us lie open to view, then we can allow ourselves to evolve in an unfettered way.

Wittgenstein wrote: 'A philosophical problem has the form "I don't know my way about" ' (*PI* ¶123). This is remarkably like a psychotherapeutic problem except that here pain and despair are involved. Perhaps this is why it is seen as more to do with medicine than philosophy. Nevertheless, psychotherapy is a cure by means of language and other symbolic systems which act very differently from chemical cures or physical interventions.

Neither Wittgenstein not psychotherapists are interested in language as linguists. They are concerned with the relation of the word to things in the world and to others. This relation is not a connection between words on one side and things on the other, as occurs when we start learning a foreign language. A child learning to speak has to be initiated into language as it does not know what language is, and does not have words to connect to things. Language is not self-generated, a ready made machine in the brain that we learn to use. It depends on others; it is a gift, so its acquisition involves genuine selfhood, that is, acknowledgement of our separation from others and our dependence upon them.

In neurosis and psychosis there is an inability to speak of experiences that were traumatic or important but 'unspoken'. When this happens language 'goes on holiday'; we employ words but fail to express the experience, and so produce false appearances which are not integrated in the life of a person. The victim is mystified and not able to understand the reasons for her unhappiness. 'I feel dread whenever I have to meet new people but I know it is unreasonable.' To that extent the person cannot fully participate in the human world as herself.

The talking cure does not involve learning new facts, explanations and theories but rather involves reminders of what we have overlooked. Saying what can be said clearly reveals what cannot otherwise be made manifest. It attends to the particular person and what they have to say, rather than subsuming them under a theoretical generalisation and its technique. It is by coming to see the particular in a fresh way that enables the change of attitude which consists of a shift in understanding.

This book is a response to these insights. It is not a compendium containing thoughts, techniques and answers but is a tool to rethink the talking cure.

Acknowledgements

I would like to thank a number of people who helped in the background of this book and those who helped in writing it. The psychoanalyst James Home, one of my supervisors and later friend, taught me that it was logic and not psychoanalysis that should be the ground of psychotherapy; he got me to read and discuss B.J.F. Lonergan's *Insight* with him. Peter Lomas has been a long time friend and we have shared a common interest in the importance of the 'ordinary' in psychotherapy. Ronnie Laing was a colleague from whom I learned much and I still miss his skepticism and wit. Roger Money-Kyrle was one of the few psychoanalysts who agreed with me on the importance of Wittgenstein and suggested there was an interesting relation between him and Bion. Peter Winch, when he was at Kings College, encouraged me and thought that the connection between Wittgenstein's thoughts on therapy and the experience of a practicing psychotherapist were important and worth pursuing. Peter Hacker kindly read and commented on my early writing on Wittgenstein and poured some judicious cold water on it.

Onel Brooks, Miles Clapham, Kate Gilbert, Miranda Glossop, Lucy King, Barbara Latham, Jake Osborne, Luke and Jude Heaton all attended discussions on the chapters of the book over some years and made valuable contributions to it. Mike Harding, Rupert Read, Susanna Rennie and the anonymous reader for the publisher read drafts and made valuable comments. Barbara Latham and William Shone suggested many corrections of expression on the final draft. Fatima Raja helped with computer matters.

I owe most to those people who chose to consult me, especially those who came in the first 20 or so years of my practice as they had to suffer my inexperience.

Abbreviations

The following abbreviations are used to refer to Wittgenstein's published works, lecture notes by others and conversations referred to in this book.

AWL   (1979) *Wittgenstein's Lectures, Cambridge, 1932–35*, Alice Ambrose, ed. Oxford: Blackwell.

BB   (1958) *The Blue and Brown Books*, R. Rhees, ed. Oxford: Blackwell.

BT   (2005) *The Big Typscript: TS 213*. C.G. Luckhardt and M.A.E. Aue, ed. and trans. Oxford: Blackwell.

CV   (1998) *Culture and Value*, rev. ed., G.H. von Wright with H. Nyman, eds, rev. A. Pichler, P. Winch, trans. Oxford: Blackwell.

LC   *Wittgenstein Lectures and Conversations on Aesthetics, Psychology & Religious Belief*, C. Barrett, ed. Oxford: Blackwell.

LPP   (1988) *Wittgenstein's Lectures on Philosophical Psychology 1946–7*. Notes by P.T. Geach, K.J. Shah and A.C. Jackson. P.T. Geach, ed. Hemel Hempstead: Harvester.

LW1   (1982) *Last Writings on the Philosophy of Psychology*, G.H. von Wright and N. Nyman, eds. C.G. Luckhardt and M.A.E. Aue, trans. Oxford: Blackwell.

LW2   (1992) *Last Writings on the Philosophy of Psychology: The Inner and the Outer*, G.H. von Wright and N. Nyman, eds. C.G. Luckhardt and M.A.E. Aue, trans. Oxford: Blackwell.

NB   (1961) *Notebooks, 1914–1916*, G.E.M. Anscombe and G.H. von Wright, eds. G.E.M. Anscombe, trans. Blackwell, Oxford.

OC   (1993) *On Certainty*, G.E.M. Anscombe and G.H. von Wright, eds. G.E.M. Anscombe and D. Paul, trans. Oxford: Blackwell.

PG   (1974) *Philosophical Grammar*, R. Rhees, ed. A. Kenny, trans. Oxford: Blackwell.

PI   (2009) *Philosophical Investigations*, 4th ed., P.M.S. Hacker and Joachim Schulte, eds. G.E.M. Anscombe, P.M.S Hacker and Joachim Schulte, trans. Oxford: Wiley-Blackwell.

PO   (1993) *Philosophical Occasions 1912–1951*, J. Klagge and A. Nordmann, eds. Indianapolis: Hackett.

PPO   (2003) *Public and Private Occasions*, J.C. Klagge and
        A. Nordmann, eds. New York: Rowman and Littlefield.
PR   (1975) *Philosophical Remarks*, R. Rhees, ed. R. Hargreaves and
        R. White, trans. Oxford: Blackwell.
RFM   (1978) *Remarks on the Foundations of Mathematics*, rev. ed.,
        G.E.M. Anscombe, R. Rhees and G.H. von Wright, eds.
        G.E.M. Anscombe, trans. Oxford: Blackwell.
RPP1   (1980) *Remarks on the Philosophy of Psychology*,
        G.E.M. Anscombe and G.H. von Wright, eds.
        G.E.M. Anscombe, trans. Oxford: Blackwell.
RPP2   (1980) *Remarks on the Philosophy of Psychology*, G.H. von
        Wright and H. Nyman, eds. C.G. Luckhardt and M.A.E. Aue,
        trans. Oxford: Blackwell.
TLP   (1951) *Tractatus Logico-Philosophicus*, C.K. Ogden, trans.
        London: Routledge; (1961) D.F. Pears and B.F. McGuiness,
        trans. London: Routledge & Kegan Paul.
VW   (2003) *The Voices of Wittgenstein: The Vienna Circle*, notes
        taken by R. Waismann G. Baker, ed. London: Routledge.
WVC   (1979) *Wittgenstein and the Vienna Circle: Conversations
        Recorded by Friedrich Waismann*, J. Schulte and B. McGuiness,
        trans. Oxford: Blackwell.
Z   (1981) *Zettel*, 2nd ed., G.E.M. Anscombe and G.H. von Wright,
        eds. G.E.M. Anscombe, trans. Oxford: Blackwell.

1
The Problem

Over a century ago Freud's and Breuer's patient, Anna O, called their practice 'the talking cure'. Various analytical practices have arisen since using 'talk' to cure. But how can talking cure people of certain conflicts? And why talking and not writing?

Psychoanalysis first developed as a practice. Free association in adults and play therapy in children were not theoretically driven but were found by Freud, Klein and Anna Freud to be effective in practice. Such activity was not rationally deduced from a theory of the mind. However, Freud and his followers believed that the scientific method was the way to increase psychological knowledge and was necessary for credibility that their practice was a rational cure; so they created theories to explain behaviour.

Freud's basic method was free-association. He encouraged the patient to say whatever came to mind without censoring anything, or keeping it back because they thought it unimportant. This came to be called the talking cure. However, he did not construe the material freely; rather he used it to confirm his theories of the aetiology of neurosis and the early experience of children. Thus, he would lead his patient's attention to *repressed sexual ideas in spite of their protestations* (Freud 1895, pp. 273–4; 1940, p. 259).

Freud framed the patient's associations as material for finding the causes of their troubles. Instead of allowing the patient's language itself to make clear how it signifies or fails to, he used his own ideas and language to say how things 'really' are. He did not distinguish the use of language, on a particular occasion, to describe how things are, from the more therapeutic use of clarifying how expressions are being used. He assumed there is a psychological interior where the causes of neurosis could be found, and elaborated theories on this basis. He treated the patient as an evidence-exhibiting body – rather than a speaking human being. He attended more to the content of what was said, than to the nature of the saying. This was understandable because he saw himself as a natural scientist, whose job was to find the causes of phenomena.

The other important group of psychological therapies that has been developed is cognitive behavioural therapy (CBT) (Dobson 2001). This grew out of traditional behavioural therapy. Aaron Beck, the primary founder of cognitive therapy, was originally trained in psychoanalysis. He observed that cognitive factors in neurosis tended to be ignored by psychoanalysts and that patients exhibited systematic distortions in their thinking patterns. He generated a typology of cognitive distortions and ways of correcting them (Beck 1976). He assumed that cognitive agents are information processors which take input and manipulate it internally in such a manner as to produce output, that is, behaviour. The information processors are a collection of hierarchically organised systems, rather than one big information system.

As, in part, cognitive therapy is a reaction against psychoanalysis, the two share common assumptions. They both claim to be scientific and rational. They assume that while well-adjusted people like themselves have a realistic appraisal of life events a neurotic distortion of reality leads to psychological disorder. They assume that the therapist is rational and so can claim the authority to decide what is to be considered valid reality and then correct the patient by some technical means.

Both forms of psychotherapy are dualistic – there is the theory and the practice. In psychoanalysis, on the one hand, there is the practice of free association, which was not rationally deduced, and on the other explanatory theories. Freud thought the latter would be his permanent legacy (Freud 1929). Psychotherapy, he thought, would probably be replaced by chemical treatment but his theory of the mind would be of permanent importance (Freud 1940, p. 416).

It is theory, and allegedly a scientific theory, that gives authority to the practice of psychoanalysis and of CBT, hence for both authority lies outside of the practice. If we practised without theory it would seem we practised blindly, perhaps just using suggestion. However, the clinical practice of psychoanalysis is not logically deducible from its theory (Fonagy and Target 2003, pp. 283–301). Nor is theory deducible from practice, for the practice of both psychoanalysis and cognitive therapy is theory-driven. Freud and most cognitive therapists believe in the metaphysical dogma that 'reality' is scientific reality. The requirements for intelligibility are some sort of causal process, mechanisms such as objects and processes in the unconscious or complex computational processes. For example, psychoanalysts assume that the way to understand infants is by observation; yet we ordinarily understand infants by interacting with them as human, not just by observing them. Neither Freud nor cognitive therapists raise the question as to the difference between problems that require observations and theories and those that do not. Both take up the place of the scientist, whose authority lies in his knowledge, forgetting the place from which patients speak, which is not that of a scientist seeking knowledge, but of one struggling with pain, confusion and despair which lie open to view.

Representation

Causal explanations in science depend on how we represent nature. If we look at a sunset we may describe it. We describe it directly *as being thus or so*. However, we may be interested to represent or structure the world in such a way that the causes of phenomena become important. We may then seek the cause of the sun going down. Since psychoanalysts and cognitive therapists represent the mind and behaviour in such a way that causal explanations are called for, it is important to clarify what is involved in representation.

There are many puzzles about representation although it is a basic human ability. Language, the arts, sciences and politics depend on it. As everything resembles something else in some ways, representation is by selective resemblance and selective non-resemblance. There can be no perfect representation, as any representation must trade on unlikeness and distortion. Representations are made for a purpose and are governed by the criteria of adequacy to it. There can be no general valid inference from what the representation is like to the represented.

History shows us that measurement procedures and theory evolve together.

Measuring, like theorising, involves representing, for a measurement is a representation of what is measured. The theory locates the target in the logical space in which all the measurements can be located. It tells us what is measured, the physical correlate of the measurements.

Scientific representation is by means of artefacts, whether concrete ones such as statements, models, diagrams and computer monitor displays, or abstract ones such as mathematical models. There can be no representation unless certain things are used, made or taken to represent things as thus and so. Representations have many uses: a photograph to serve as a reminder, a map to find one's way or a theory to make predictions. Perhaps most importantly for our purposes, scientific representation involves indexicality, that is, we cannot draw on our representations until the user is located with respect to it, where the user is necessarily outside the representations (van Fraassen 2008).

A scientific representation is like a map or model. To draw on this map, to test it or to use it to explain, the scientist or scientific community must supply something extra which does not come from the map itself. A map is for use; we can use it to get around a region in which we find ourselves if and only if the map is the thing *we* use and locate ourselves in. Indexical terms such as 'I', 'we', 'here' and 'now' are not in the representation but must be used (Ibid., pp. 59–88).

The totality of scientific information could be written in a co-ordinate free and context-independent form. However, to test it, or apply it there must be an agent who does not come from within that body of science. As Fraassen puts it, '*describing the having of it* is no substitute for *the having*' (Ibid., p. 83).

A brief look at the history of geometry may help explain this point. Geometry is concerned with the description of space. Greek geometers created Euclidean space. It was believed for over 2000 years that space *is* Euclidean. It was not that this geometry described space, but that the nature of space is inseparable from Euclidean geometry. No distinction was made between Euclidean geometry and the real world described by that geometry. In the nineteenth century the creation of non-Euclidean geometry showed that there are rational alternatives to this description of space. It became possible to design geometries that were highly non-Euclidean. The question arose as to which geometry is true. It was found that Euclidean geometry was adequate for distances in our solar system but non-Euclidean geometry was necessary to represent the huge distances outside it. No longer was space identified with one particular geometry for different geometries *represent* it, and were understood to have different *uses*. Thus, if we want to find out where a rocket to the moon will land, then Euclidean geometry suffices, while the movements of galaxies require non-Euclidean geometry.

All geometry presupposes fundamental notions which are undefined and 'outside' geometry. Position is basic. Relations of position can be expressed by means of direction and distance and a geometry can be designed. But what is position? Anything that can move itself must move from a position. Human beings are the absolute source of their spontaneous movements. A baby can move its limbs or reach out for objects and lives in space but cannot represent it; it has no concept of geometry. There is then a primary lived experience of space which is 'outside' any representation of it. We can only use our representations of space if we are 'outside' them. Geometry does not describe space but represents it.

Most psychotherapists are similar to people who thought that space *is* Euclidean. They assume that the nature of the mind is inseparable from their descriptions of it. Hence their tendency to identify with a particular theory – 'I am a Freudian, Kleinian, a cognitive therapist, etc.' – instead of attending to the most fruitful way of understanding human action and its disorders. How do I describe *my* mind? With what do I describe it? Like space, our 'minds' are primarily lived. I am a living human body that has the capacity to speak and think about myself and others. This capacity is primary to any description of a mind. Psychotherapist's theories and descriptions are better understood as *representations* of the mind, useful for certain purposes, but not to be identified with.

Psychoanalysts create representations of the psyche by inference, and create models of it. These form a dynamical system, psychodynamics. The representations and their objects and processes are models of each other: they reflect each other. There is no distance between the representation of the psyche and its object: one models the other.

These representations of the psyche are abstract structures. What does it mean for them to be true to reality? Do they have causal power? A painting of an angel has representational *content*: it depicts an angel. But whether it has a *referent*, something that exists that it depicts, is another question. We can map two sets of structure if we define their domain and range, plus the relation between them. But if the target is the psyche, how can we speak of an embedding or isomorphism between the representations and their target?

Hertz, a physicist who was an important influence on Wittgenstein, pointed out that when we make scientific representations,

> We form for ourselves pictures or symbols of external objects; and we make them in such a way that the necessary consequents of the pictures in thought are always the pictures of the necessary consequents in nature of the things pictured. In order for this requirement to be satisfiable at all, there must be certain agreements between nature and our mind .... The pictures of which we are speaking are our conceptions of things; they agree with the things in *one* respect which consists in satisfying the above-mentioned requirement, but for their purpose it is not necessary that they are in any further agreement with the things. (Hertz 1956, p. 1)

So our representations and their objects are two systems that are models of each other. We seek to understand the world scientifically through our representations. This is well put by Heisenberg:

> The atom of modern physics can be symbolized only through a partial differential equation in an abstract space of many dimensions.... All its qualities are inferential; no material properties can be directly attributed to it. That is to say, any picture of the atom that our imagination is able to invent is for that reason defective. An understanding of the atomic world in that primary sensuous fashion ... is impossible. (Quoted in van Fraassen, p. 201)

Surely the nature of psychotherapeutic understanding should be a crucial question for therapists. Do theoretical explanations lead to it, or does it involve understanding the limits and uses of theoretical explanations and pictures of the mind in therapy? A scientific theory models objects in the world, but we, the users of the theory, cannot be represented in that theory. Yet it is *we* who seek therapy. It is clear that for most therapists the theory is very important; they tend to identify with, and define themselves by, the one they hold. Theories, however, are representations, ways of ordering observations and making predictions. None of them have been shown to have better predictive or therapeutic power than ordinary human understanding. People with special experience, such as forensic psychiatrists who work with violent people, will be better than the rest of us at predicting their likely behaviour, but this is due to their special experience, not a theory.

Theories in psychotherapy are mostly used as persuasive explanations, giving reassurance and authority to their holder as well as having a placebo effect on the person he seeks to help. But there is the question of their truth, for most therapists believe their theory to be true and not a representation. Does truth matter? Is a theory which fulfils contemporary epistemic norms more curative than one which makes a good soothing story? Is an interpretation true just because it seems to have a therapeutic effect? It has a use but is it true? Can we distinguish the effect of the way it is put to the patient, from its content? Can we tell the difference between what objectively seems to be the case and what a theory says is the case? Is a theory more important than words and gestures which show attention to the patient's suffering? Are there a set of definite facts in the matter of psychotherapy that can be determined? (Jopling 2008)

The theoretician pays selective attention to the phenomena, attending to certain aspects, *representing* them in certain ways, and to an extent; their link to reality is *his* use of them and here representing is equivalent to not being present. They are not descriptions of reality but for a use. Their plausibility comes from speaking in a general way and abstracting from particular cases; but *our craving for generality* and *the contemptuous attitude with the particular case* leads us astray (Wittgenstein *BB*, p. 18).

Therapy is a craft and ought not to be understood as the mastery of a set of theories. This does not imply that therapists should have no use for theories. Rather part of the craft depends on being able to choose which theories are helpful in certain contexts, and to take account of ways in which, as representations, they are limited. It is judgement and timing, identifying the *kairos*, the moment that must be seized, the ripe time for intervention, that a good therapist exhibits. Any theory or representation must take indexical terms into account and these are outside the theory, as is the sense of *kairos*. *We* have a theory or picture of the cause, or possible cause of our troubles. As it is a view of ourselves, it is apart from our own life. We think it *must* be that way yet it is *we* that seek therapy.

One of the roots of Wittgenstein's thought is the importance of respecting the difference between factual statements, which are contingent, and expressions of necessity, of what must be so. False doctrines, theories and dogmas arise when the two are confused. We then imagine that reality must be a certain way, projecting our theory onto reality, forgetting that any empirical theory only makes sense if its user locates herself outside the theory, or representation. This is most easily forgotten when we construct theories of the mind. Since theories and representations are created to explain and perhaps control things, it makes no sense for the user of the theory to be represented in her theory. What can it mean to explain and control *myself*? Who controls me as I try to control myself? What sense is there in explaining *myself* to myself? The user, if she is to understand herself and her place in the world, must not identify with any theory, least of all one about herself if she is to avoid theoretical totalitarianism.

Psychological concepts such as thinking, feeling, desiring, and intending are practices grounded in the kinds of life we lead and inconceivable apart from our ordinary lives with other people. We need to be reminded of the various ways in which these concepts are used in everyday circumstances. Humans have the capacity to create theories and may create theories of the mind for certain purposes. However, these theories are not expressions of necessity of what must be so.

> One predicates of the thing what lies in the mode of representation. We take the possibility of comparison, which impresses us, as the perception of a highly general state of affairs. (*PI* ¶104)

It is like an optical illusion: we seem to see within things what is drawn on our glasses. We trace the form of expression, the method of representing, and think we have drawn the thing itself. We need to remove our glasses.

I will argue that neurosis and psychosis involve a misunderstanding of the nature of oneself; the sufferer is locked dogmatically in the terms of some theory, belief or dogma, instead of being mindful that she is 'outside' any possible representation of herself. Self-understanding requires realising that it is *we* who have made such representations of ourselves. You cannot understand the meaning of many neurotic or psychotic utterances without being attentive to the way they are being used. It is not just a matter of plotting how they came about. Nor is it a matter of what the particular words might or might not be referring to, rather the aptness of this language to the person's life. Failure to understand this leads theorists of psychotherapy as well as their patients to become identified with a theory and fixed on some representation of themselves and others which confuses factual statements with necessary expressions. Thus, because someone was abused as a child (a fact), then he must act (a necessary expression) in certain ways. To the victim it may seem to be an absolute necessity.

To make the problem more apparent, consider one's own mind. There are many theories of the structure of the human mind. Since I am human, presumably one or other of these theories applies to me. But which one? Perhaps I am attracted to the theory that I have an unconscious and an ego. But what does this mean? For what purpose do I use it? And in what way? I can understand the words of the theoretician who propounds this theory, he seems to mean something definite by his words, but where do I find *my* ego and unconscious? The terms 'ego' and 'unconscious', being determined by acts of meaning, have the meaning the theorist gives them. If I understand them in the same way, then where is *my* evidence that they occur in *my* mind? Where do I find my ego? Do I look into my mind and find it there? Supposing I say I cannot find it, does that mean I have no ego? Does 'the ego' represent 'I'? 'I' is a pronoun resistant to representation and knowledge; it is a manifestation of my power of choice, of self-movement, of the possibility of bringing something into existence, of going for a walk or constructing a theory. The ego, on the other hand, is an objective agency and we may talk of it as a thing a person may have – he has a big or small ego, etc. It is senseless to talk in this way about 'I'.

If we believe that a theory of the mind truly represents us, then it is not a truth that we can confirm or reject. We may believe it because we have been told that everyone has an ego and an unconscious; we may then make a convincing story for ourselves using these characters. If we do so, then whatever seems right is right and the distinction between truthfulness and mere agreement with the theoretician evaporates.

That this confusion is at the basis of psychoanalysis is made clear by Freud in one of his most important essays. 'Consciousness makes each of us aware only of his own states of mind; that other people, too, possess a consciousness is an inference which we draw by analogy from their observable utterances and actions, in order to make this behaviour of theirs intelligible to us' (Freud 1915a, p. 170). He goes on to say: 'all the acts and manifestations which I notice in myself and do not know how to link up with the rest of my mental life must be judged as if they belonged to someone else' (Ibid., p. 171).

Freud takes for granted the Cartesian tradition that consciousness is the mark of the mental. He argues on the basis of an analogy. He assumes that other people possess a consciousness on the analogy between himself and them. But what is the criterion of the sameness between my consciousness and other people's? I can imagine that others are conscious in the way I am but this is just to imagine myself being in the same place as them. It fails to take account of the criteria by which we can decide the sameness between my consciousness and another's. Can I objectify my consciousness and other people's and compare them? In parallel, it is assumed that some hidden contents of our own mind are hidden away in our unconscious and we cannot link them up with the rest of our mental life. We have to treat them as if they belonged to someone else and infer them.

Self-deception

Wittgenstein wrote: 'Nothing is so difficult as not deceiving your self' (*CV* p. 39). Self-deception was of central interest to him, as it has been to many people in different cultures. However, psychoanalysis and CBT are interested in curing neurosis which is a medical term that only began to be used in the nineteenth century to refer to ailments for which physicians could find no organic cause.

Psychoanalytic interpretations and CBT may be useful in particular cases in so far as they throw light on relevant confusions and relieve mental pain. Nevertheless, they are not based on a fixed truth about reality. The analyst is not in a position to observe reality and put it into words without representing it. Although he should strive to be just, he is not neutral.

To Wittgenstein the speaking of language is part of an activity or of a life-form (*PI* ¶23). Therefore, clarity about its use and concepts involves clarity about our life. We are misled by the pictures and theories we create if we dogmatically hold onto them. The question arises as to whether such pictures fit our life as it is lived, or are we self-deceived, attached to imaginary pictures and unable to realise ourselves?

'Philosophy is a struggle against the bewitchment of our understanding by the resources of our language' (*PI* ¶109). The ambiguity of the sentence is important. Language is both the source of our confusions and the means by which we seek to cure them – the talking cure.

Wittgenstein's methods are for loosening the grip of misleading pictures and analogies, which hold our thinking in a cramp and stand in the way of our recognising the extraordinariness of the ordinary. The particular pictures that we fix on are rooted in our human way of life and culture, and therefore connected to our desires, fears and aspirations. They may be the expression of a wish to control the seemingly arbitrary world, especially if our childhood experiences were chaotic and unjust. Because they are heavily influenced by the problems and beliefs of our culture, in the present day the scientific and technological picture of the world has great power.

> One must start out with error and convert it into truth
>
> That is, one must reveal the source or error, otherwise hearing the truth won't do any good. The truth cannot force its way in when something else is occupying its place.
>
> To convince someone of the truth, it is not enough to state it, but rather one must find the *path* from error to truth. (*PO* p. 119)

When we seek knowledge and explanations of mental conflict, we are caught in a confusion whose character is not transparent to us. We are driven by a wish to find an explanation for the conflict, as if that will enable us to cure it. But this search for an answer is also the driving force in the conflict; we need to be liberated from the persistent inclination to seek answers to all questions. It is the conditions in which conflicts emerge; and the confusions which arise that need attention. Instead of rooting around for psychological explanations in the contents of an inner container, called 'the mind', we can attend to the way we are seeing things, as well as to the way language is being used.

The motto Wittgenstein chose for *Philosophical Investigations* is instructive. It is from the play *Der Schützling* (The Protégé) by the Austrian playwright Nestroy (1802–62). In translation it reads: Anyway, the thing about progress is that it looks much greater than it really is (Trans. Stern 2004, p. 58). Nestroy ranks as one of the greatest authors of supremely intelligent farce. The play was written at the beginning of the industrial revolution in Austria and was critical of the still current hysterical optimism that with the aid of technology we can make continual progress in eradicating evil from this world. Modern society was, Nestroy thought, governed by *the categorical imperative of money*.

Wittgenstein also considered our civilisation bewitched by the word 'progress'. This word contains the idea of a continuous, ongoing solution to all problems. We can measure technical progress but by what measure can we assess human well-being? The form of progress is constructive: it realises itself by making structures, such as theories, that are ever more complex. It plays into our greed for satisfaction. Psychoanalysis and cognitive therapy are examples of this tendency, as they construct complicated models of the mind, mere explanatory hypotheses, to solve the problems of neurosis and psychosis, instead of showing the need to expose human problems by unravelling the actual knots which are preventing movement.

Wittgenstein was an aeronautical engineer by training and had a deep appreciation of science and technology. But he was acutely aware of their limits and of the fact that many spheres of human flourishing are not touched by them. His disengagement from the idea of universal progress and the system of rationality driving it was due to his insight that in building structures to reach pre-determined goals there was blindness to the non-constructive foundation. It was this he sought to render evident. 'Anything that can be reached by a ladder does not interest me.... For the place to which I really have to go is one that I must actually be at already' (*CV* p. 10).

He avoided being a spokesman for a special school to which he was trying to convert people. 'The philosopher is not a citizen of any local community of ideas. That is what makes him into a philosopher' (*Z* ¶455). 'If one tried to advance *theses* in philosophy, it would never be possible to debate them, because everyone would agree to them' (*PI* ¶128). This applies to the talking 'cure'. Of course therapists may be stimulated by famous therapists – Freud, Jung, Lacan, Beck, etc. – but these should provoke him to thought, not to being a follower who

identifies with their theories. This would be to encourage people to identify with some idea, rather than spurring them to understand what it is
to be responsible and live a life in good spirit. 'Pretensions are a mort-
gage which burden a philosopher's capacity to think' (*OC* ¶549). The
danger of pretensions is that we remain locked in the cage of the opinions of our particular school of therapy. Wherever we look we see with
our own theories and the values on which they are based; the otherness,
the strangeness of our own life and that of others, is reduced to fit what
we value.

This can be illustrated from *Middlemarch,* by Dorothea's response to
Mr Casaubon after their visit to Rome. Dorothea had never been to
Rome before. Casaubon, a learned man, showed her round, explaining everything in a measured official tone and with a blank absence of
interest, or sympathy, in the glories of the ancient city, or in Dorothea's
relation to it. This had a stifling, depressive effect on Dorothea. Her artist
friend Ladislaw points out:

> Language gives a fuller image, which is all the better for being vague.
> After all, true seeing is within; and painting stares at you with an
> insistent imperfection. I feel that especially about representations of
> women. As if a woman were a mere coloured superficies! You must
> wait for movement and tone. There is a difference in their very
> breathing: they change from moment to moment. (Eliot 1965, p. 222)

Wittgenstein helps us to see that critical rigour can be part and par-
cel of practice; but it is a flexible rigour. In free association everything
is contingent and temporalised. Therapy involves apparently arbitrary
and superfluous factors that characterise the encounter: the agreed time
and place, the nature of the persons involved and what culture they
come from, the hurly-burly of life. Theory abstracts from all this and
creates 'a mind' which is ruled by necessity – psychic determinism. It
fails to take into account that it is by means of words we make ourselves.
Freud is doing this 'unconsciously' when he tells us what he thinks rules
us. When we speak, we are giving expression to a way of life; this is
as true of neurotic or psychotic speech as of psychoanalytic theorising.
The talking cure follows the movement, the becoming, of thought and
speech. Therapy begins in *medias res* and not in a technique based on a
foundational theory.

The work of Wittgenstein shows the way for this shift in focus. He
wrote: 'The philosopher treats a question; like an illness' (Trans. Mulhall
2007, p. 89; *PI* ¶255). This semicolon, as Erich Haller pointed out, is a

profound one as it makes the statement ambiguous. It can mean that the philosopher treats philosophical questions as one treats an illness. But it can also mean that what is like an illness is not the question but the way the philosopher treats it.

The first meaning implies that the philosopher is sane and rational and treats the questions he is asked as if they were put by someone confused. The second meaning implies that the philosopher is confused and afflicted by the question and this is shown by the way he seeks to answer it (*PI* 109).

Attending to people who we encourage to say what they feel they have to say can dissolve knots in their understanding when we remind them of the pictures, analogies and assumptions they are using which mislead them. The skill required is not to argue for a different point of view, or to claim to be making discoveries about the causes of the neurosis. We untie *knots in our thinking* (*Z* ¶452) and take care not to replace them by further knots from dogmas fuelled by ambition. We use appropriate questions, similes, pictures, forms of representation, reminders and humour; these may enable the person to overcome his cravings and demands, see their absurdity and so live more freely. Blindness and prejudice are healed when we freely acknowledge previously unrecognised possibilities.

Therapy is a dialogue between two particular people, one of whom is complaining of suffering from conflicts and confusions. It can only occur when he recognises his own need for it. To recognise a need is to acknowledge a lack in himself. It is this lack which provides the dynamic for therapy.

> I must be nothing more than a mirror in which my reader sees his own thinking with all its deformities and with this assistance can set it in order. (*CV* p. 25)

Wittgenstein would have been familiar with Lichtenberg's remark:

> A book is like a mirror: if an ape looks into it an apostle is hardly likely to look out. We have no words for speaking of wisdom to the stupid. He who understands the wise is wise already. (Lichtenberg 2000, p. 71)

Wittgenstein's writing is very different from most works of psychotherapy. He shows his manner of thinking, which does not proceed step by step in a linear fashion. His writing is repetitive, disjunctive and, often, recursive. There are many voices in it and it can be difficult to identify his from those of his students, or teachers, such as Frege and Russell. One false notion is driven out and then another threatens to take its place. He is constantly changing his position showing new aspects to the problem and different ways of presenting it. As one scholar put it, he wanted to show in a book that nothing can properly be shown there. His dilemma was like the one described by Plato in the *Phaedrus*, a dialogue infused with a sense of mystery which shows his way of thinking could never reside in a book (McGuiness 2002, p. 197).

The therapist is more like a midwife, as the philosopher is in Plato's *Theaetetus*, whose presence is necessary to respond and elucidate. Clarity takes place through the dynamic of need in the patient and the use of language by both parties. The therapist is attentive to the tricks language plays upon us, the way language may not allow us to speak for ourselves. Words are spoken at particular times and places, but can we ever say all we mean? Is there a totality of meaning? The connection between using words and meaning what we say is not automatic. We easily chatter away about ourselves and others forgetting the disjunction between being silent and speaking. To express ourselves responsibly, to allow the word to regain its power, requires us to be clear about our use of language and this is difficult, especially when we are talking about ourselves. We imagine that we, or some 'expert', can stand outside of ourselves, or our context with others, look into our minds and proclaim to know the real meaning of what we or others say and do. Psychotherapists advertise their expertise and squabble as to which school is the most expert. However, we seek to understand the difference between chatter about reality and untying knots in our thinking.

Service users of psychiatry and psychotherapy repeatedly state that it is not knowledge but being treated with respect which is important to them. 'I couldn't care less really whether they knew about it (*the "illness"*) or not, what I care about is how well they can listen to me and treat what I say with respect, and acknowledge that I'm an expert in what's going on with me' (Nisha et al. 2009).

Wittgenstein wrote: 'The philosopher strives to find the liberating word, that is, the word that finally permits us to grasp what until then had constantly and intangibly weighed on our consciousness' (*BT* p. 302). This is a joint task for the therapist and the patient; it is a matter of 'seeing' and 'hearing' aright, not an intellectual one of seeking and applying knowledge. Authority lies in the actual practice of therapy rather than in the ability to construct and apply psychological theories to cure people.

2
Fearless Speech

As I have said, in the talking 'cure' we attend to the dialogue itself, to the use of language, avoiding explanations which depend upon dogmatic assumptions. I shall give a brief account of psychotherapy in the ancient world of Greece and Rome, as it is close to the talking cure and can be fruitfully contrasted with modern therapies, such as psychoanalysis and cognitive behaviour therapy, which are reductionist and modelled on natural science.

Ancient therapies in Europe were based on a 'Socratic' conception of philosophy and took Socrates as a more or less adequate model to follow. Philosophy was not something you simply learned, it was to be practised. The discipline of philosophy sought to promote a way of life that led to tranquillity and the fulfilment of human potential. A philosopher's life was the definitive expression of his philosophy.

Following this, Aristotle argued that norms, right living, are potentially present in practices rather than in theory. Practical, truthful reasoning is linked to desire and tends towards an end. Confusing practical matters with the sorts of things that can be best explained on the basis of theory is not a matter of ignorance but a sort of folly which can be destructive. Virtuous knowledge, he argued, is a *knack for* acting, in which we can distinguish between too little and too much with respect to pleasure and pain, and exert self-control. It is the ability to distinguish not simply what is right or wrong in the abstract but what is right or wrong for me in a particular situation. This is learned not through formal education but by gaining insight into the fulfilment experienced from appropriate action.

This insight is immanent to the activity itself. It cannot be systematised as it involves knowledge of my personal limits; nobody can be a decent person for me – I am responsible for that. It cannot be forced on me but is an exercise of my freedom.

The practice of free speech was an important notion in ancient Greece and was an important part of learning how to live a fulfiling life. For example, Diogenes of Sinope, a cynic influenced by Socrates, when asked what was the most beautiful thing in the world, replied '*parrhesia*', the Greek word meaning free speech. The *parrhesiastes* was someone who said everything she had in mind, who opened her heart and mind completely to other people through discourse. As emphasised by Foucault (2001), the word *parrhesia* refers to the type of relationship between the speaker and what she says. The *parrhesiastes* uses the most direct words and forms of expression she can find. She does not use rhetorical devices to help her sway people's minds, as many politicians, advertisers and 'spin' doctors do; instead she acts on people's minds by showing them where she stands. This implies that the *parrhesiastes* must have courage and be living in a social situation where it may be dangerous to expose her commitments. Thus a tyrant could not be a *parrhesiastes*, for he risks nothing by what he says. Similarly, it is unusual for today's 'expert' to be in a position of a *parrhesiastes*, provided he keeps within the bounds of his expertise, it is assumed he is unquestionable, except by another expert.

Two types of *parrhesia* were distinguished. There is the pejorative sense of the word which meant 'chattering', that is, saying everything that comes to mind without any sense of its value. And there is the positive sense in which the *parrhesiastes* expresses her personal relationship to truth which she stands behind. The proof that she is open to truth is her courage and the fact that she can say where she stands. However, this is difficult and cannot be done to order.

Galen, who lived A.D. 130–200, was a famous physician. In his essay 'The Diagnosis and Cure of the Soul's Passions' he argued that for a person to cease being a slave to his passions he needs a *parrhesiastes*. One of Galen's patients was Marcus Aurelius who, in his *Meditations*, praised 'free speech' as it was employed by Old Comedy and by the Cynics. He used it for himself to cut away illusions and hypocrisy (Marcus Aurelius 2006, Book 11, ¶6). Galen thought, as did most philosophers and physicians in antiquity, that we are our foremost and greatest flatterer and as such deluded about our own nature. There is no way that a person in love with himself can make a fair and impartial assessment of himself. 'The lover is blind in the case of the object of his love. If, therefore, each of us loves himself most of all, he must be blind in his own case' (Galen 1963). If our relationship to ourselves is one of lying, and our most common lie is that we imagine we are far more important than we actually are, then we cannot take proper care of ourselves and are not free. The genuine *parrhesiastes* will not be a flatterer of herself, or others, and will have the courage to help us recognise our self-delusions.

The recognition of a genuine *parrhesiastes* was of great importance and was discussed by Plutarch (1992), Galen and others (Foucault 2001). There must be harmony between what she says and how she behaves and there must be steadiness of mind in that a self-deluded person tends to shift their thoughts and opinions according to what they consider would be to their advantage. Galen also thought that a potential *parrhesiastes* should be tested by carefully directed questions about herself, to see if she is severe enough for this role.

> When a man does not greet the powerful and wealthy by name, when he does not visit them, when he lives a disciplined life, expect that man to speak the truth; try, too, to come to a deeper knowledge of what kind of man he is (and this comes about through long association). If you find such a man, summon him and talk with him one day in private; ask him to reveal straightaway whatever of the above mentioned passions he may see in you. *(These were anger, wrath, fear, grief, envy, and violent lust)* Tell him you would be most grateful for this service and that you will look on him as your deliverer more than if he had saved you from an illness of the body. Have him promise to reveal it whenever he sees you affected by any of the passions I have mentioned. (Quoted in Foucault 2001, p. 140)

In spite of the fact that Galen was a physician and often cured people of disordered passion, he did not think the *parrhesiastes* need be a physician nor have any professional qualifications.

Wittgenstein too thought that vanity and pride are the greatest obstacles to truthfulness.

'The edifice of your pride has to be dismantled. And that means frightful work' (*CV* p. 30. cf. pp. 41, 53, 54, 77). His private diaries show how he struggled with his vanity. Thus:

> When I say I would like to discard vanity, it is questionable whether my wanting this isn't yet again only a sort of vanity. I *am* vain & in so far as I am vain, my wishes for improvement are vain, too. I would then like to be such & such a person who was not vain & whom I like, & in my mind I already estimate the benefit which I would have from 'discarding' vanity. As long as one is on stage, one is actor after all, regardless of what one does. (*PPO* p. 139)

Although the death knell of Galen's vision of medicine was William Harvey's anatomical demonstration of the circulation of the blood, he continued to be influential in medicine until about 1850. His demise in medicine has not been wholly beneficial. Galen was both a very able logician and interested in language realising that the way the physician speaks is important in cure. He thought, like Wittgenstein, that confusions in speech bedevil clarity as much in medicine as in philosophy (Hankinson 1994; Drury 1996; Galen 2008).

He says of the doctor: 'He must study logical method to know how many diseases there are, by species and by genus, and how, in each case, one is to find out what kind of treatment is indicated. The same method also tells us what the very nature of the body is' (quoted in Hankinson 2008, p. 69).

He thought that reasoning logically from first principles is required to merit being a doctor, properly speaking. So the attitude to logic is fundamental to the integrity of a proper doctor. This is quite unlike modern medicine which is almost purely empirical. Nowadays, studying the nature of logic or language is thought to be pointless even in psychiatry where people mostly *talk* to patients who have troubles with *reason*.

> Words are wise men's counters, they do but reckon by them; but they are the money of fools, that value them by the authority of an Aristotle, a Cicero, or a Thomas, or any other Doctor whatsoever, if but a man. (Hobbes 1996, p. 29)

The relationship with a *parrhesiastes* is not like a relationship with someone claiming to be a scientific expert. Just as it would be absurd for an ordinary person to argue with a neuro-scientist about the structure and function of the brain, it would be equally absurd to argue with a psychoanalyst about the unconscious or inner world. Part of the genius of Freud was to make the mind a special subject that only experts can understand, thus shifting responsibility for understanding ourselves over to the expert. Ordinary people may understand what is conscious but the expert understands the unconscious, which to Freud is by far the most important part of the mind. This expertise is licensed by a group who have their own interests to pursue, yet the authority conferred means patients cannot question it in any serious sense. Psychoanalysts take great pains to remain as anonymous as possible to encourage the patient to idealise them and so submit that they are resistant if they question the analyst.

Nevertheless, words, even those of an anonymous expert, can be duplicitous. As Francis Bacon put it:

> More trust be given to countenances and deeds than to words; and in words, rather to sudden passages and surprised words, than to set and purposed words. (Bacon 2002, p. 273)

Bacon was aware of the revelations of slips of the tongue.

In the talking cure it is as important for the patient to assess the therapist's truthfulness as it is for the therapist to judge the patient's. This is one of the most important features of the cure, for we can be unsure that people are making sense even when they claim to be an expert. They may be merely mouthing theories. Truthfulness has to be uncovered in a dialogue and does not belong to the 'expert'. Truthfulness, in contrast to truth, is not a matter of expert knowledge and cannot be judged by a committee. It is dependent on the context between people, on the nature of the situation, and how they react to the demands it places upon them. We can be truthful to one person yet lie to another, or lie to get out of a difficulty. Worse still, we can delude ourselves we are being truthful.

> Is there such a thing as 'expert judgement' about the genuineness of expressions of feeling? – Even here, there are those whose judgement is 'better' and those whose judgement is 'worse'.
>
> Corrector prognosis will generally issue from the judgements of those who understand people better. Can one learn this knowledge? Yes; some can. Not, however by taking a course in it, but through 'experience'. Can someone else be a man's teacher in this? Certainly. From time to time he gives him the right tip. – This is what 'learning', and 'teaching' are like here.—What one acquires here is not a technique; one learns to judge correctly. There are also rules, but they do not form a system, and only experienced people can apply them right. Unlike calculating rules. (*PI PPF* 355)

The practice of *parrhesia*, fearless speech, is clearly similar to the fundamental rule of free association, which is the basic principle of psychoanalytic treatment. But there are important differences. As psychoanalysts have noted, a patient may not speak freely, although he has been invited to do so. He may try to impress, hide certain feelings, try to get sympathy and so on. The analyst may be doing much the same. The patient is instructed to speak freely but the analyst interprets dogmatically according to a rule. He assumes that any deviation in free associations is caused by unconscious processes in the mind. He ignores the influence of external and physical factors.

In the talking cure, on the other hand, the patient is invited to say what he wants to say and the therapist makes appropriate remarks that are not dogmatically ruled by the belief that any deviation must have an internal cause. Free speech may take place although there is no forcing the matter, no instructions to follow and chance is allowed to play its part.

Freud psychologises the fundamental rule, in that he sees it as a mode of access to the unconscious – a theoretical entity which he and only people trained in his method understand. He introduces concepts such as repression, instincts and the unconscious to explain the various data concerning memory that he came across in his practice. He takes these concepts to be empirical facts. He claims we repress certain memories as if they were entities and that repression is some empirical mechanism which actually pushes these into the unconscious. This is a confusion. Concepts are not facts. People certainly can forget, wish to forget, suppress and censor memories. They may be unable to recall them except under special circumstances and may produce false memories. These are the data which are met in practice. We can enquire as to why a particular person forgets an important memory, by asking that person appropriate questions and describing their responses. We do not need to turn concepts into facts by positing some mechanism – a mental apparatus.

Freud thought that the associative chain of ideas is unconsciously determined; the fundamental rule allows the products of the unconscious to become available to the analyst, which he can then interpret to the patient. Therefore, it is not free speech as far as the analyst is concerned. In fact Freud sometimes forced or coaxed the 'right' association from the patient (*SE*, Vol. 2, pp. 279–80, Vol. 3, p. 204). An American psychiatrist who had been in analysis with Freud in the 1930s reported: 'Freud would wait until he found an association which would fit into his scheme of interpretation and pick it up like a detective at a line-up who waits until he sees his man' (Wortis 1940).

When free speech is taken to be rule governed, it invites a certain view of words and meaning. It implies that in any occurrence of speaking, the thought the words express is fixed. Real meaning is in everything that is said. Meaning and truth are collapsed into one another. Truth, however, depends on a suitable sensitivity to the surroundings in which words are spoken. Understanding what given words express requires more than knowledge of the concepts involved and acquaintance with the objects spoken of. Thus if someone says, 'Pass the mustard please' when he has run out of food while crossing a desert on a camel, we need to know his circumstances to understand him. Even if he is eating beef at a meal he may not mean that he wants mustard, but instead he may be being sarcastic, thinking the host should have politely asked him if he wanted mustard. If everything is supposed to be channelled into words and words are understood as somehow containing the whole meaning, then we are led to the belief that only the unconscious contains real meaning and correspondingly only the analyst can know it. But meaning and truth are not psychological properties contained in the mind, or in words; rather they depend on the role words, gestures, pictures and action play in our life.

Confession

The talking cure can be compared to the rite of confession. Of course, it differs in some ways, in that the therapist has no authority to give absolution or penances and the person freely comes for help. Freud recognised this but claimed that in a confession the sinner tells what he knows, whereas the neurotic has to tell more (Freud 1926, p. 289). He was referring to his belief in the unconscious causes of neurosis. A psychoanalyst must concern himself with the structure of the mental apparatus, the conflict between the conscious and the unconscious, the inner world and the concept of repression. It is discovering the unconscious forces which drive this apparatus that will bring us to the origins of neurosis and enable us to cure it.

This belief that the cause of mental disorder lies in the unconscious is in many ways a demonology – there is a dark power in the unconscious that must be coaxed out by an expert. This is an ancient and highly suggestive picture. Freud made good use of this as in his famous motto to *The Interpretation of Dreams*: *Flectere si nequeo superos, Acheronta movebo* (If I cannot bend Heaven, then I will arouse Hell) (Virgil 1918, *Aeneid* Book 7, line 312).

Confession can involve a very different understanding if it aims at clarity. This involves careful attention to what we say and do. If we attend carefully to our practices, we may become more truthful. If a person confesses a sin, then he is 'conscious' of the sin but might merely be reporting it. As Freud rightly said, he merely tells us what he knows. That does not mean he is not self-deluded. He may be behaving correctly in confessing his sin yet have no sense of its full meaning. This would involve understanding the consequences in his and others' lives and *expressing* contrition for the sin, not just telling what he knows. The ancient and medieval confessors were well aware of the power of self-delusion and self-love to occlude truthfulness. But they had no concept of consciousness and so of the unconscious. They were not concerned with causes, rather with truthfulness.

In ancient literature moral thinkers such as La Rochefoucauld show how self-love leads to self-delusion. Thus, to give a short quotation from Maxim 563 on self-love:

> No man can plumb the depths or pierce the darkness of its chasms in which, hidden from the sharpest eyes, it performs a thousand imperceptible twists and turns, and where it is often invisible even to itself and unknowingly conceives, nourishes, and brings up a vast brood of affections and hatreds. Some of these are such monstrosities that on giving them birth it either repudiates them outright or hesitates to own them. (La Rochefoucauld 2007)

To give another example, Diogenes Laertius tells us that Diogenes of Sinope was invited to Plato's house and trampled on his carpets saying, 'I trample on Plato's vainglory.' Plato replied, 'How much pride you expose to view, Diogenes, by seeming not to be proud' (Diogenes Laertius 1925, Vol. 2, p. 29).

Plato is showing that Diogenes does not really understand pride. Diogenes imagines it is a behavioural trait, Plato has fine carpets, and therefore he is proud. But a person who is very rich is not necessarily proud because of self-love. He would certainly be aware he is very rich but would not necessarily impute this to some superior inner property that he alone possesses.

An interesting case discussed by Foucault (2001, pp. 150–60) is from Seneca who tells us that a young man called Serenus consulted him, as he felt restless and lacked tranquillity. Tranquillity was a state in which one was disturbed neither by external events nor by agitation and conflict due to involuntary movements of mind. Serenus tells Seneca:

> When I made examination of myself, it became evident, Seneca, that some of my vices are uncovered and displayed so openly that I can put my hand on them, some are more hidden and lurk in a corner, some are not always present but recur at intervals; and I should say the last are by far the most troublesome, being like roving enemies that spring upon one when the opportunity offers, and allow one neither to be ready as in war, nor to be off guard as in peace.
>
> Nevertheless the state in which I find myself most of all – for why should I not admit the truth to you as to a physician? – is that I have

neither been honestly set free from the things I hated and feared, nor, on the other hand, am I in bondage to them; while the condition in which I am placed is not the worst, yet I am complaining and fretful – I am neither sick nor well. (Seneca 1932)

In short, Serenus was what we might call neurotic and this would be cured by talking to a *parrhesiastes* such as Seneca. He was clear that it is not activity that makes men restless, but false imagination renders them mad (*Non industria inquietas, sed insanes falsae rerum imagines agitant*) (Seneca 1932, Book 12, ¶5). Seneca was not looking for causes but for lack of clarity. He saw Serenus had difficulty in being truthful.

One's responsibility for the care of oneself was widespread among the Greeks and Romans (Foucault 2001). To be mindful of one's own nature and learn to take pleasure in oneself was a responsibility. This pleasure was differentiated from *voluptas*, which is a pleasure whose origin is outside us and so uncertain. '*Disce gaudere*, learn how to feel joy', wrote Seneca to Lucilius; '*verum gaudiam severa est*, real joy is a stern matter since we are too readily satisfied with ourselves substituting pleasure for real joy' (Foucault 2001, pp. 66–7). In these writers it is not observation of the inner world by an expert that is required for self-knowledge but right judgement and dialogue. They seek to muster the patient's own resources rather than give him knowledge which has been discovered by an expert.

Pyrrhonian scepticism

An important school of ancient therapy were the Pyrrhonian sceptics who influenced the thought of physicians for over a thousand years as scepticism was close to empiricism (Heaton 1993, 1999; Hankinson 1995). There were deep connections between philosophy and medicine in the ancient world. Pyrrhonian scepticism was essentially therapeutic in nature and our main source of information about it is through Sextus Empiricus who was a practising doctor (Sextus Empiricus 1994).

The aim of Pyrrhonian scepticism is the final object of desire: 'that for the sake of which everything is done or considered, while it is not itself done or considered for the sake of anything else' (Ibid., pp. 1, 12, 25). It was not knowledge or belief they sought so they refused to be seduced into any kind of theoretical stance and opposed all doctrinaire beliefs. There were no specifically Pyrrhonian doctrines and no views which they had to accept. Scepticism was not a doctrine that could either be accepted or refuted. The Pyrrhonist's intention was not to bring about universal doubt. *Aporia is* a state of bafflement, perplexity, being at a loss, when confronted by dogmatic *beliefs* (Mates 1996, p. 30). The Pyrrhonist is aware that a criterion is lacking for deciding whether a dogma is true or not. He points out that the dogmatist's theories and definitions lack clear criteria. So he withholds assent from all categorical assertion. The sceptic relies on what seems to him to be the case, while he suspends judgement on how things are 'in reality', that is, the fantasy that we can know the essence of things beyond what can be expressed in human language.

Dogmatic craving for security leads to conflict. Attachment to dogmatic beliefs about reality creates a permanent state of inner torment, since any subject of enquiry turns out to present conflicting impressions – to adopt one position is to condemn you to being permanently troubled by it (Frede 1997). A Pyrrhonist discourse involves exposing the dogmas at the root of the conflicts in order to suspend judgement, the *epochē*, and to become untroubled and tranquil. This state cannot be forced or hunted; it does not depend on argument, although it has its place, nor on any system, or technique. *Ataraxia* (peace of mind) is not a state of mind that can be obtained. It happens by chance, as it were, when we come to see the pointlessness and torment of chasing after an imaginary good and running away from the bad. Sextus gives this analogy:

> *The painter Apelles* was painting a horse and wanted to represent in his picture the lather on the horse's mouth; but he was so unsuccessful that he gave up, took the sponge on which he had been wiping off the colours from his brush, and flung it at the picture. And when it hit the picture, it produced a representation of the horse's lather. (Sextus Empiricus 1994, pp. 10–11)

In other words, all talk about how to obtain tranquillity is *sinnloss*, senseless; like logical symbols, it presents no possible state of affairs.

The sceptics are disturbed by natural things – they may shiver when cold, be thirsty, feel pain, mourn when a loved one dies, etc. – but they claimed that most people dogmatically believe that natural responses are bad. This puts them in conflict and so they often resist pain or are afraid to mourn. By contrast, the sceptic who has freed herself from the judgement that such beliefs are true comes off more moderately.

It is judgements that can deceive, not the senses. When we see a stick, which in water appears broken, the visual impression itself does not deceive. Only in that moment, in which a conclusion is made about the stick itself, and which involves an act of judgement, can one speak of deception. This is an example of the sign/symbol confusion that Wittgenstein claimed riddled philosophy, as it does psychotherapy (*TLP* ¶¶3.32–3.328). For what do we mean by the 'stick itself'? It is a sign which has no sense but only the appearance of one. Whoever saw a 'stick itself'? We see sticks which are not in water and they are straight. We can feel a stick in water and it looks bent but feels straight. In all these cases the stick is being perceived in a situation; it is not an isolated 'itself'.

Many scholars have pointed out the closeness of Wittgenstein to the Pyrrhonian sceptics (e.g. Fogelin 1987; Palmer 2004; Stern 2004; Nordmann 2005). As Fogelin (Ibid., p. 234) pointed out traditional sceptics, down to at least Hume, held that philosophical problems are in principle unsolvable as they involved doubts which can never be satisfied.

> Scepticism is *not* irrefutable, but obviously nonsensical, when it tries to raise doubts where no questions can be asked.
>
> For doubt can exist only where a question exists, a question only where an answer exists, and an answer only where something *can be said*. (*TLP* ¶6.51)

Wittgenstein's method has similarities to Montaigne's, although, as far as I know, he never read him. Montaigne was influenced by the Pyrrhonian sceptics. He became depressed after the death of a friend; so to shame himself he decided to write down his thoughts and emotions. He wrote mostly about himself and his essays were 'assays' of himself by himself. He understood that he lived in time so it was senseless to try to capture himself as a unity. 'I do not portray Being, I portray Becoming; not from one age to another ... but from day to day, from minute to minute' (Montaigne 1991, Book 3, essay 2). His essays are very like free associations but, unlike Freud, he did not theorise over them and did not try to create a unity. He adds: 'If my soul could only find a footing I would not be assaying myself but resolving myself. But my soul is ever in its apprenticeship and being tested. I am expounding a lowly, lacklustre existence' (Ibid.).

Freud's self-analysis

There is a marked contrast between the struggles many people have over the delusions of self-love and Freud's self-analysis, which was the exceptional event that founded psychoanalysis. It mostly took place between 1895 and 1901 and involved discussions with his friend

Wilhelm Fliess, an Ear, Nose and Throat surgeon. Both men were seeking the causes of neurosis. Fleiss thought they lay in disorders of the mucous membrane of the nose, while Freud thought they were in the unconscious. They never confronted each other as to the possibility of self-deception, but only agreed or disagreed with each other. Much of the time it was a *folie de deux* (Anzieu 1986).

This 'analysis' provides the standard and defines the concepts and can measure the degree of self-knowledge achieved in psychoanalysis. Thus Jones, Freud's colleague, friend and biographer, emphasised that the task of self-knowledge had been attempted before by Solon, Augustine, Montaigne and many others; however, no one else had succeeded, as their inner resistances barred advance. He gives no evidence for this extraordinary statement. He tells us that only indomitable intellectual and moral courage along with flawless integrity had enabled Freud to enter the Promised Land – the realm of the unconscious (Jones 1953–57, Vol. 1, pp. 351–60). In analytic circles no other self-analysis is authentic if it differs in any significant way from Freud's 'discoveries'. It is therefore discouraged. Experts know best.

Jones assumed self-knowledge has the one meaning it had for Freud. That is, knowing the causes of one's actions which lay in the unconscious. He never questioned the dogma of mentalism, believing that meaningful actions are caused by inner processes and states (Bouveresse 1995; Elder 1994; Cioffi 1998). He, like most psychoanalysts, never showed any historical or anthropological awareness, like reflexive questioning over what is meant by 'self-knowledge' in various cultures for example.

Freud was interested in universal theoretical knowledge so he sought for causes in the mind. He was an ambitious and authoritarian man who had little insight into this aspect of his personality (There are many biographies of Freud which expound this; Breger 2000 is one of the most judicious.). During his self-analysis he 'discovered' the meaning of dreams, the Oedipus Complex, the primal scene and castration anxiety. In addition he acquired many other psychoanalytic notions (Anzieu 1986). It also had a therapeutic effect. He had been easily depressed, resentful, moody and hypochondriacal. After his self-analysis he was more at ease with himself and was certain psychoanalysis was on the path to truth. His phobias of taking trains, crossing the street and his fear of death had not disappeared but had waned. As Anzieu points out (p. 562), he was now aware of their mechanisms. Freud himself wrote that after his 'analysis' with Fliess, 'a part of homosexual cathexis has been withdrawn and made use of to enlarge my own ego. I have succeeded where the paranoic fails' (Jones 1953–57, Vol. 2, p. 92). He defined self-knowledge purely in terms of his own theory!

Freud observed himself and his patients and wrote down his observations and 'discoveries'. He produced a long string of formulae which explained what he had observed. Dreams are wish fulfilments, perversions are the negative of neuroses, superstition and religion are psychologies projected onto the external world, we identify with a lost object in order to keep it, happiness is the achievement in maturity of a childhood wish and so on.

At the same time he gave names to many 'psychical events' that he thought he observed such as repression, regression, horror of incest, family romance and sexual stages such as the oral, anal, urethral and phallic. He created a special vocabulary which enabled him to found a special science exclusive to him and those who followed his procedures. Thus anyone who did not know about his anal-sadistic stage could be claimed to be seriously lacking in self-knowledge.

Procedure in the practice of psychoanalysis involves setting up an unusual situation in which the patient faces away from the analyst while the analyst remains neutral, observing and interpreting. This creates deep anxieties in the patient as it is artificial. It is an experiment but the patient's permission is not sought nor is it explained to him what will be done as would happen in the practice of medicine. As Foucault has argued, psychoanalysis can be read as a major form of depsychiatrisation but also as the reconstitution of a truth-producing medical power so that the production of truth is exactly adapted to that power (Foucault 2006, pp. 342–4). The psychoanalyst has an external relation to her patient. She aims to extract from the individual his inner subjectivity through a particular technique and the subject is supposed to interiorise the norms imposed upon him (Ibid., p. 362). Instead of throwing light on the person's confusions, it creates theoretical chatter behind their back. It is concerned with the production of knowledge rather than truthfulness between people.

Freud invented a procedure and a system that he thought was scientific. As he idealised science so he idealised his 'discoveries' about himself, and his followers have idealised him and his 'discoveries'. His assessment of his self-analysis was entirely dependent on his theoretical assumptions. It meant enlarging his ego and increasing knowledge. He imagined he had made discoveries about the human mind. But a discovery is finding something by searching, or by chance. It assumes there are things in the world that are already there, waiting to be discovered or inferred, and so known. Freud thought that we only know of the existence of others by inference (Freud 1915, pp. 170–1). But does the mind consist of things and processes that are present to be discovered by inference?

> Does a child believe that milk exists? Or does it know that milk exists? Does a cat know that a mouse exists? (*OC* ¶478)

Does a child infer that its mother exists?

Self-knowledge has many different meanings depending on culture and beliefs. It can mean universal theoretical knowledge of man 'in abstacto'. Its traditional meaning, *gnothi seauton*, meant to know what it is to be human in a personal sense. This usually implied certain humility because we are frail, mortal, and our understanding is limited. The oracle of Apollo said that Socrates was the wisest of men because he had found out for himself that human wisdom has little or no value. (Apology) Much of Wittgenstein's writing was concerned with studying our limits and showing the incoherence of attempts to describe anything beyond them. This was similar to Pope's understanding:

> Know then thyself, presume not God to scan:
> The proper study of mankind is Man.

The contrast between ancient ways of self-knowledge and the techniques of psychoanalysis is enormous. For them self-knowledge was best obtained in the presence of someone who was critical, not in the sense of finding fault, but someone who helped us examine our reasons in order to determine their presuppositions and limits especially when we think about ourselves. They emphasised the importance of responsibility for the proper care of oneself; it cannot be left to the techniques of an outside expert. There are many ways in which we can deceive ourselves, depending on our culture, intelligence and much else.

The technique of giving names and formulae to what has been observed, the nominalising tendency, in which nouns are derived from verbs, is an example of the ascendancy of the object and the concomitant mystification of reality. It is characteristic of the formal and impersonal prose of media news, reports and bureaucratic discourse. It is ideally suited to a discourse which places a premium on the transference of information in as economical way as possible (Orwell 2004). It elides the voice that, active or passive, participates in a particular action and leaves a reified, intransitive and obscure given in its place. My 'ego' acts; my unconscious blinds me.

The elision of agency encourages an unquestioning acceptance of a mystified authority. It provokes uncritical obedience before what is ultimately a political construct. It removes the dignity of self-understanding and covers the tracts of power. It creates a structure as a given, a self-generating and unquestionable system, for example, the psychic apparatus. It conceals human reality which involves events in time, removing the personal from itself. Instead of helping the person to understand his own problems, engaging in his thought in its own sphere and sense, Freud moves it into the universal sphere of theory.

The result is that psychoanalysis becomes an ideology. Freud presents his beliefs, theories and pictures of the mind as inherently connected with universal interests when in fact they are subservient to his desires and the particular interests of psychoanalysis. The ideological illusion is then fostered by the configurations of power set up by the psychoanalytic institutes.

Wittgenstein wrote:

> Psychological concepts are just everyday concepts. They are not concepts newly fashioned by science for its own purpose, as are the concepts of physics and chemistry. Psychological concepts are related to those of the exact sciences as the concepts of the science of medicine are to those of old women who spend their time nursing the sick. (*RPP2* ¶62)

Psychological concepts are developed in the interactions between the child and its carers. A child learning its mother tongue is not learning a psychological theory or a theory of meaning. The human capacity for language depends on the ability to recognise other persons as having intentions like her own and so having an orientation to the world. This ability emerges around 1 year of age across all cultures. Mastery of language depends on many cognitive and learning skills, some of which we share with other primates. The child observes and understands that others have an orientation to the world and can express sounds that make sense, so it wants to join in.

We teach a child 'that is your hand', not 'that is perhaps your hand'. That is how a child learns the innumerable language-games that are concerned with his hand. An investigation or question, 'whether this is really a hand' never occurs to him. Nor, on the other hand, does he learn that he *knows* that this is a hand. (*OC* ¶374)

Discourse concerning the mind is full of verbal pictures, figurative expressions that become part of the regular currency of language. We lose our memories, contain our thoughts, explode with anger, bubble over with happiness, feel horny, have heavy scenes with people, feel there is a void in our life, have lofty thoughts and so on. These words can be expressive when aptly applied and may capture something vital about people. But they do not express a discovery of some entity or process. They are constructions of language which have emerged over time and from the experience of the individual. We use metaphors and figurative expressions about the mind precisely because it does not consist of things and processes. When we use metaphors we are contrasting literal language with what is being said; they show aspects of things but do not literally say what they are.

It is in the way we refer to ourselves in the written or spoken word that offers an insight into our nature. We reflect on what we say and do, or fail to do. It is the immediately seen, heard or felt that is important. We deny the primacy of individual initiation into language once we allow the theoretical and universal to take precedence over the particular and when we infer rather than understand. This can constitute a verbal smoke-screen, which prevents contact with what we actually do, or fail to do.

The talking 'cure'

The talking 'cure' is an exercise in truthfulness; it exposes the ways our imagination can lead to delusion when we are disorientated in our relation to the world. In ordinary experience what is true is thought to be true in so far as it is not actually falsified. Thus, as long as my beliefs about myself are not defeated in experience, I may consider them to be true. I may believe myself to be a reasonable person who is constantly treated unfairly by my employers. In the talking cure it may become evident that I am actually envious and that this accounts for my unhappiness far better than my beliefs. The talking cure undermines conventional beliefs by undoing the framework upon which they are based. It is a destabilising dialectic involving two truths: conventional beliefs, which are expressed in propositions, and the acknowledgement of who we are, which does not depend on conventions and cannot be expressed in propositions but can be revealed by reflection. It is liberating in that it promotes freedom of thought and opens the way to exploring new aspects of ourselves (Baker 2004).

Wittgenstein pointed out:

Our language can be regarded as an ancient city: a maze of little streets and squares, of old and new houses, and of houses with

extensions from various periods, and all this surrounded by a mul-
titude of new suburbs with straight and regular streets and uniform
houses. (*PI* ¶18)

What is needed is clarity in making perspicuous what is obscure because
it is too familiar. This can enable us not to confuse the straight streets
of science with the little winding streets in the city, where we can feel
at home.

Care of oneself calls for the plainest, homely language in which no
word is wasted since it is intimate and the language of the little streets
in the heart of the city. It calls for a response from the therapist using
words perspicaciously, which are simple, and are ideally spoken without a touch of ill-feeling, contempt, arrogance, bias, frivolity, jargon or
word intoxication. This transformational discourse does not call for theories explanations and a technical vocabulary, as it is fundamentally an
ethical struggle.

This struggle is displaced when we construct theories about the 'psychical apparatus', mental processes and suchlike. Take fear. There are
important conceptual differences between reporting one is afraid, in
which we are tempted to imagine we observe a state of mind – our fear –
expressing our fear by trembling and using a shaky voice and confessing
that we are afraid or admitting we are a bit cowardly. All these differ
conceptually from when we pretend to fear, say in acting, or tell lies
about it. Such conceptual differences are important to distinguish in
psychotherapy and depend on tone of voice, gestures, the context and
our knowledge of ourselves and others. Since 'fear' has many meanings,
according to the language-games in which it occurs, reducing them to
psychical processes occurring in a mental apparatus in the inner world
is a gross simplification (*PI* pp. 160–1; Canfield 2007).

The twisty streets of the old city must not be blown up in the belief
that there should be an inner extension of the straight ordered suburbs. Artificial languages and the formalised constructs of science can
help us map sub-personal structures but to understand a person living
her life we must respect the tangled and contradictory structures of the
old city.

> The criteria for the truth of the *confession* that I thought such and
> such are not the criteria for a true *description* of a process. And the
> importance of the true confession does not reside in its being a cor-
> rect and certain report of some process. It resides, rather, in the special
> consequences which can be drawn from a confession whose truth is
> guaranteed by the special criteria of *truthfulness*. (*PI*, PPF ¶319)

Much of Wittgenstein's writing can be read as a confession. He often uses phrases like 'I want to say ...', 'I feel like saying ...', 'Here the urge is strong ...'. The voices of temptation and truthfulness are the antagonists in his dialogues. He confesses he is subject to inclinations and compulsions that one can recognise and question. Like most ancient philosophers and in marked contrast to psychoanalysis, he thought that pride is one of the greatest obstacles to understanding. It is not lack of intelligence but the presence of pride that gets in the way of genuine understanding in much philosophy and therapy. For pride involves lying to oneself because we may want to be something we are not, or conversely, not want to be something we are.

> One *cannot* speak the truth; if one has not yet conquered oneself.
> One *cannot* speak it – but not, because one is still not clever enough.
> (*CV* p. 41)

It is truthfulness rather than discovery that we are concerned with in the talking cure, and this requires dialogue, confession and acknowledgement. As Ben Jonson wrote, 'Language most shewes a man, speake that I may see thee' (Jonson 1947, line 2520).

3
Talking versus Writing

The fundamental practice of psychotherapy is an activity in which people speak and listen to one another, trying to be truthful. Reading books and giving instructions are secondary. Freud acknowledged that psychoanalysis is a talking cure; but he was a prolific writer and creator of theories, which involve writing. He tended to elaborate his theories at the end of the day after seeing his patients. Instead of attending rigorously to the practice of the talking cure, where the full resonance of oral utterance, imbued with the personality, gestures, tone of voice and physical presence of the speaker is at play, he conjured this away into the abstract impersonality and sheer silence of marks on paper, depicting theories and explanations of what he imagined had taken place.

The literature on psychoanalysis and psychotherapy is vast. The authors of this literature usually distinguish themselves by the particular theory they hold and presumably believe that their theories can convey directly what is essential to their thought and practice. Writing rather than talking prevails.

It may be helpful to remind ourselves of the development of writing, what it can and cannot convey, to see some of the losses and gains of the change from an oral culture to a literate one.

Development of writing

Writing systems had multiple origins. The earliest known developed in the fourth millennium B.C. probably in southern Iraq and Egypt, in China prior to 1000 B.C. and in early Mesoamerica around 500 B.C. It is likely that each culture developed it independently, as a product of social practices within particular cultural settings and power structures. Small-scale societies used signs, as mnemonic devices to represent ideas and signs to record names, long before writing itself developed. Writing, however, records speech. It was an invention, a technological break-through, not a result of evolution as was once thought (Houston 2004). As the Sumerians put it, spoken language is the gift of the gods, whereas writing is a human creation (Glassner 2003, p. 9). In modern terms, speech developed over thousands of years, being heavily dependent on changes in the brain and evolution, whereas writing was invented and designed over a few hundred years, used at first mostly for administrative purposes to record information and calculate as cities were being built. But it was also used for display and prestige. Writing looses much of the expressive powers of speech. The invention of writing was rather like the current development of information technology. Both require a rigorous system of rules and conventions which inform the creation of signs to form a system. The scribes who invented writing, like computer programmers, had to be fully aware of these. Languages standardise when they are written down. The grammar and phonetics of speech have only been articulated in the last two thousand years or so by specialists. For thousands of years before, people spoke but had no rules of speech, pronunciation or grammar although, of course, they could recognise deviations from the norm. Language was then a network of dialects.

Writing was not a mere transcription of oral utterances; it was a delib-erate attempt to create a new mode of communication involving signs and it led to a reshaping of our understanding of the world. Before writ-ing people had graphic systems: dancing, cave paintings, tattoos on the body, drumming, etc. These developed at the same time as speech. The earliest scripts consisted of picture signs, that is, greatly simplified pic-tures of objects such as the sun, moon, rivers, trees, people, etc. Then phonograms developed, which were marks for particular sounds, such as 'b' and 't' in 'bat'. Some of the earliest writing combines writing and figures. The Narmer palette, an early example of writing, combines a pic-ture of the King of Egypt smiting his enemies, with his name, Narmer, in hieroglyphs.

Mathematics led the way to writing; no society that could not count beyond three ever achieved writing by its own efforts (Harris 1986, p. 133). The human race had to become numerate in order to become literate. Numbers have no natural existence; they require the ability to count, which rests on the repetition of an identical act and making marks, such as |||| or - - - -, to record these acts. Numbers are an amal-gam of identifying, naming and making marks. These are requisite for literacy. The use of marks on bones to record numbers, say of sheep or goats, was an early use of writing. Later a separate sign was made for groups of numbers; so instead of having a picture of a sheep with 60 marks after it, one could have a sign for a sheep with a mark for 60. The rebus principle was vital in later developments: for example, in English the picture of the sun, say a circle with rays coming from the circumference, could be employed as a rebus for the word 'son'. So graphic signs could be endowed with syllabic value.

As writing developed it tended to become more abstract. Thus Egyptian hieroglyphs are mostly pictographic signs, representing people, animals, plants or buildings. In the 'alphabetical' revolution they were rendered in Greek-derived alphabetical script (Coptic). Coptic is the ancient Egyptian language rendered alphabetically by the Copts who were Christians. It is significant that it was the script, rather than the language, that became a symbol of heathendom, of the old religious order, which the new-revealed religion of Christianity aimed to overcome. Christianity and therefore the West became obsessed with the superiority of alphabetic writing. They believed words accurately represented sounds, repressing the fact that writing involves its own signs and is creative in its own right. It is not just a reflection of speech. Even the most phonetically consistent and efficient alphabet cannot completely spell out an intonation, or a tone of voice or the context of irony. Spelling does not consistently reflect pronunciation – for example, compare 'fluff' with 'enough'.

Many cultures, such as Chinese, Japanese and ancient Egyptian, kept the graphic element in their writing and can reveal meaning without recourse to rigid phonetic structures. The word is not exclusively a matter of sound or sight. Graphic writing encourages a different relation to language from an alphabetical script. There is a greater fluidity of meaning in their texts than in the more literal alphabetical scripts which tend to encourage simplistic notions of meaning such as 'this (a word) means that (an object pointed out)'. The visual text has an artistic dimension, a fact recognised by oriental and Islamic cultures which developed calligraphy to a fine art. Hand writing, as opposed to print, does however reveal character, as in the craft of graphology, for example. Modern techniques of word processing are transforming writing again. It is becoming an exploration of verbal possibilities made available by electronic word processors, rather than a mere reflection of verbal communication.

The signs in writing are graphic differences; we must be able to distinguish one letter or character from another. These signs must be written somewhere, usually on paper, and must be able to be seen. We cannot read an illegible hand. The signs constitute a notation, such as the alphabet. But reading and writing require more than a notation; they require a script. A script is a structure which is a system of differences determined by tradition. Thus English, French and Italian have the same notation but are very different scripts (Harris 2000). A script may not bear any relation to pronunciation; thus Chinese characters can be read throughout China, in spite of big differences between the dialects which in speech are mutually unintelligible.

The main point about writing for our purposes is that it was primarily designed for the storage of information and calculating for administrative purposes. Since it decontextualises from the to-and-fro of dialogue, meaning can become divorced from use. It was only after long experience in using writing that societies began to learn to use it to express themselves in poetry, novels and so on (Houston 2004, p. 83).

Reading

Writing involves reading. In the early days of writing reading was essentially passive. It involved reading tallies, dispatches, legal documents and proclamations. It enabled the reader to retrieve simple accounts or information, or to recall something that had been committed to memory. Legends, myths and incantations were rarely written down. But with the consonantal alphabet and writing's diffusion from the Middle East, reading became easier and more advanced ways of reading developed. Instead of being read to by trained slaves or reading aloud to friends, one read silently to oneself. The scope of literacy gradually enlarged to reading religious texts or novels.

But in the ancient world reading was by no means regarded as an innocuous process in which we can 'take in' the truth about ourselves. The reader was seen as 'passive' in that he is 'subjected' to the writing. Thus on a kylix vessel found in Sicily and dating from 500 B.C. we read, 'The writer of the inscription will "bugger" (*pugíxei*) the reader' (Svenbro 1993). There is plenty of evidence that the Greeks and Romans saw the relation between the writer and the reader as a pederastic relationship between a lover and his beloved. The dominant and active partner is in opposition to the dominated and passive. Among the Romans there are many inscriptions such as 'the one who will write is the lover, the one who will read gets buggered (*amat qui scribet pedicatur qui leget*)' (Ibid., p. 190).

The responsibility of the dominant partner was to improve and educate, while the dominated had to submit, to give pleasure without seeking it and to remain faithful. As Dover observes, 'acceptance of the teacher's thrusting penis between his thighs or in the anus is the fee which the pupil pays for good teaching' (Dover 1989, p. 91).

To read was to submit to what the writer had written, therefore to be dominated. So reading among the Greeks tended to be done by slaves. A free man, a citizen, had to be sure not to identify with the role of reader. It was best to remain 'poor at reading', that is to say, capable of reading but no more.

Reading was a topic which Wittgenstein repeatedly discussed, as it involves questions about meaning, understanding, and learning skills (e.g. *PI* ¶¶156–78, 375–6). He shows that neither mechanical nor mentalistic theories help us to understand the vast terrain involved in reading. He noted the difference between a person who serves as a 'reading machine', vocalising correctly but without understanding the text (a slave), and one who understands. This raises the question as to just what understanding is and how to spot it. What is the relation between the sound of a word and its meaning? Is there a causal connection between the two? Can we identify the first word that is read and not imitated by a child learning to read? Does the child then have the feeling 'now I can read'? When we read a text without sound, does it change its meaning? Wittgenstein shows there is a huge variety of subjective phenomena that can accompany reading aloud but there is no uniform type of experience which would serve as a definition of reading. It is a skill that is connected with the situation in which it takes place. It is a capacity in which we must be free to make up our mind as to whether we are reading. (A good account is given in Ammereller and Fischer 2004, pp. 86–126; Harré and Tissaw 2005, pp. 90–107.)

Writing enables meanings to be created that are not possible with speech alone. Mathematics, most modern science, and large parts of literature could not develop without it. For example, how could one represent the square root of minus one on an abacus? Mathematics depends on its notations, figures, graphs and equations, which are manipulated according to rules that determine the meanings. Or how could one convey the meanings of Joyce's *Finnegans Wake* if it were not written in a book, since it would be impossible to memorise? Writing enables the storing of vast amounts of information and encourages the forming of lists and elaborate classifications. The signs are detached from the writer so they survive through time and can be distributed over space (Goody 1987). It enabled people to 'speak' from beyond the grave. For example, a fifth century B.C. Greek inscription goes:

> Salutations, O passer by! I rest, dead, under here. You who draw near, read out who is the man buried here: a stranger from Aegina, Mnesitheos by name.... (Svenbro 1993, p. 48)

At this early stage in history the readers have to lend their voice by reading the letters aloud, so that these letters can transmit the words that the inscribed object is saying. The words are not divorced from a speaker.

Speaking and writing

Societies that do not use writing do not readily assume that the speaker is an individual author as do literate ones. In ethnographic societies narrative is never assumed by a person but by a mediator, shaman, or reciter. The reciter or shaman is seen as a voice in the service of some other. He was a master of truth and his 'truth' was a performative truth, that is, it was a truth that did not depend on agreement between a proposition and its object (Detienne 1996). Thus a shaman in a trance does not simply tell stories of gods and men of the past; he reactivates them.

Similarly the reciter does not claim to be a speaking subject, or the originator of his words. The voice is separated from the shaman's person; he is a conduit for the words of an other, perhaps the Muse. The heroic epic poet, for example, Homer, understands his words to be a verbal monument that effects 'undying fame'. He is a master of the code of Greek epic, and his words invoke a tradition, but he is not its source. The speaker of the Homeric poem is totally dependent on indexicals for their identity, as for example, *Tell me Muse* .... Whoever activates the narratives of the *Iliad* and *Odyssey* is no one and everyone (Kahane 2005). His words embody power regardless of any speaker. The referend of the indexical is merely the activator of the power of words, not their source. The words themselves are assumed to contain power to produce certain effects that can be released if they are said rightly.

The concept of an author who was solely responsible for what he wrote emerged in the Middle Ages (Foucault 1977, pp. 113–38). Foucault argues that the author-function is not formed spontaneously but depends on complex operations, whose purpose is to construct a rational entity, called an author. Thus a 'philosopher' and a 'poet' are not constructed in the same manner; what is decided to include in their works differs. A poet's love letters may be of great importance in understanding him but few would think a philosopher's of interest.

The place a text was written in was also important: The context in which it was recorded became part of its meaning. Thus in ancient Egypt, texts were not in books but on mummy bandages, shrouds, coffins, tomb walls, papyri kept in special places, stelae, statues, offering tables and so forth. Their place and context correlated with what they were supposed to say and do. Texts in the coffin, where they were inaccessible, were magical, whereas texts that were accessible to the living were to be recited as part of a liturgy.

Writing and speech are related through scribbles. In a famous experiment by Luria (quoted in Harris 1998, p. 263) some illiterate children were, with the help of pencil and paper, able to recall and distinguish sentences more accurately than when relying on aural memory alone. The marks on the paper were mere scribbles, apparently undifferentiated, but they enabled the child to identify and distinguish between dictated items. The puzzle is, can we say the child is making an attempt at an objective recording of what it hears or are the set of marks a creative expression of the texture of things between the child and the reader? It would be question begging to insist that a sentence cannot be written down unless the written marks reflected the linear structure of the spoken sentence.

A similar phenomenon is found in Winnicott's Squiggle Game which he used as a way of communicating with children (Winnicott 1971a). He would make a squiggle on a piece of paper and then invite the child to add another squiggle to it and so they would create various images together. They would talk about what these squiggles reminded them of, which would often be of considerable significance. As Winnicott acknowledged (ibid., pp. 9–10), this was a creative achievement between the two and not an interpretation of the unconscious, which is assumed to exist in a prior form, in psychoanalysis.

Speaking enables us to determine what the *speaker* expresses by his utterance. The musicality, pitch, rhythm and timbre of the voice reveal him to those who can hear. Writing and print, on the other hand, are detached from their sender and have a stable physical presence on paper, or computer disc. The focal question then becomes what the *words* mean, as they are detached from their original context. This provokes a gradual shift from the intentional to the conventional aspects of linguistic meaning. The preliterate equation of language and speech is destroyed. Reification becomes a temptation, as the words can be seen as self-sufficient interpretable objects and language as a complicated object, which has an existence in its own right apart from people. Dictionaries and grammar books, if not properly understood, reduce language to an apparent stable form, the words and rules being taken as representing a fixed meaning. Thus in an oral culture people tend to think in practical units, in a context, that is, what is a good thing now, rather than abstract notions such as THE GOOD.

Meaning and writing

When meaning is cut loose from the speaker or writer, writing easily becomes a substitute for thinking which it displaces, and usurps its truth. This was an important theme in Plato's *Phaedrus* (274c–275e) in which he makes the Egyptian King Thamus say to Theuth, the mythical inventor of writing, the following:

> For your invention will produce forgetfulness in the souls of those who have learned it, through lack of practice at using their memory, as through reliance on writing they are reminded from outside by alien marks, not from inside, themselves by themselves: you have discovered an elixir not of memory but of reminding. To your students you give an appearance of wisdom, not the reality of it; having heard much, in the absence of teaching, they will appear to know much when for the most part they know nothing.... (Trans. C.J. Rowe)

Plato begins the third section of the *Phaedrus*, which is concerned with the relationship between the written and spoken word at 257e where he observes, 'the proudest of statesmen are most fond of writing and of leaving documents behind them in order to perpetuate their names for wisdom.' He points out, however, that no man who is serious about wisdom and self-knowledge will write about them in ink, or sow his thoughts with written words (276c). For words, once written, preserve a solemn silence when questioned, or they keep on saying the same thing. 'For when you ask a piece of writing what it means, it can only answer you with the words that you read in the writing' (275c). At best the words are a reminder to the man or woman who knows the subjects to which the things written relate. For Plato, truthfulness is no dead word and no authority, however venerable, is a substitute for the *living and breathing word* (Cushman 1958, pp. 305–9; Szlezak 1999, pp. 39–46).

Plato wrote that those who are enamoured with the written word, or are overcome by the rhetorical power of speech, suffer 'paralysis of the head' (*paraluein-kephalos* 227a), an immobility and enfeeblement of the mind. It is an illness; the person is 'ravished' or 'carried away' (*harpasai* 229b5) by the word, for the word has erotic power. This ravishment leads nowhere, except to 'paralysis of the head', or, as we now say, 'being in the head'. Compare: 'One of the most dangerous of ideas for a philosopher is, oddly enough, that we think with our heads or in our heads' (Z ¶605).

This mad demand to read books, absorb what is written, and consequently suffer 'paralysis of the head' requires a cure. Plato sketches a way. It involves a critical consideration of speech and writing, especially the art of rhetoric. Only by seeing what the spoken or written word *cannot* say will enable us to move out of our heads into the world. Philosophical writing, Plato suggests, should stimulate our neglect of remembering what words cannot say. The written word must encourage us to discover its dangers and deficiencies. The charm of the written word must be transformed from lulling us into dogmatic slumber to what awakens thought. One way is to use the form of dialogue as Plato and Wittgenstein often do (Geir 2002, pp. 143–215).

Memory and thoughtfulness are linked; it is this link that prevents the destructiveness of mere ideas. Memory (Latin *memor*, mindful) is 'thinking back', and thinking back is remembering. Many cultures respect the intimacy between memory and thought, especially scholastic ones. Thus European Medieval and Tibetan contemporary culture combine both writing and orality in a creative way. Dreyfus (2003) observed that in the education of a Tibetan monk, learning texts by heart was an important discipline. They would recite texts out loud, rocking their body back and forth, often to a tune to which the words were set. This makes the text penetrate the mind and become near to gesture. At this stage they were not expected to understand the text. Later, for some, the deeper meaning becomes apparent; knowledge becomes active and thoughtful rather than being itemised bits of information, which have to be taken from storage somewhere in the mind. This way of learning develops the attention span and encourages knowledge to become embodied. Debate on the texts is also part of the curriculum. There is relentless questioning of the meaning of the text, reconstructing the question to which the text is a reply. This helps students to understand the limits of concepts and ideas and encourages a dialogical exchange between reader and text, orality and literacy.

As Wittgenstein wrote in his diary:

> One often thinks – and I myself often make this mistake – that everything one thinks can be written down. In reality one can only write down – that is, without doing something that is stupid & inappropriate – what arises in us in the form of writing. (*PPO* p. 35)

Psychoanalysis and writing

The contrast with psychoanalysis is very great. Freud mostly wrote for everybody, like a scientist who communicates facts directly to readers. The psychoanalyst has special knowledge and questioning by an ordinary person is often seen as a sign of resistance and neurosis. Freud, in contrast to Plato, ignored the erotic power of his own writing and authoritarianism, even though he wrote a lot about sexuality, seeming to believe that because he wrote 'scientifically', it would have no erotic attraction. He made repeated claims that only psychoanalysis has the 'real' scientific truth about what drives us, ignoring the suggestive power of these claims. Truth shows itself if we attend rightly, to be persuaded of a truth is not to see it.

Freud created a highly suggestive special vocabulary which required technical knowledge to understand and emphasised the special position of the analyst. We do not question experts on a subject we are unfamiliar with. Thus the neurotic 'would become healthy if the conflict between his ego and his libido came to an end and if his ego had his libido again at its disposal' (Freud 1916–17, p. 383). This sounds very neat and learned yet is difficult to bring down to earth, as it is an enormous generalisation and filled with metaphysical implications.

'What *we* do is to bring words back from their metaphysical to their everyday use' (*PI* ¶116). This is done by persuading us to look and see how we use particular words to describe things. We talk about being happy and enjoying life, finding what we do as fulfiling and seeing our friends as being fulfiled. There are subtle criteria which help us to judge. So what does it add to say our *ego had his libido again at his disposal?* Can we dispose of our libidinal impulses just as we like? Why is Freud not content to stick to the familiar use in its particular context? Why is he *driven* to say something different? Why does he not see that there are many ways of describing happiness and mental pain depending on context, culture and much else?

Freud was subject to the metaphysical urge to seek the essence of things; to dig down to a once-and-for-all answer, which is above all particularity. This diverts attention from the particular case with its unique context, which is, above all, seen in dialogue with people. It is blind to the way psychological concepts are dependent on patterns of life. When, for example, is a smile a smirk, a pretence, a 'fixed' smile or genuine? It is difficult not to see the motive for this in Freud's life, his craving for fame and his belief, shared by many in his culture, that the scientific method was on the way to possess the final truth about the human mind.

The metaphysical urge to seek the essence of things, hidden by the use of jargon, is often used to denigrate opponents. Thus in Winnicott's review of Jung's *Memories, Dreams, Reflections*, he states that Jung is a 'recovered case of infantile psychosis' (Winnicott 1964, p. 483). He asserts that, 'whatever Freud was, he had a unit personality, with a place in him for his unconscious. Jung was different. It is not possible for a split personality to have an unconscious, because there is no place for it to be' (Ibid.). Of course Jungians could make Freud equally pathological by using their jargon.

The seductive powers of the written word are especially obvious in psychoanalysis. Books containing 'original ideas' about it are extremely popular. A well-known example is Masud Khan, an eminent psycho-analyst, who wrote many books admired by the psycho-analytic community. But after his death it came to light that he had behaved appallingly to his patients and to others. He had numerous affairs with his patients, took control of them and their families and was a chronic liar and alcoholic (Hopkins 2008). There is little understanding in psychoanalysis that bright ideas put forth in books have little to do with therapy.

The idealist stance towards language shared by psychoanalysts abolishes answerability and so truth. Truth depends on answerability. In the natural sciences, it depends on how nature responds to observation and experiment; among humans on how we answer a claim to a truth about ourselves asserted by someone. But psychoanalysts assume their language is true in itself, by definition. They have no place for *agreement in judgement* (PI ¶242). So they can explain anyone who disagrees with them without recourse to investigation. Examples are the 'primitiveness' of tribal people, without bothering to learn their language and talk to them; religious beliefs without attempting to understand what they may be trying to express; and of course rival psychotherapies.

Writing easily encourages this metaphysical urge as it reminds us of its ancient magical use to carve the ruler's unquestionable edicts in stone. Since it isolates from the context of speaking it is not bound to the interactional contexts in the way speech is. A conversation is 'loose'; we do not usually know what we will say before we have said it; misunderstandings and disappointments of communication come by chance; we may not know what to say, how to answer. These gaps show the space between us, the reality of our being neither one nor two.

The exaltation of writing over speech leads to the obliteration of timeliness by space. Freud tried to map psychological space where the various structures in this space served to explain behaviour and determine what it is like to be a particular person. Writing and reading about people tell us what they are.

Writing encourages the idea that language is an object, a self-contained system that is context free. It leads to a focus on finding internal mechanisms by which it is supposed to work as a device for encoding and decoding information about an objectively given extra-linguistic world. However, every oral utterance is unique in respect to its context, pronunciation, and meaning. Theoretical units of language such as phonemes, morphemes and sentences are not. These invariants are difficult to pin down, especially in speech, and there is no general agreement among linguists as to what these are when all the thousands of languages in the world are considered. What we count as a word in English may be very different from what might count as a word in Zulu. Many early manuscripts use *scriptio continuo*, which is a continuous stream of letters. 'Words' are not marked off in this form of writing, any more than they are phonetically in speech with silences.

The introduction of writing and its propagation in the mechanically produced written book, in which the text supplies its own context, opened a conceptual gap between sentence and utterance (Harris 2000). As a written sentence has a physical existence that is independent of a speaker or writer, we cannot refer to them to understand what is meant. Once meaning comes to be understood as residing in the words themselves, the text takes on a life of its own. The relevance of intimacy between speaker and hearer to the meaning of the exchange is forgotten. This leads to a change in the notion of meaning. It is cut loose and assumed to lie either behind both sentence and utterance, for example, in psychoanalysis in the unconscious, or in cognitive therapy meaning becomes purely functional. The contribution to meaning of gestures, silences and the shifting patterns of tempo, stress and pitch in speech is ignored.

Freud was wedded to the written word. Not only did he produce a vast amount of writing telling us the meaning of his patients' dreams and symptoms, but also grand generalisations about the meaning of civilisation, religion, art and morality. He was a prolific writer – it has been estimated that he wrote about one letter every 2 days of his 83 years (Eissler 1980). He listened to his patients' words, but what any of us hear cannot be described and written about in the same way as it is heard.

The reduction of language to precise lines in the development of the printed book allowed only a narrow segment of sense to dominate the other senses (McLuhen 1962). It has been suggested that the rise of the 'discovery' of the unconscious was a result of this restriction of conscious life within the limits of print technology (Whyte 1960).

Oral culture makes it difficult to make a rigid separation between 'body' and 'mind'.

Psychoanalysis distinguishes verbal from nonverbal communication, the body from the mind. In order to recognise these distinctions, we have already adopted a perspective which assumes it is legitimate to identify one communication system by implicit reference to another. It assumes that our communicational universe is determinate and can be mapped into discrete types of communication – verbal and nonverbal, reporting and acting (Harris 1996, pp. 25–8). But to be involved with a child learning to speak should destroy this myth; gestures, grunts, actions and speech come together as she learns to speak. What counts as a word is very arbitrary and what counts as reporting is only one use of language. Our judgements as to the truthfulness of speech or not depends on the coming together of speech and gesture, 'body' and 'mind'.

Speaking and gesture

Language is radically indeterminate. It is not a set of containers in which to bottle up meanings. The traditional description of speech by analysis breaks it into units that are static, discrete and context-free. The theory of meaning that underpins psychoanalysis is that these units are combined by a finite set of rules which give structure to our speech. This in turn generates specifications of statements such that for each there is exactly one structure to determine a given meaning.

There are many difficulties with this way of understanding language and meaning (Kripke 1982; Harris 1988, 2003; Travis 2008), the chief being the problematic of the passage from the semiotic to the semantic. It would appear that the structures that constitute the semiotic would generate exactly one statement to fit. So to understand *the* meaning of a statement we need to only look at the structure determining it. Semiology would map directly onto the semantic. It is questionable if this makes sense. Linguistic elements such as phonemes subsist without any real denotation since they acquire this in actual discourse. The sign is constituted in the context of the situation. Meaning is occasion-sensitive. We need to look outside the speech circuit to understand meaning. Much of what we say is conventional so we take the context for granted. Thus if someone says 'I am at home,' it may mean she is in her flat, but what if there is an earthquake and her block of flats is sliding down a precipice, would she feel at home? Or what if she is in a foreign hotel but she feels at home there, etc.? If we are to understand meaning, language cannot be segregated from all forms of non-linguistic communication, for speech is underpinned by it.

A consideration of American Sign Language (ASL), mainly used by deaf people, may make this clearer. It has been established that ASL is a natural human language, more or less independent of the spoken language in the same region (Armstrong et al. 1995). It has its own syntax and grammar which are not grounded in the phonetic structures of speech. The link between language and sound is not indispensable. The question arises as to what is common to spoken and signed language? Is this meaning? Gestures are perhaps the earliest events that are meaningful. Gestures are visible and sign language uses visible actions rather than sounds to make words. These actions signify directly and show their meaning. Signs for eating, drinking, hitting with a fist and throwing a small object seem to be universal. Other ones, such as the sign for a gun, depend on the particular culture.

Speech is profoundly gestural. Infants are very sensitive to the sounds and patterns of speech. They learn to respond to the rising pitch of question and surprise, the falling pitch of declaration and the music and dance of language. They are attentive to the gestures that go with gender, position in the social hierarchy, affection, rejection and so on, and these are accompanied by particular patterns of speech. Dance, too, is gestural and infants respond to simple dances and catch onto their meaning. Babies use gestures long before they can speak. They can point, grab, pull, yell, make animal noises and creative gestures meaning 'no', 'up' and many others. Even young blind children gesture while communicating. Gestures may well constitute the roots of language.

Language development studies show that what is acquired at first is not a grammar consisting of a complex system of units and the combinatorial relations between them. A basic urge in humans is to communicate with one another. We first learn to speak to one another; in time certain patterns of speech become customary and so can become grammatised.

The symbolic dimension of language is equally important. Thus, deaf children acquiring a signed language learn it as quickly as hearing children learning a vocal language (Tomasello 2003, pp. 35–6).

Language is a normative activity, a vital activity of human beings. It is part of the human organism that arose in the course of evolution from the pre-existing social activities seen in chimpanzees. From about 9 months of age, children, in contrast to other primates, are able to share attention with and imitatively learn from another human. They both know that they are attending to the same thing; it is not joint attention if they are both focussed on the same thing yet are unaware of the partner. Joint activities are necessary for language to develop (Tomasello 2003). This was noted long ago by Aristotle:

Therefore a man ought also to share his friend's consciousness of his existence, and this is attained by their living together and by conversing and communicating their thoughts to each other; and this is the meaning of living together as applied to human beings, it does not mean merely feeding in the same place, as it does when applied to cattle. (Aristotle 1926, 1170b, 10)

The child is subject to the adult who initiates him; he cannot question his authority or humanity. This is of huge importance. For supposing the authority is deviant, for example, beating the child whenever it smiles. Here the child will learn a very different language of feeling and emotion than is usual. Similarly if children are treated 'like cattle' they will have difficulty in developing the human language of love and desire.

Gesture and ritual

Gesture and ritual are closely entwined. Small children love ritual – the ritual of going to bed, having a story read, etc. Ritual is vital in early learning. For example, the ritual of nursery rhymes, such as 'One two, buckle my shoe, three four, open the door...', is the beginning of our initiation into mathematics.

Rituals cannot be explained in functional terms as Freud tried to do, following Fraser (Freud 1912–13). They are not done for a specific purpose – they are not primarily means to some specific end, although they can be used for that. When a ritual is meaningful its rules are not felt to be imposed by the participants. This contrasts with obsessional 'rituals' in which the sufferer feels compelled to act, or think in certain ways. If I say a prayer, wishing that my child will recover from a serious illness, this would be superstitious and obsessional only if I believed the prayer useless should it fail to fulfil my wish. A prayer is not the same as a medicine; God is not a super-doctor. A ritual of kissing the picture of someone we love is not based on opinions, hypotheses, or beliefs that it will have a specific effect on the person in the picture. It aims at nothing at all but is satisfying as it is part of our natural history; it is instinctive. 'In the ancient rites we have the use of an extremely developed gesture language' (*PO* p. 135). They are a matter of *rite words in rote order* as Joyce put it. There is a good deal of evidence that the sacred, the numinous and the divine are creations of ritual (Rappaport 1999).

There is a strongly ritualistic element in psychoanalysis – the regular sessions, the same place and person, the analyst confined to his chair, concentration on a few unquestionable themes such as the Oedipus Complex. The analyst behaves like a highly sanctified sign in the discourse of a liturgical order. Thus in Polynesia the high chiefs, the ali'is, are

> thought to be free of desire, precisely like the gods. That is why they are characterized by immobility and inactivity...the highest point of etiquette among illustrious Hawaiians was, not to move. Laziness for a high ranking ali'i is a duty not a vice; it is a manifestation of his absolute plenitude, of the absence of any lack, and moreover, of perfect self-control. The prescription of immobility helps explain why divine ali'is do not walk but are carried.... (Rappaport 1999, p. 333)

This is not far from Bion's ideal that psychoanalysis depends on disciplined denial of memory and desire (Bion 1970, p. 41). The psychoanalyst is confined to his chair, the patient to the couch; this is part of the ritual. Another part is that everything must be put into words while gesture tends to be seen as acting out. Freud was blind to the logic of ritual and gesture. Thus ritual was explained by him as being obsessional, its meaning lying in the unconscious. The therapeutic frame, however, creates a space and a legitimating *gravitas* which is very much like the set-apart spaces of ritual that enable the evocation of invisible agents. In psychoanalysis these agents are internal objects and archetypes (Davies 2009, pp. 81–3).

Gesture and ritual are not referential, in contrast to propositions. Our first utterances are gestures and so logically cannot be an utterance about something antecedently given. Suppose we point to a doll and say 'dolly' to a child being initiated into language. Are we telling him what a doll is or what the word 'dolly' means? The child, at this stage, does not know what naming is – it cannot ask: 'What is this called?' while pointing to it. Nor does it have a concept of an entity such as 'doll'; for to know that, it must be able to distinguish dolls from teddy-bears and other toys, know that dolls are not alive, and so on. It seems that we cannot answer the question in the intellectual terms of teaching them either what a name is or what the concept of doll is.

This is why it is better to say the early learning of language is an initiation as the child is learning to take part in the human way of life. The child begins to understand both what a name is and what the names of things are, that is, what a dolly is and what it is called. It is learning how to express the wish for a dolly and what expressing a wish is. It is not learning in the ordinary sense in which we know what it is we are learning; here the things we are learning are already constituted. It is by taking part in human life that a child becomes initiated into the use of language.

Language is woven into our actions. Our relation to the world is neither primarily cognitive, nor is our language representational. Language arises from our practical involvement with the world and people. The meaning-bearing elements of language do not mirror the world but depend on our involvement in practices from which meaning is acquired. When we say 'dolly' to the child it initiates certain actions: perhaps it puts out its hands to cuddle it and as the child reacts in certain ways, we respond using more words and gestures. By its actions the child shows us that it is getting the hang of how we speak about and treat dolls. It is only much later in development that the child learns how to ask the name of things and perhaps invent its own name for them (Cavell 1979, pp. 168–90). Speaking can remind us of this weaving between language, gesture, and action much more than writing. This is why speech is important in psychotherapy.

Wittgenstein, speaking and writing

Wittgenstein was very aware of the advantages of speaking over writing in philosophy. He very rarely gave a lecture and mostly taught in his rooms or those of a friend, to small groups of interested people. His talks were informal, he seldom had any notes and often would ask for help from his audience or answer their questions. Gesture, long silences, plain language, fairy stories, humorous descriptions and analogies all played a part in his teaching. He made full use of the expressive power of speech.

Both the *Tractatus* and *Philosophical Investigations* were crafted by him at length and painfully to convey the limits of knowledge and the limitations of language for expressing the world. Electronic editions of Wittgenstein's papers show how his remarks form a complex network of interconnected structures, far more like a conversation than a structured book. The clarification of concepts in Wittgenstein also involves changes of context, seeing different patterns of use, negotiating and renegotiating expressions, all of which may open different ways of thought (Baker 2004, pp. 179–204; Schulte 2006).

Attention to conceptual patterns and linguistic commitments are an essential part of the talking cure. This fluidity contrasts with the case history in psychoanalysis in which the analyst gives a linear story of what he thought happened, and how it fits his theory.

The importance of truthfulness, the living and breathing word, is shown in Wittgenstein's basic distrust of thoughts that did not come spontaneously. His friend Engelmann wrote: 'the "spontaneous idea" was so decisive for him that he would only recognise a philosophical proposition of his own if it had spontaneously occurred to him in the right words' (Engelman 1967, p. 89). Of course it might need a long struggle before the right words come. It is style that reveals whether the words are truthful and the thinker at one with his language; whether the words are grounded or artificial, abstract and technical.

Writing the right style means, setting the carriage precisely on the rails. (*CV* p. 44)

4
The Critical Method

Wittgenstein was concerned with the place of language in human life and the ways it can mislead. He uses various methods for the clarification of language use. Their task is the removal of illusions and dogmatic beliefs, not to make discoveries. They do not depend on developing a specialist technique or vocabulary for describing peculiar mental objects and processes. Ordinary language is good enough. Language is a historically changing phenomenon, where problems arise and re-arise in particular historical and personal settings and have to be dealt with in these. There can be no fixed set of methods for clarification.

> There is not *a* philosophical method, though there are indeed methods, like different therapies. (*PI* ¶133)

An important point for Wittgenstein was not so much the matter but the manner of speaking and thinking. This brings him into touch with literature and music, as well as mathematics. He wrote more on mathematics than on psychology and considered that his investigations in mathematics were analogous to those in psychology (*PI* ¶¶372). In both the nature of logic and rule-following were of central concern. Thus, in mathematics, a short proof is usually better than a long one and elegance is important. Much the same could be said of psychotherapeutic interventions. The nature of signs, notations, diagrams and codes is critical to both. To give a simple example, try dividing a large number using Roman numerals and then Arabic ones! Mathematicians freely invent new numbers: when certain polynomial equations cannot be solved with natural numbers, or even with real numbers, they construct complex numbers and, thereby, solve the equation. Sometimes it is convenient to consider a straight line as part of a circle, so they may define a straight line as the circumference of a circle with an infinite radius. Psychotherapists too invent new theories and pictures to help clarify confusion.

Many scientists and philosophers have thought of mathematics as a building whose foundations are solid. The philosophy of mathematics, however, is a wonderful proof-field for general epistemological ideas, as it shows most of our doctrines founder in one way or another (Putnam 1995, pp. 499–511). The emergence of modern mathematics is linked to the abandonment of traditional claims of absolute truth about its axioms, proofs and body of knowledge. Computer proofs have uncertainty built into them. It is the complexity of mathematical practice which has opened the question as to the nature of mathematical knowledge. A frequent mistake of both mathematicians and psychotherapists has been to assert the existence of things, without being clear as to what they mean by existence. Neither mathematics nor psychotherapy are idealised collections of theories, with mathematical objects in an ideal space or internal objects in an ideal mind, waiting to be pinpointed by human beings. Both are practices (Ferreiros and Gray 2006, Introduction). If this is understood we would be sceptical of claims, such as Bion's (1970) that psychoanalysis could be a system of eternal truths waiting, in some third realm, to be discovered.

> Philosophical clarity will have the same effect on the growth of mathematics as sunlight has on the growth of potato shoots. (In a dark cellar they grow yards long). (*PG* p. 381)

This applies equally to psychotherapy.

Wittgenstein sought to *change the aspect* under which we look at mathematics so we no longer see it as something that needs foundations but as a motley of techniques and practices we employ when we use mathematical signs (Monk 2007). Psychotherapy, too, is a motley of techniques and practices employed to help people in mental pain and distress. It does not need a foundation in any science or theory. The psychotherapist gives people 'space' to think and feel and, together with them, uses pictures, analogies, metaphors or humour to develop their thinking.

Psychotherapists create theories without careful attention to the concepts they use in making them. They use category terms such as 'process', 'state' and 'entity' with little or no explanation of how they are to be understood. They describe the mind without paying attention to the different uses of descriptive terms. Thus there is a considerable difference in the use of words between describing a room and describing a state of mind (*PI* ¶¶290–1). They are held captive by pictures, such as the idea of mental states and cognitive processes, but their nature is left unclear. They assume that the main use of words is to refer, failing to achieve an overview of their complicated patterns of use of words and so blurring distinctions in how symbols symbolise. They reduce our life with language to a theoretical model.

Psychoanalysis classically studies the mind in an individual who is isolated as much as possible in the consulting room, lying on the couch being observed but not allowed to see the face and gestures of the observing analyst. This is a highly artificial position. Much cognitive science too depends on putting people in artificial situations and observing them. These are static situations which do not encourage therapeutic action. No wonder patients feel lost and resigned to having their minds described by a stranger.

Freud was fond of emphasising that psychoanalysis is based on prolonged observation. His empiricism led him to believe that if you look long enough and hard enough you will really *see*. However, this easily encourages us to become captive to a fixed image. Looking hard at your king in chess will not tell you why you are check-mate. Freud was not aware that observation in science depends on theory, on assumptions. An experiment cannot be performed, or even conceived, outside of a theory. It is theory that structures the world of the experimenter, and which governs how he interprets what he can do and has done.

Therapy is an activity which must be timely and moving, not depending on definitions and experiments, as it explores neglected possibilities, bringing about changes of mind and modifying how we *want* to see things (Baker 2004). The person in confusion together with the therapist have to find the right timing for each other. This requires judgement rather than theoretical knowledge. Most therapists would agree that the 'correct' interpretation given at the wrong time is useless. Therapeutic action is more like dancing which involves both restraint and movement, than looking hard at something that is fixed and isolated.

Therapeutic action occurs when both parties in the conversation are orientated by the subject matter in question, not by dominant opinions. We can only understand a neurotic complaint when we have understood the question which it is trying to answer. Much theory in psychotherapy answers questions posed by the theorist rather than the patient. Instead of thinking through the problem together with the patient, the therapist takes the easy way, bypassing the problem by appealing to theories.

The technical language of psychoanalysis encourages us to believe that we know what we are resistant to, that is, our unconscious sexuality and 'primitive instincts'. Human vanity and self-deception are not mentioned. Psychoanalysis is the technique devised to enlighten us and if we have specialist training in its technique we become experts on the unconscious. Freud wrote perceptively of himself: 'For I am actually not at all a man of science, not an observer, not an experimenter, not a thinker. I am by temperament nothing but a conquistador – an adventurer, if you want it translated – with all the curiosity, daring, and tenacity characteristic of a man of this sort' (Masson 1985, p. 398). He goes on to say success in discovery is what is esteemed by such people. He did not consider that his desire for achievement may not be what is required by the patient.

As I have said, Freud and Klein claimed to be empirical scientists, making discoveries which could be learned, repeated and applied. They were infectiously enthusiastic about their discoveries, yet had neither a natural scientist's discipline of doubt nor a sceptic's sense of irony. Can one discover oneself? Is knowing things *about* oneself knowing oneself? Is being subject to a desire for achievement the way to self-knowledge? Is oneself some 'other' that one can discover and hold fast? Or is knowledge of oneself intrinsically practical, existing only in action, in particular situations?

Much psychotherapy is a modern version of the ancient technique of 'healers' using symbols and other magical practices to provide a system of reference, in which confusing and contradictory elements can be integrated (Lévi-Strauss 1968, pp. 167–85). Lévi-Strauss described the method of treatment of a famous Vancouver Island Kwakiutl shaman Quesalid. He used an elaborate ceremony of cure, the high point of which involved extracting a hidden tuft of blooded down from his mouth, and telling his patient that he had successfully sucked out the cause of the illness in the form of a bloody worm.

Lévi-Strauss wrote that the shaman accepts the beliefs of the society in which his patients live, one of which is that disease is caused by some entity in the body. The patient, however, does not accept the pains and symptoms of the illness. The shaman's actions re-integrate them into the system of beliefs, which makes them meaningful for the patient and others concerned. Modern therapy has much the same pattern. It is a common belief in our society that the cause of mental illness must be *in* the mind, or brain. Psychoanalysts and psychiatrists accept this belief and elaborate theories about entities and processes in the unconscious or the brain and use methods of treatment to deal with these 'causes'.

These methods may be understood as rhetorical devices or forms of magic. Therapists, however, often believe their own rhetoric and forget the enormous importance of the placebo effect, which is not causal but symbolic. It is rare for a control study to be done to check the worth of a new psychotherapeutic technique. There is no evidence that psychoanalytic or cognitive techniques work better than an equally experienced psychotherapist who uses neither. To argue that it is not possible to use a control as everyone is unique does not prove that the new technique gets its results because of the technique and theory behind it, rather than by a placebo effect.

A mathematical analogy may make this clear. Take the Euclidean proof for the three internal angles of a triangle. If we measure hundreds of triangles and find the sum of the angles is always the same, this would not prove that it were so for all triangles. But the construction of the proof *shows* all that is essential if we can understand it. 'The essential point in all these cases (Euclidean geometry, Russellian proofs etc.) is that what is demonstrated can't be expressed by a proposition' (*PR* ¶131).

Psychotherapy is much the same. The confused person has to be with the therapist who may *show* him his confusions. This may enable him to 'go on' with his life. Nevertheless, neither the therapist nor the patient can demonstrate in propositions exactly what enabled him to do this; they cannot extract a cause or make a rule, as with an empirical problem. The patient has to see for himself. It is similar to understanding a mathematical proof, seeing the humour in a joke, and the task of seeing the humour in our absurdities. The Pyrrhonian sceptics had a similar point when they described the peace of mind following the *epochē* as just befalling one, although, of course, after a lot of hard work (Chapter 2).

Literature, especially poetry, is concerned with language as the medium of expression. Think of the huge variety of love poetry. In this the facts are much the same but the meaning is unique. It is deeply concerned with the use of language. Irony, metaphor, rhetorical devices, temporality and silences are of huge importance. Wittgenstein used them all (McGuiness 2006). The style of writing, the right word and the liberating word were of crucial importance to him. It is said he read *Tristan Shandy* about a dozen times (Redpath 1990, pp. 50–1). It is a witty book concerned with the various ways to write a story.

> We speak of understanding a sentence in the sense in which it can be replaced by another which says the same; but also in the sense in which it cannot be replaced by any other. (Any more than one musical theme can be replaced by another.)

> In the one case, the thought in the sentence is what is common to different sentences; in the other, something that is expressed only by these words in these positions. (Understanding a poem) (*PI* ¶531)

In an empirical science we are concerned with the discovery, the result, which can be described in many ways. A large specialist vocabulary may be developed to describe discoveries as these usually involve a special domain, such as the brain, with which most people are unfamiliar. But when we want to express ourselves, the precise expression that fits the occasion is vital as it is in wit where the nuances of accent, gesture and looks are at play to produce a specific effect.

In therapy a person is in the grip of a problem. Being grabbed around the throat by a set of apparent impossibilities can provoke him to find the way through. Only then will the necessary steps of understanding appear, and the concepts that find a path between impossibilities be created. Everything depends on his free acknowledgement; there must be no bullying, so it is not adversarial. If he does not agree with an elucidation, the appropriate expression has not been found (*PI* ¶128; Baker 2004).

This contrasts with much psychotherapy which is addressed to the problem as diagnosed by the therapist rather than the *grip* of the problem on the individual.

> Teach me to speak to men's hearts without what I say doing what I did not intend to the fragile system of their convictions. (Lichtenberg 2000, p. 44)

A few of Wittgenstein's remarks may indicate a different way of thinking about therapy which speaks to the heart rather than to convictions.

> Where others go on ahead, I remain standing. (*CV* p. 75)

> One *cannot* speak the truth; – if one has not conquered oneself. One *cannot* speak it – but not because one is still not clever enough.
>
> The truth can be spoken only by someone who is already *at home* in it; not by someone who lives in untruthfulness, & does no more than reach out towards it from within untruthfulness. (*CV* p. 41)

This way of thinking is characteristic of the Pyrrhonian sceptics. Thus Montaigne, who was influenced by them, wrote: 'All men gaze ahead at what is confronting them: I turn my gaze inwards, planting it there and keeping it there. Everybody looks before himself: I look inside myself;

I am concerned with no one but me; without ceasing I reflect on myself, I watch myself, savour myself' (Montaigne 1991, p. 747). By 'self' he is not referring to the modern idea of self as when we say someone is 'selfish' or self-centred. He is referring to what we mean by 'I' in its expressive use, of being where one is; the first person pronoun is repeated insistently. Many of his essays are concerned with the illusions of self-love, which is nearer to our concept of selfishness.

The characteristic unit of Wittgenstein's teaching was not the book, treatise or lecture, but the 'remark' (*Bemerkung*). This is a unit that can be as short as a sentence or as long as a page or two of a book. Central to it was his custom of writing up his thoughts in a journal day by day. He used the term *freie einfall* (Trans. Free fall, the idea occurred to me, it struck me) for this activity (Nordman 2005, Index *einfall*). It was extremely important that the thoughts 'struck' him, that they were alive. He would select the better remarks, improve them, rearrange them a number of times and then have them typed out; sometimes he would cut up the typescript, pasting the remarks in a new order. 'For only at the right place do they perform their whole work!' (*PPO* p. 219). The result is more like an album, 'criss-crossing in every direction', covering a 'wide field of thought'. Modulations and transitions, moods and feelings, are crucial. He did not think that philosophy can be neatly divided into systems – metaphysics, logic, ethics, etc. This classification has a hidden academic agenda – specialisation.

He wrote:

> The best that I could write would never be more than philosophical remarks; my thoughts soon grew feeble if I tried to force them along a single track against their natural inclination. – And this was, of course, connected with the very nature of the investigation. For it compels us to travel criss-cross in every direction over a wide field of thought. (*PI* Preface)

Freud also used the term *freie einfall*, which is translated as 'free association' and is a basic psychoanalytic method. Since he was in the grip of a picture of the nature of rule-following and meaning, he was led to believe in psychic determinism. The patient's free associations were interpreted according to this picture, as Freud sought to demonstrate the determinate order of the unconscious. He assumed that, when purposeful ideas are abandoned, concealed purposive ideas, determined by the unconscious, assume control of the current of ideas (Freud *SE* 5, p. 531). These give *the* meaning of dreams, parapraxes and symptoms, as meaning is determined. He never examined the concept of meaning and why he assumed that it must have a determined sense.

Words sometimes seemed to pour out of Freud with little attention to meaning. As he wrote, the Traumdeuting 'completely follows the unconscious... it is obviously not written for the reader; after the first two pages I gave up any attempt at stylization' (Masson 1985, p. 319). Klein, perhaps the most influential analyst after Freud, dictated without notes. Thoughts poured out of her. She stopped when a new idea occurred to her, which she would immediately term 'a discovery'. Winnicott called her a 'Eureka shrieker' because of her tendency to regard every insight as the ultimate truth! (Grosskurth 1985, p. 121).

This attitude to words rather than meaning is a rhetoric. We are persuaded to learn the truth about things according to the words given them. There is the illusion that words are merely terms with sense which we use to describe something objective. The reader is led to assume that they are looking through the words to the truth but, in fact, are viewing what the speaker has painted with his words. They are rendered impotent to question this because of the claim of expertise to a special region of the mind. This is particularly seductive when the subject is 'the mind' because of its elusive nature.

If language is treated as a medium through which we can immediately describe the structure of the mind and of relationships, then form, style and whom they are addressing are of little importance. In this relation the writing up of results and explanations are impersonal since its findings are assumed to be universal.

Wittgenstein's way of writing combats this. For him writing involved wrestling with the temptations that seduce us in language. According to Kenny (1973, p. 20), *Philosophical Investigations* contains 784 questions and only 110 answers, and by his account *70 of the answers are meant to be wrong!* Posing a question places what is questioned into a particular perspective; it reveals the questionability of what is questioned and so makes it pass through a state of indeterminacy. A rightly posed question can lead to knowledge, as a thing is known only when the counter-arguments are seen to be correct. Just as in the physical sciences, an experiment is a question posed to nature which must be repeated by different people in different circumstances. Opinions, on the other hand, suppress questions; they are free-floating answers to questions, produced by the seductions of language that have not passed through the state of indeterminacy in which a decision can be made.

Wittgenstein wrote in many voices, undermining the traditional demand that the author be consistent. His reflections are thought experiments rather than statements of position. His writing is rather like Montaigne's *Essais* or Nietzsche's aphorisms, and they reflect Deleuze's remark that some writers are stutterers in language, in that they make language as such stutter. This is not an affection of the one who writes but they are using an affective and intensive language (Deleuze 1997, pp. 107–14). 'My writing is often nothing but "stammering" ' (*CV* p. 16).

Wittgenstein sought to undermine the common belief that philosophy gives us a privileged perspective to see the world as it really is, if we climb on the shoulders of those we believe know more than we do. Instead he tried to clarify thinking; he tried to draw attention to the many temptations, urges and prejudices in our use of words. His writing reflects these difficulties inherent in human cognition. Truth is elusive as are Wittgenstein's texts which seek to alert us to this. The secret lies in how to characterise this uncertainty. Some beliefs are to be discarded; others are necessary but not true or false.

He emphasised the importance of 'imponderable' evidence in psychotherapy. Thus, can we prove that a certain expression is genuine? It often has to be felt. Subtleties of glance, gesture, tone of voice and familiarity with the person all play a part. It may be very difficult to put into words the difference between, for example, a genuine loving look and a pretend one. 'Ask yourself: How does a man learn to get an "eye" for something? And how can the eye be used?' (*PI PPF* 361).

Theorists simplify, and their adherents become tempted into believing that their models reflect or approximate the underlying structure of life. Wittgenstein, on the other hand, was concerned to do justice to the indefinite and multicoloured filigree of our ordinary life which lies open to view and this we must see for ourselves. For this: 'You don't stand on stilts or on a ladder but on your own bare feet' (*CV* ¶10). To find one's way we must first know where we stand.

How could human behaviour be described? Surely only by showing the actions of a variety of humans, as they are all mixed together. Not what *one* man is doing *now*, but the whole hurly-burly, is the background against which we see an action, and it determines our judgement, our concepts, and our reactions. (*RPP2* ¶629)

Philosophy does require a resignation, but one of feeling, not of intellect. And maybe that is what makes it so difficult for many. It can be difficult not to use an expression, just as it is difficult to hold back tears, or an outburst of rage. (*BT* p. 300)

Some remarks by Proust on style are relevant here:

> For style... is a question not of technique but of vision: it is the reve-
> lation, which by direct and conscious methods would be impossible,
> of the qualitative difference, the uniqueness of the fashion in which
> the world appears to each one of us, a difference which, if there were
> no art, would remain for ever the secret of every individual.
>   ... this struggle to discern beneath matter, beneath experience,
> beneath words, something that is different from them, is a process
> exactly the reverse of that which, in those everyday lives which
> we live with our gaze averted from ourself, is at every moment
> being accomplished by vanity and passion and the intellect, and
> habit too, when they smother out true impressions, so as entirely
> to conceal them from us, beneath a whole heap of verbal concepts
> and practical goals which we falsely call life. (Proust 1983, Vol. 3,
> pp. 931–2)

For Wittgenstein, therapy should help us to see that the world does
not present itself as a collection of objects to be known, possessed or
rejected. We have no direct access to the world. For us humans, thinking involves language. We may come to understand the world through
clarifying the differences in how symbols symbolise. This is mirrored
in their use and cannot be captured in pictures or models. We must
proceed obliquely to depose the play of appearances and opinions. It
is because therapy is oblique that we are obliged to enter into it, rather
than use it to solve problems or be seized by it. We have to enter therapy,
not in order to know what it is about, but to think what happens in it.
Therapy addresses our capacity for thoughtfulness and involves restraint
in the therapist. At no point must it be the realisation of pre-existing
knowledge, even though knowledge has been painfully acquired by the
therapist. This restrained intensity on the part of the therapist allows the
disclosure of thought. So we experience the enigma of thought, the mur-
mur of the indiscernible. For the world is at once multiple, contingent
and untotalisable.

He often used aphorisms as he was concerned with boundaries that
move rather than facts. An aphorism (*aphorizein* to define, *horos* a
boundary) responds to limits and boundaries; it frames a thought yet
grows with what it frames. It is not a representation, as it leaps out of the
frame; it is a play of forces. It appeals to the individual rather than the
collective since it invites careful reading. It shows rather than explains.
It contrasts with the way we represent knowledge set down in a series of

propositions where there is the risk of taking the representational view of language dogmatically.

Aphorisms were first used in the Hippocratic writings. They came into being as a way of reporting personal experience and for the purpose of promoting good health. In the Corpus Hippocraticum we are told that *'chronos* is that in which there is *kairos*, and *kairos* is that in which there is not much *chronos*. Healing happens at times through *chronos*, other times through *kairos'* (Hippocrates 1923–31, Vol. 1, Precepts 1). *Chronos* is clock time; many diseases just need a certain length of time to heal. *Kairos* means 'due measure', 'fitness', 'occasion' or 'critical time'. Psychotherapy depends on the right timing of remarks and interpretations, on *kairos* as well as *chronos*.

An aphorism unites the singular and universal in a unique judgement. It is not a report on universal laws extracted from individual observations. It does not fit an authorial ego of one who knows. It makes one pause, and its tone and texture make one pay attention to the actual language used. Aphorisms open the text to new readings and new connections. They are enigmatic.

Consider the maxims of La Rochefoucauld (2007). He presents *a portrait of man's heart*. His technique is mostly descriptive. He uses ordinary language and most of his reflections are a few sentences long. He is concerned with the difficulty of knowing oneself. But, as the translator of the new O.U.P. edition writes: 'Few books as widely read have provoked as much resistance' (Ibid., Introduction, p. 1). As La Rochefoucauld ironically wrote:

> The reader's best policy is to start with the premises that none of these maxims is directed specifically at him, and that he is the sole exception to them, even though they seem to be generally applicable. After that, I guarantee that he will be the first to subscribe to them, and that he will think them only too favourable to the human heart. (Ibid., p. 147)

Is the resistance we have to these maxims, or to Wittgenstein, the same as that resistance to psychoanalysis, which Freud so emphasised? In the latter the mechanism of repression is at work, whereas in the former there is an inability to be moved.

La Rochefoucauld wrote: 'Self-love is cleverer than the cleverest man in the world' (Ibid., p. 5). He wrote ironically and, as the psychoanalyst Jonathan Lear points out, irony is not the same as sarcasm with which it is often confused (Lear 2003, p. 70). Sarcasm expresses contempt towards an individual – it is aggressive. On the contrary, *irony*, says Quintilian, is a figure of speech 'in which something contrary to what is said is to be understood' (Quintilian 2002, Book 5, Section 2, p. 15). It is not aggressive but provokes the reader to attend to the saying of what is said. Its great importance for therapy was seen by Kierkegaard, whose writing Wittgenstein was familiar with.

> Just as scientists maintain that there is no true science without doubt, so it may be maintained with the same right that no genuinely human life is possible without irony .... Irony limits, finitizes, and circumscribes and thereby yields truth, actuality, content; it disciplines and punishes and thereby yields balance and consistency. (Kierkegaard 1989, p. 326)

Irony is a practical skill, an excellent surgeon, as it helps us to beware of any language that claims to tell us what we are or what we should become. Irony is absent from theory as it questions the authority of facts and theory; it points to their 'unthought'. There is no fixed answer to what anyone is.

This is why the talking 'cure' cannot be taught systematically in the way of natural sciences. It is grounded in practice rather than theory, apprenticeship rather than lectures. It must remain open to the hurlyburly of human life. Its language is incomplete and changes according to the speaker and the person addressed.

Wittgenstein's writing is designed to show his practice, not to just talk around it. In this it is like a work of art where form and content are one. In his later work he draws us into a complex play of scenes and voices so we are not always sure which of these voices is his. Language is a shared human practice; it is against this background that we become aware of what is clear and what is not. He writes to discourage a passive reading of his work, for we would then be tempted to absorb what we might take as his observations and theories and try to apply them. And this would turn it into an expert's propositional knowledge, not a shared understanding. Clarity may be obtained by reminding us of how we learned to speak and of the variety of uses of language. Satire and dubious philosophical theories are intertwined.

> This book is a collection of wisecracks. But the point is: they are connected, they form a system. If the task were to draw the shape of an object true to nature, then a wisecrack is like drawing merely (just) a (one) tangent to the real curve; but a thousand wisecracks (lying close

to each other, closely drawn) can draw the curve. (Wittgenstein MS 119, p. 108)

In the talking 'cure' we do not distinguish between the saying and the content of what is said. It is not a discourse in which we say things about the patient which is independent of the way we say it or of the subject who hears it. We do not make statements about the patient that may be verified and believed by him. It takes place according to trust and enacts its effects through weakness rather than force.

> If someone were to advance *theses* in philosophy, it would never be possible to debate them, because everyone would agree to them. (*PI* ¶128)

The same applies to the 'talking cure'. We become aware of how both our pictures of the mind and the patient's confusions interfere with our actual use of words about our minds and feelings and so confuse our relationship.

Wittgenstein wrote: 'I believe I summed up where I stand in relation to philosophy when I said: really one should write philosophy as one *writes a poem*' (*CV* ¶28). I do not take this to mean that philosophers, or psychotherapists, should write poetry but that there are important analogies between the two activities. Poets attend carefully to the use of words and the way sense depends on their placing in a composition. The physicality of words through sounds, modulations, tonality and tempo is in play in poetry. In this it is like the actual meeting of people in therapy where their physicality – gesture, looks or body movements – are important. This is lost in the traditional case history. A poem is a singularity, a truthful expression, a resuscitation of language from banalisation, lethargy and mechanisation – all of which are common in neurotic and psychotic speech as well as in much psychotherapy talk. Self-knowledge is revealed in the singular use of language, by both the expression and its truthfulness, not in propositions based on pictures of the mind. It is expressed in how a life is lived, not on theories we believe.

5
Reasons and Causes

Wittgenstein thought it was Freud's confusion between reasons and causes that led his disciples into making an *abominable mess* (*PO* p. 107). This has been much discussed (Bouveresse 1995; Cioffi 1998; Schroeder 2006, pp. 219–33). Wittgenstein's critique has had little or no effect on psychoanalysis, it being taken as a mere academic point and having no relevance to the practice of therapy. I shall try to show that the distinction is highly relevant to the practice of all forms of psychotherapy.

In ordinary talk we say of a neurotic person that they are unreasonable in certain areas of their life and that a psychotic person has lost their reason. So reason seems important in understanding these conditions. In the last few hundred years, however, it is the natural sciences that have become the main authority on the nature of knowledge and reason. As they are empirical and give a causal account of nature, it is understandable that many have attempted to explain neurosis and psychosis in causal terms, thus neglecting the place of reason.

An important language-game that human beings develop is asking the question 'why?' The ability to ask this question seems to be fundamental. The answer, as a person develops, may take different forms, including causal explanations and giving reasons. Each of these categories evolves in complicated ways and depends on history and culture.

Cause

Wittgenstein suggested that the most primitive concept of cause is a reaction; it is like pointing and saying '*He's* to blame!' that is, we instinctively look from what has been hit to what has hit it (*PO* Cause and

Effect, p. 373). A child is both passive and active. He is acted on by the impact of objects and by adults or children who may pick him up, put him down, feed him, push or pull him. He is active in that he can move, pick things up, drop them and can see that these activities have an impact. All this will often be in the presence of adults who remark on his activity. These basic forms of interaction form the background of learning causal discourse. Simple expressions develop, such as, 'Uh! Uh!' and pointing at something wanted, or cries of pain and gestures of refusal. Cause and effect are not differentiated. Doubt about the link between cause and effect is not involved at this stage. So cause and effects are not just temporal coincidences but an influence, an experience we instinctively react to. They are practical, part of our life and not a matter of speculation.

Later the child learns to apply the term 'cause' to a variety of circumstances. 'Push', 'pull', 'bend', 'burn' or 'make' are a few of the causative verbs. From these prototypes, diverse forms of causal discourse develop. They become highly developed in the natural sciences. We learn to look for a cause in itself; causes may then be separated from effects. When we become more sophisticated we observe mechanisms to see how levers and wheels cause movements. Thus mechanics is developed. We discover causes using experiments and observations that can be repeated by others to develop natural science. Natural regularities are noted, for example, noting the presence of a particular micro-organism associated with certain signs and symptoms gives the cause of a disease.

Causes, however, have no end. For any event that is cited as a cause, we may ask for its cause and so the chain of causes has no end in theory. In practice this does not usually matter. Why did he develop a sore throat? The streptococcus is found to be the cause and as it is sensitive to chemotherapy, there is no need to look any further.

In the sciences we generally look for causes, as scientific explanation provides a causal account of phenomena. We say we discover causes, as they may be hidden. There is room for scepticism about the relation between cause and effect. There may be a causal mechanism, as in the machinery of a clock, but there are objects that may be difficult to detect, such as viruses causing some disease. The notion of cause implies a force emanating from some material entity, or entities, or a precipitating event such as a trauma. A causal account will identify the agent or event responsible for the effect. This will produce explanatory satisfaction which propitiates most people's need for understanding.

What we see as a cause will effect treatment. In the various psycho-analytical therapies there are many different theories as to the cause of psychological disturbance. Some believe it is caused by maternal deprivation, others that there was no proper respect for the phallus, others that there are inborn, instinctual disturbances which affected the infant's experiences, others that there was an unbearable trauma and so on. There is no objective evidence for any of these theories of cause and mostly they are not causes anyway, for an efficient cause must be separate from what it causes. They are usually a theoretical justification of the therapist's particular skills and interests as well as what is popular and sells. Such causal explanations assume that at root all mental patients are essentially the same. In fact, it is the beliefs of the therapist that are in common, not their patients.

We can make causal laws to predict what is going to happen in the future, because the natural world displays enough regularity for us to engage in making predictions and generalisations about nature. It is a contingent fact that we can do this; we cannot say we do this because it is a *fact* that 'nature is uniform'. To create natural laws we need induction and this involves assuming the *simplest* law which fits the evidence. Necessity is not involved. To assume this would be to take an omniscient position in which we rise above our experience. Nature has not got a real essence that is uniform and neither advanced physics nor biology requires this (*TLP* ¶6.371).

Wittgenstein argued that 'the main source of superstition results from belief in the causal nexus' (*TLP* ¶5.1361). Like Kant he argued that we need causal laws to make objective empirical judgements; they are part of the syntax for scientific language but they are not laws that nature obeys.

The success of contemporary biology depends on respect for the diversity of life not on some grand theory of 'life'. The models, metaphors and machines which have contributed to biology do not bring us any closer to a unified understanding or theory of the nature of life. The world is too complex to fit neatly into any of our models, theories or explanations (Keller 2002, p. 301). Much theoretical work in science depends on the productive use of novel metaphors and models because scientific work is directed at understanding new entities and processes. We must, therefore, find new ways of talking about that which we do not know very much. Increasing knowledge depends on the techniques available, the kind of data that we are able to acquire and the wit of scientists. It satisfies certain needs while failing to address others. *We* find uniformity because we can make predictions under certain conditions that usually turn out to be true. 'It is always by favour of Nature that one knows something' (*OC* ¶505).

Freud was fond of Heine's quip against philosophers:

Mit seinen Nachtmützen und Schlafrockfetzen
Stopt er die Lücken des Weltenbaus.
(With his nightcaps and the tatters of his dressing-gown he patches up the gaps in the structure of the universe.)

In *The Interpretation of Dreams* (p. 490) he uses this analogy to describe 'secondary revision' which makes the apparent absurdity of a dream appear intelligible. He also used it to contrast what he thought were the illusions of philosophy with the scientific *Weltanschauung* of psychoanalysis (Freud 1933, p. 161).

But many philosophers from antiquity to the present did not think that it was their job to describe the structure of the universe. Thus Russell wrote:

The essence of philosophy is analysis not synthesis. To build up systems of the world, like Heine's German professor who knit together fragments of life and made an intelligible system out of them, is not, I believe, any more feasible than the discovery of the philosopher's stone. (Russell 1971, p. 84)

Russell, like his student Wittgenstein and many other philosophers, especially sceptics, focused on logical analysis and a piecemeal approach to the plurality of things and so rejected metaphysical speculation (Landini 2007). Freud, with one hand rejected philosophy, closing his eyes to the sceptical and critical traditions, but with the other brought grand theories back under the name of a unified science, using the philosopher's stone of a scientific *Weltanschauung* applied to the mental field. So psychoanalysis has moved in the opposite direction of modern biology.

Freud was mesmerised by a metaphysical dogma into which everything has to fit. As Sulloway wrote: 'Freud's entire life's work in science was characterised by an abiding faith in the notion that all vital phenomena, including psychical ones, are rigidly and lawfully determined by the law of cause and effect' (Sulloway 1992, p. 94).

Dispositions

An obvious way to account for human actions and where they go wrong is to give a dispositional account of them, for a disposition befits a mechanico-causal way of answering the question 'Why?'.

A disposition is a permanent tendency which actualises itself occasionally. Thus diamonds are hard, water is disposed to run down hill, fire burns things and a car will make certain movements if the engine is turned on. Inanimate things may possess dispositions which are not usually actualised. Not every soluble thing dissolves; the hardness of a diamond may never come to be tested. Human dispositions are usually of temperament and character such as cheerfulness, melancholy and excitability. In contrast to inanimate things they must manifest the disposition at times. A melancholy person who was never melancholic would not be said to have that disposition. They are aspects of the nature of the person that are relatively abiding.

In psychology a disposition may be thought of in terms of something being present, a cause, from which certain behaviour follows. It assumes that thoughts, feelings and behaviour are caused by structures underlying the surface phenomena. Internal states, emotions, instincts and thoughts drive behaviour. These assumptions are found in psychoanalysis with its drives and defences and in cognitive therapy with its cognitions and schemas, and structuralist family therapy. This picture seems obvious to many people.

It depends on an analogy between the structure of a machine and the behaviour that follows from it. Thus a pocket calculator has a disposition to carry out certain calculations because a decision procedure for true or false equations in arithmetic has been encoded in its circuit. It has a structure such that it can carry out certain calculations. A Turing machine, which can follow a set of finite rules slavishly without having a reflective grasp on the operations it is performing, is such a structure. This can be a model which leads us to imagine a mental apparatus as an immaterial mechanism determining all mental processes.

We easily move into science fiction and magic. Analogies easily mislead; a model of a mechanism is not the mechanism. There is an internal relation between the properties of a model; they persist unalterably in the whole they constitute. A model is a symbol and not subject to contingencies; it will not break. On the contrary, an actual machine is a physical object and may succumb to external forces. If my calculator becomes very hot, for example, it will loose its disposition to calculate. No physically real mechanism in the brain or mind can be found which is programmed to unwind the logical consequences of symbolic expressions. A programme is a system of rules dealing with signs which apply to models, enabling us to make sense of them; they cannot be in the brain or anywhere else.

Wittgenstein argued in the *Tractatus* that the law of causality is not a law but the form of one; it is a general name about the form in which the propositions of science can be cast (*TLP* ¶¶6.3–6.3751). Science is an activity in which we look for causes; it provides a causal account of phenomena. But 'There is no compulsion making one thing happen because another has happened. The only necessity that exists is logical necessity' (*TLP* ¶6.37). In particular, future events cannot be inferred from present ones. This does not mean that they cannot be forecast on the basis of scientific laws. But what it does mean is that those laws, together with the available observational data, give no logical guarantee for such predictions to be true; they are hypotheses.

There can be no unrestricted universal laws which either belong to observational evidence or necessarily follow from it. If this were so, future occurrences and events could be known by deducing them from universal laws and initial conditions. If the causal nexus were endowed with a necessity which was matched to that of logical entailment, then we could have no concept of choice and freedom. The relation cause–effect must not be confused with the necessary relation: premise–conclusion. This would combine a causal role of the agent's motives with a rationalistic conception of causality. There is an epistemic difference between knowledge of the causes of physical events, which is based on experiment and observation and is hypothetical, and knowledge of the motives of actions. The latter are kinds of reason and depend on the development of language. The child learns to gesture towards what he wants, then perhaps scream 'want', and later says, 'I want'. In time he learns to describe what he is doing, and why, and what he is going to do; he learns to describe desirability characteristics – reasons which provide others with a way of understanding his behaviour.

Psychic determinism is basic to psychoanalysis. It is assumed that there are mental processes which are over-determined by many causal chains, in which each link is sufficient for its successor. Thinking is a mental process in which some thoughts cause other thoughts to follow. This is why Freud could claim to discover *the* meaning of dreams, neurosis, etc. and claim that free will is an illusion. He rightly saw all this followed from his belief in the universal validity of the law of determinism. Belief in chance and free will is a superstition, he claimed (Freud 1901, pp. 300–44).

Thus Freud claimed that Luther's declaration at the Diet of Worms, 'Here I stand: I can do no other', was an expression of psychical determinism (Ibid., p. 253). He had no conception that it could be an expression of freedom, that Luther was standing by a decision *he* had made.

Freud collapsed causes and reasons together. He imagined the relation cause–effect is a necessary one. This led him to imagining that dreams and neurosis have a determined meaning. He confused genetic explanations with causal ones. A genetic explanation directs our attention to the relatedness of facts. Thus one might illustrate the internal relation of a circle to an ellipse by gradually converting one into the other. This would not show that a certain ellipse had originated from a circle, it is not a causal relation, but it sharpens our eye to the formal connection between the circle and the ellipse. Mathematics is full of such examples (*PO* p. 133).

Freud was very good at sharpening our eye for connections. To give one example out of hundreds: in an essay on the psychology of love he describes 'sexual enlightenment' in boys (Freud 1910, p. 231). According to him, a boy learns that there are women held in contempt – prostitutes – however, he is far from feeling this contempt. When he learns he can be initiated by these 'unfortunates' into sexual life, which has been reserved for 'grown-ups', he regards prostitutes with longing and horror. He thinks 'with cynical logic' that there is not much of a difference between his mother and a whore. This awakens memory traces of the wishes of his early infancy and he begins to desire his mother and hate his father as a rival. He cannot forgive his mother for granting favours, not to himself but to his father, and so the story goes on. This is a story which may have relevance for some. But it has such suggestive power that it imposes itself on many with irresistible self-evidence. It is then declared as a causal explanation, which is universally true.

Freud was led to think of the mind in terms of a machine – the mental apparatus.

The mind, according to his picture of it, is an entity. The instincts in it predetermine its activities. These are dispositions to act in certain ways; thus birds, for example, are disposed to structure their nests according to the species and all mammals have a sexual instinct. He conceived that instincts are in the unconscious and the pressure of an instinct is the force for work which it represents. Its aim is satisfaction; it has an object which is the thing in regard to which it is able to achieve its aim. Instincts are in the mind but are determined by their origin in the body, presumably the brain. They cannot become an object for consciousness; only the idea that represents the instinct can. Mysteriously they are supposed to be *lying on the frontier between the mental and physical* (Freud 1905, 1910). Thus an instinct is both a real biological entity, presumably in the brain, and a rule determining future behaviour.

If we think of the mind as a machine, the mental apparatus, then it seems to follow that there is a mental reservoir inside the mind, in which everything it will do in the future is already stored up in it. It assumes that all its future movements, in their definiteness, are like objects lying in the mind. For we are prone to think that a machine has particular possibilities of movement predetermined in advance; the mechanism determines the agent's every move (*PI* ¶193).

There are two senses of determine. There is a logical sense and a causal one. In the former, we speak of determine where 'a = a', '3 + 2 = 5'. Here we are in the presence of rules which are part of our language. We do not get them by observation. I do not observe that I am identical to myself or that anyone else is! I may observe that if I add 3 apples to 2 then I can count 5 apples but this does not mean I understand the mathematical proposition: $3 + 2 = 5$. Causal determinism depends on the observation of regularities in nature. Pure mathematics does not.

A machine has such-and-such possibilities of movement. These possibilities are distinct from the movements themselves. If we think of a model of a machine, we cannot doubt that the model shows the exact possibilities of this or that movement. We can draw the model and thereby show the possibilities. When we do this, we are using the model as a symbol, illustrating the laws of kinematics which is the geometry of motion and is timeless. Thus a pair of cogwheels can be used to demonstrate that one *must* revolve clockwise if the other turns anti-clockwise. This is an empirical observation but if the cogwheels were inside the sun they certainly would not revolve. The logical 'must' is symbolic; the model is an ideal object which does not exist in space or time but does show us what it makes sense to say about its movements.

> A *picture* held us captive. And we couldn't get outside it, for it lay in our language, and language seemed only to repeat it to us inexorably. (*PI* ¶115)

Freud's misunderstanding about mental mechanisms and human action is a result of his confusing the real with the ideal, the empirical with the place of rules. His beliefs are not open either to empirical or to conceptual investigation. His is a reductionist thesis in which human actions are reduced to the actions of their brains, or to historical laws, or to psychological processes. He forgets that it is people who have brains who also are embedded in history. It is people who calculate, speak, dream and act – all of which involves meaning and understanding (Bennett and Hacker 2003, pp. 355–77).

Freud portrays psychology mythically and tries to explain myth psychologically.

Thus he recommended to Ernest Jones: 'the simplest way of learning psychoanalysis was to believe that all he wrote was true and then, after understanding it, one could criticize it in any way one wished' (Jones 1953–57, p. 204). Conjuring tricks and most forms of deception depend on the initial moves being unquestioned. The conjuring trick appears magical if we are seduced by the picture it presents and remain unaware of how it is set up.

If one tries to understand psychoanalysis without questioning the initial moves, one invites confusion. It is the hidden initial moves that set up the picture Freud wants us to stare at but it is the logical analysis of these moves that can prevent us from being seduced by his picture.

Wittgenstein sums this up: 'Every empirical proposition may serve as a rule if it is fixed, like a machine part, made immovable, so that now the whole representation turns around it and it becomes part of the coordinate system, independent of facts' (*RFM* ¶¶7, 74, p. 437).

Idealization

One of the neurotic defences discussed by Freud is idealization. This is supposed to be a mental process by means of which an object is overvalued. It occurs notably in sexual overvaluation. When we are in love, Freud assumed we overvalue the loved object. This certainly may happen, but people may value love highly and not necessarily overvalue the one they love. He did not differentiate between the object of love and love. In the practice of analysis idealization is important. Thus a patient may idealize the analyst, for example, imagining he would get something from her what so far he had failed to find in an ideal way, that is, without waiting too long, without stimulating anxiety or guilt, envy or jealousy, or wounding his narcissism. Klein developed the concept and imagined that the breast may be idealized as a good object that the infant wants to possess and have 'inside' him. This may result in 'splitting', as if the 'good' is a possession, there is the danger of it being taken away, and so the phantasy of a 'bad' object which might do this may arise. The various ways that this 'bad' object may be dealt with are discussed in the psychoanalytic literature.

It is notable that both Freud and Klein invert the traditional meaning of 'good'. As Aristotle puts it: 'every action and pursuit is considered to aim at some good. Hence the good has been rightly defined as "that at which all things aim"' (Aristotle 1926, 1094a). Hence it is absurd to imagine we can possess the good; that it is a mental agency in the mind constituted through the internalisation of parental prohibitions and demands. It would mean that there can be no free judgement as judgement would depend on identification and internalisation. A good marksman does not possess the target, but when he aims at it he usually hits it. His skill is not a mechanism depending on objects he possesses inside himself. It is an ability which he may or may not exercise.

The good is not an ideal to be identified with or internalised. It is not *in* the mind or *in* anything. A person may possess Euclid's proof of Pythagoras' theorem in a book or interiorise it in his mind but if he does not understand it, it is not true for him. It has been said that you cannot understand a proof in mathematics until you construct your own proof (Chaitin 2007, p. 128). It is the same with judgements as to what is good or not.

Wittgenstein is reported to have said:

> The disciples of Freud have produced nothing but nonsense. They have been fascinated by his means of expression. No one has allowed his thought to be more overlaid by his means of expression than has Freud. There are deep strata, as it were hundreds of feet thick, of means of expression overlying and obscuring the original facts of observation. One cannot see the original facts because they are hidden by the means of expression. (*PPO* p. 395)

Psychoanalysts idealize their theories, which they claim to possess, as they confuse the real with the ideal. Theories are seen as something to be identified with. But theories are made for a purpose and cannot belong to anyone; they are for use, not for possession. As stated earlier, any theory involves indexicality if it is to be used. The ideal has a logical and ethical sense; it is a normative notion and not an empirical one.

> The ideal, as we conceive of it, is unshakable. You can't step outside it. You must always turn back. There is no outside; outside you cannot breathe. – How come? The idea is like a pair of glasses on our nose through which we see whatever we look at. It never occurs to us to take them off. (*PI* ¶103)

Kafka puts it thus: 'The true path is along a rope, not a rope suspended way up in the air, but rather only just over the ground. It seems more like a tripwire than a tightrope' (Kafka 2006, p. 3).

Reason

Order is of great significance in human life and human order may be expressed in terms of reason. The laws of nature describe the natural order and these are based on natural regularities. Reasoning and reasonableness, on the other hand, concern human order and making sense of human action. They show the path we are taking. They include the ability to draw conclusions from grounds, to pursue ends and see the means to pursue them, to understand human behaviour and to be sensitive to whatever are reasons or poor reasons. Perhaps most importantly, they include sensitiveness to the limits of reason.

Suppose someone is calculating and writing down a series of equations. We can ask him: 'Why did you write down these equations?' He may answer in terms of causes, or reasons. In the former he would talk about processes in his brain, the nerves and muscles to his fingers. In the latter he would answer by giving the rules which allow the transition from one equation or proposition to another. The causal account requires a knowledge of natural science, which most people do not have, whereas the mathematical account assumes that the person knows the rules and can apply them correctly. Of course, he may have got them wrong or disobeyed them, but an authority can correct him and lead him to see where he went wrong. The reasoning required for the equation has then been specified. In other words, in giving reasons we stay within language; we do not have to make empirical observations to see if some further experience can confirm or contradict us.

Thus $2 + 3 = 5$ is a mathematical statement and is correct according to reason. For given certain principles, laws of deduction and the practice of mathematics in which they are embedded, we can say certain things and not others. They determine our judgements of what is correct or not. Thus if I added 2 pears to 3 apples in a basket and counted 6 pieces of fruit, I would conclude that I had made a mistake in counting or perhaps someone had added a piece of fruit without my noticing; I would certainly not query arithmetic. If someone said $2 + 3 = 6$, he would not be making a mathematical statement; neither would he be making a false statement about anything in the world. Instead he might be playing a game with numbers.

Mathematics and logic do not involve space and time, so they are not concerned with objects. An intelligent being on a planet in another galaxy might not understand that $2 + 3 = 5$, as she might not have a language that can be translated into any human language but might get on with her life very nicely without being able to count. But if she could understand human language and could count, then she would 'see' that $2 + 3 = 5$. The objectivity of mathematics depends on understanding rules.

On the other hand, saying 'I believe or think that $2 + 3 = 5$' or 'I believe that $2 + 3 = 6$' are statements about my psychology and would require an investigation of me to see if they were true. We usually understand truth either as a relation to reality or with saying what is so. We can move from a statement about what was said or thought or judged to such statements as, that A judged correctly or that the proposition 'aRb' (e.g. Jack loves Jill) is true or not. When we read Judge Schreber's account of his madness, in which he tells us of all sorts of weird and wonderful things he experienced, there is no means of judging what is so, as he has lost his reason. We cannot determine what is correct or not. Are his statements empirical or logical?

Reasoning is bound up with the use of language. Animals and small children can have purposes but cannot give reasons, balance them, or understand and answer questions like 'Why?' and 'What is to be done?' We have to master a language before we can engage in reasoning, for reasoning involves language, thought, feeling, judgement, action and sensitivity to others. It is the most distinctive form of understanding human action.

Reason does not drop from some logical heaven onto humans, or onto a special group of them, such as white males, logicians or psychoanalysts. There is no autonomous order of reason that tells us how we must talk, or act. There are only ways of talking and acting, people who understand or fail to understand them and, above all, people who are involved in various forms of power, seeking to impose their understanding of what is reasonable and what leads to truth.

What makes power hold good, what makes it accepted, is simply the fact that it doesn't only weigh on us as a force that says no, but that it traverses and produces things, it induced pleasure, forms knowledge, produced discourse. It needs to be considered as a productive network which runs through the whole social body, much more than as a negative instance whose function is repression . . . .

There is a battle 'for truth' or at least 'around truth' – it being understood once again that by truth I do not mean 'the ensemble of truths which are to be discovered and accepted', but rather 'the ensemble of rules according to which the true and the false are separated and specific effects of power attached to the true', it being understood also that it is not a matter of a battle 'on behalf' of the truth, but of a battle about the status of truth and the economic and political role it plays. (Foucault 1980, pp. 119, 132)

Freud wrote: 'The ideal condition of things would of course be a community of men who had subordinated their instinctual life to the dictatorship of reason' (Freud 1932, p. 213).

This ideology is still very powerful in Western societies. It indicates a deep confusion about the nature of reason. Reason and rationality are value-laden notions with a long history and the cause of much bitter conflict. Thus 'classical' psychoanalysis claims to be the most rational of therapies – claiming that others use suggestion and are merely supportive. Cognitive therapy, in its turn, claims to be the most rational as it is based on empirical science.

What constitutes this picture of a perfect rationality for which we should strive? A perfectly rational person will have a set of beliefs and desires. She will believe and intend all and only those things she ought to believe and intend, in the light of her original set of beliefs and desires. She will specify her reasons in accordance with the rules of the propositional and predicate calculus, or perhaps use an even richer logic, such as modal logic. As she is likely to have to cooperate or compete with others, then decision theory and games theory will play a part in her deliberations. There is also the question as to whether she should use intuitionist or classical logic.

This perfectly analysed person may have to revise her beliefs and theories at some point; she may, for example, fall in love. But how should she proceed? Just what new beliefs should be added and what discarded, and how and when? Logicians, epistemologists and philosophers of science debate this, novelists give us stories illustrating it and psychoanalysts explain what is 'really' happening, but there is no consensus (Heal 2008).

It is difficult to make any practical sense of reason as an ideal which dictates. It is people who dictate when they identify with a particular picture of reason.

But it would be a pity to dump the word 'reason' as it has a use in ordinary discourse. Roughly it is the ability to engage in conversations and discussions in which there is the possibility of agreement, or at least understanding. Humans are mammals that have an instinct to learn language and seek order and understanding, so there is no necessity for a dictatorship of reason. Reason is never dictatorial, it is dialogical. The game of giving and asking for reasons is not logically replaceable by forcing 'reason' on people. There should always be room for deviance and questions as to what is reasonable. The task of reason is to understand, negotiate and clarify the forces, conditions and problems of human possibility. It is not something abstract that can be defined.

Ironically those therapies that claim to be most rational are irrational, as they do not allow for free discussion. Only if we submit to their version of therapy would we be rational. They see themselves as experts on a special field of knowledge, rather than as participants in the drama of reason. Few of us could have much of a conversation on sub-atomic physics with a specialist, but physicists do not claim we should. Whereas many psychotherapists assume they are experts on 'reason' itself, they are actually participants.

The particular culture that she is born into and the nature of her initiation into language will influence how a person understands what is reasonable. Before I enter a public toilet, would it be reasonable if I checked first whether I was a man or a woman? Perhaps I should undress first to make sure. But then how can I be sure I am seeing right? Can I give reasons to make this reasonable or unreasonable?

> The child learns to believe a host of things. I.e. it learns to act according to these beliefs. Bit by bit there forms a system of what is believed, and in that system some things stand unshakeably fast and some are more or less liable to shift. What stands fast does so, not because it is intrinsically obvious or convincing; it is rather held fast by what lies around it. (*OC* ¶144)

> I do not explicitly learn the propositions that stand fast for me. I can *discover* them subsequently like the axis around which a body rotates. This axis is not fixed in the sense that anything holds it fast, but the movement around it determines its immobility. (*OC* ¶152)

This insight is critical for the talking 'cure', where meaning is explored by careful attention to the use of language to get a clear view as to what is necessary and what is contingent. It contrasts with both psychoanalysis and cognitive therapy where rationality is assumed to be contained in the practitioner's theories and techniques. Most psychiatrists and psychotherapists agree that arguments are of little use in neurosis or psychosis. In fact, people with phobias and obsessions, for example, are usually well aware their troubles are irrational. They have to be helped in other ways than showing them their irrationality. In the talking 'cure' this involves helping them to *develop* reason in the particular area where they have lost it. This includes undermining assumptions and destroying idols, not replacing them by others. It involves helping the person to 'see' rather than identifying with a fixed point of view or theory. Rhetorical methods besides argument have to be used (Morris 2007, pp. 66–87).

Rule following

The ability to make and follow or disobey rules is a mark of reason. Other mammals cannot do this. They may display complicated forms of repetitive and regular behaviour and may alter it to get what they want, but there is no evidence that they have a concept of 'ought'. Rules depend on human ability as well as certain general facts of nature. Thus, we do not make it a rule that we ought not to jump 20 feet in the air in cities, as none of us are able to do that. Rules are a vehicle for spelling out what is essential. Thus grammatical rules are tools for the description of language. They are not statements about how we must speak, and they are not the source of necessity. We cannot change them easily by rational decision, however, as they depend on deep-seated customs. We may revise some of our beliefs but not all at once; perhaps some psychotic language is the result of a change that was too absolute. When we are familiar with rules we can make them up, change, debate, rebel against, obey or disobey them. Rule following involves freedom, for we may choose between obeying and disobeying them. We have the potential not to follow them. The laws of nature cannot be disobeyed; they have no potential. But they can be made use of, for example, when we use chemotherapy to treat an illness, or a parachute to alter the consequences of gravity.

To follow a rule we must be able to understand and apply it; we must understand what it means and what it accords with. We cannot follow a rule just once, as a rule is meaningless until we can apply it. The instance of application is part of the rule – there is no 'gap' between the rule and its application. If we are familiar with the rules of chess, we seamlessly follow them when we play. As the rule is not independent of its applications, the two are constitutive of each other. There is an internal relation between the rule and its application. If this were not so, we would have to have a rule as to how to apply the rule and then a rule as to how to apply that rule and so on. A rule may encounter uncertainty and indeterminacy in new and unforeseen circumstances and then a creative decision may have to be made.

In mathematics certain rules are held constant by the mathematical community; so its rules appear absolute even though they have been developed. In psychotherapy, on the other hand, there may be no mutual agreement as to the application of a rule and interpretations may be necessary. But to interpret is to replace one set of signs by another, so it cannot determine meaning since each substitution of signs is susceptible to further interpretations (*PI* ¶198). Justification must come to an end, and then we simply act (*PI* ¶211).

> What happens is not that this symbol cannot be further interpreted, but: I do no interpreting. I do not interpret, because I feel at home in the present picture. When I interpret, I step from one level of thought to another. (*Z* ¶234)

Here is an example. A middle-aged lady had been consulting me for about 2 years. One Christmas she sent me a Christmas card. At the next meeting I thanked her. I presented this incident to a group of psycho-analytic therapists who were critical at what I had done, on the grounds that I should have interpreted this act and handed the card back to her, as it was obviously a manifestation of transference. To have done this would have been dogmatic on my part as it would assume there was an external relation between the lady and her act of sending me a Christmas card and I had no evidence that this was the case. To her it was a perfectly ordinary act to send Christmas cards to people she was familiar with – her family, G.P., solicitor and even her psychotherapist. There was an internal relation between sending Christmas cards and the people she knew. She never sent me a card after she had left. The psy-choanalyst tends to see all behaviour, other than his own, in terms of external relations and so interprets it in terms of his theory.

'Following a rule is a particular language game' (*RFM* p. 416). It pre-supposes a community with its ways and customs and also our human form of life. A child naturally reacts in certain ways to pain or separa-tion; her community shows her the language in which to express them. They show her what is appropriate and what is not, at first within the limits of her family. She learns when interpretations have a role to play in the use of a rule and when we must act thus and so. Much later we may come to use rules creatively and perhaps see that what has seemed correct does not now make sense of our experience of life. It is shared human responses, constituted by actions and judgements, that enable our rule-following ability.

It is tempting to imagine our understanding of meaning as a mech-anism in the mind or brain, a disposition which generates and so explains manifestations of understanding, or its lack. But mechanisms lack potentiality: no mechanism, or formula in the mind or anywhere else, could guide us in the applications of a rule unless we understood it. It could not tell us what to do if it meant nothing to us. Rules are not rails that are blindly followed; thinking is not a fixed process. To understand a rule is to be able to manifest or refuse to manifest that understanding in practice. It is not to know something outside its application, such as a theoretical structure which generates or guides these manifestations. It is a practical capacity that humans can understand and the process of learning is crucial to our understanding of understanding. Of course we must have a human brain to undertake this but there is nothing in the brain or mind that is specific to any particular act of understanding and we can always refuse to understand.

A rule, as a formula or chart, has no normative status alone. It is the human community, our *form of life*, which sustains the structure in which it is meaningful to obey or disobey rules, to name and understand them. When we engage in rule following we do not have to appeal to a rule as an objectified content, that is, a content independent of our engagement in practice. For rules are not facts, they are not statements about actualities but tools for the description of practices. We can go on in the same way without having to decide or say what is the same. We can always say 'I did not and I could have'. 'To use a word without justification does not mean to use it wrongly' (*PI* ¶289). (There is a large amount of literature on rule following. Kripke 1982 is a classic; Kusch 2006; Mulhall 2007.)

Blind obedience to following a rule is based on our upbringing and our human responses to one another. A child learns how to act by following the customs of its family; it needs to be part of a human community. 'The child learns by believing the adult. Doubt comes after belief' (*OC* ¶160). There is no question for it, at this stage, as to what is normal or not. A child can act long before it can say what a rule is, or what rule it should follow, or whether it is normal or not. As the form of our life is the basis for the use of words and this varies according to culture and upbringing, then the meaning of words depends on the spoken occasion and not on *a-priori* meaning. This is especially important with psychological words since the physical world is more stable than is human life. Think of the different ways people and cultures express grief, anger, lying, pain, sexual desire and a sense of awe (Cavell 1976, pp. 44–72).

Rules are not an internalised set of pre-ordained requirements or formulae that somehow reach ahead of us and determine of themselves their every actual and counterfactual application. They do not have a normative status alone. It is the responses and judgements of the human community that sustain them. This is lost in obsessional neurosis where certain rules become merely internalised formulae, 'in the mind' rather than embodied, and so are pointlessly followed. Thus the advice to wash one's hands after going to the toilet may be turned into a rule as a rail.

We master concepts by developing a sensibility to the similarities and differences among their different uses. People will have sensitivities to different and equally real similarities. Thus people's ability to see family resemblances is variable. We vary in our sensitivity to subtle shades of behaviour and our relation to the appearance is part of the concept. Is a person slighting us, or are they just rather indifferent? Is their glance a sign of erotic interest or not? Is the pain a pretence to get more compensation or not? We judge actions according to their and our own background, and this is not monochrome.

> The background is the bustle of life. And our concept points to something within *this* background. (*RPP2* ¶625)

The capacity to follow rules enables us to make choices. Choice requires a conceptual repertoire that a wish does not. At first a child can only have wishes for he has not yet developed reason; he cannot express a choice. He cannot endorse a particular reason for doing 'A' rather than 'B'. He just wants to be picked up, or have a sweet. He cannot take responsibility for his wishes; he cannot say or think, 'I want "A" because of "R" '. A choice involves a reason which makes it intelligible to others; it connects his purposes with his actions. It must cohere with the person's background and subsequent behaviour. Failure to cohere may cast doubt on the person's sincerity, or on his self-understanding. Others may disagree with the reasons a person gives for his action. He may be deceiving himself and perhaps trying to deceive others. Others may see him in a different light from how he sees himself or may bring in aspects of his character and past that he is unwilling to consider.

To the extent that we are neurotic, we cannot choose to be healthy. All we can do is to wish we were, or perhaps seek help. When we choose we give expression to a choice. Its truth depends logically on the criteria of how things are with us. Thus: 'I am going to go to France next year for my holiday'. If this is a free choice then it implies that I am aware of how things are with me – that I like France, it is possible for me to go there, etc. It implies that I am not deceiving myself, that my choice is intelligible. But supposing I have a phobia, say for flying. I cannot choose to be rid of it, as I can choose not to go to France, because the phobia itself is not intelligible to me. The criterion that shows I suffer from a phobia and not a fear is that it is unintelligible to me. It is unreasonable. My refusal to go on a rickety old plane might be a 'reasonable' fear and not phobic.

Rules change and develop. For example, the rules as to what constitutes sexual abuse. Freud regarded the primal scene – a child's observation or phantasy of sexual intercourse between its parents – as highly traumatic. Yet people for thousands of years have slept in a common space huddled together when it is cold; seeing sexual intercourse was not considered traumatic as it was ordinary. It is now common for people who are unhappy to claim they were abused as children, although they may not remember it. Is this an advance in our understanding of unhappiness, or just a profitable view for workers in it?

A rule does not act like a force but it does have authority. Schreber's account of his psychotic illness, even though he was an eminent judge, lacks authority. His descriptions do not use the propositions of geography; they could be altered and we would be none the wiser. Thus: 'Another time I traversed the earth from Lake Ladoga to Brazil and, together with an attendant, I build there in a castle-like building a wall in protection of God's realms against an advancing yellow flood tide: I related this to the peril of a syphilitic epidemic' (Schreber 2000, p. 79). This sort of remark can be interpreted in various ways as many psychiatrists and psychoanalysts have done, but the interpretation is always general, depending on the particular theories used. They do not and cannot tell us anything specific, such as why he went to Brazil and whether he was sure it was not Argentina.

What legitimates power and authority? What is normal and what is not? Authority is a context-dependent concept; it is not an abstract force existing independently of the field in which it is deployed. When authority and law are working creatively there is a relation between rulers and ruled; those who obey are no less essential than the one who commands. The anarchist maxim 'If no one obeys, no one can rule' is true. No rule is applicable to chaos. 'The Law' is brought in when doubt becomes rampant, and then arbitrary laws may be promulgated in desperation. If rules become abstract, apart from any determinate content other than serving the interests of a particular group, they loose significance and appear arbitrary. The indecipherability of law is equivalent to its nullity.

Rules may be forced on us by people who imagine rules are the source of necessity. Elementary arithmetic is usually drilled into pupils and children may be ordered to do things. We may resent this and see no point to the order and feel forced. In Orwell's *Nineteen Eighty Four*, Winston, who is living under a brutal dictatorship which determines the truth, says, 'Freedom is the freedom to say that two plus two makes four. If that is granted, all else follows' (Orwell 1984, p. 79). The truth of the matter is independent of what anyone says or believes. It is free of suggestion and understanding, this is freedom. Perhaps if we are in the army or learning arithmetic, we may see the point of blindly obeying certain rules, realising that this discipline makes rules and law possible. When this is accomplished, we become orientated by the rules and are autonomous in that we can decide whether to follow, ignore, change or develop them.

Capacity

A dispositional view of human understanding depends on the belief in a unitary mind, or brain, from which action causally follows. There must be a cause to make a disposition manifest. The cause is in an external relation to the action. It implies the picture of a world of order, stasis and causal determination. However, there is no normative element which enables us to justify our actions. We need to move from this picture to one that emphasises contingency and freedom: the human ability to reason, decide and learn from others. It has to include our ability to develop the skills required to see the significance of similarities and differences and create analogies across complex wholes. For this we need the notion of capacity, which involves the sense of a human world that is historical, and of language that is a vast web of mutually related elements with internal relations between them within which new forms of significance are created.

A capacity is a know-how at the agent's disposal. It is fundamentally practical, a know-how rather than a knowing. It is a way of understanding action which is not separated from the process by which it comes to pass. Riding a bicycle, having a conversation, playing games and being able to follow rules, or to refrain from doing these things, are capacities and not dispositions. A capacity does not transcend its manifestations. There is nothing that stands behind it as a particular object or structure which is necessary for the exercise of each capacity. It is a potentiality that is to be cultivated by practice and not the establishing of a model to be copied. Of course we could not have human capacities unless we had a human brain but a capacity is not reducible to it. There is no special structure in the brain that enables us to play chess rather than poker, or to refrain from doing either. These will depend on training and a way of life.

We speak of people *having* capacities. So and so can ride a bicycle, can swim, etc.; they have these capacities. But this picture can be misleading. For we cannot own capacities. A capacity is the ability to do, or refrain from doing, something and when we do not exercise it, it is not something we can store away, because it is not a thing that can be located.

This confusion is widespread. It is common for people to feel that when they think, its source is in their heads; they feel they 'think' with their heads and that their head may be full of thoughts. They may rationalise this and say they are using their brains and the brain is in their head. Some psychotic people, when they 'think', feel the 'machinery' in their head or their brain gets hot and is painful.

Analogies confuse us. A head full of thoughts does not mean we are thoughtful. We must have an active brain to think, or abstain from it, but we do not think with our brains. A less confusing picture of thinking is to say that it is the ability to operate with signs. This may help to remove the prejudice that thinking is an activity that occurs in our heads, or minds. Of course the vehicle on which the ability depends, such as the limbs and brain required to play football or to think, are things that are located, but they are not stored, nor do they belong to one in the sense of being external possessions. When we walk we use our legs but we do not walk with our legs, although we may use a walking stick to walk (*BB* pp. 117–18).

The link between capacities and their occurrences is not causal but criterial. It involves internal relations rather than external ones. Thus there are criteria as to whether someone is playing football or rugby, swimming or floundering, thinking or expressing an emotion. We attend to what is happening and see if it fulfils its criteria. We do not look for external causes as we do if we want to decide if a person has tuberculosis or not. A capacity is a possibility dependent on our use of language. There are all sorts of ways of playing football or swimming which we recognise if we have the skill and new ways may be developed that might become accepted as part of the activity.

Capacities are related to reasons and are normative – we can have various degrees of failure or success in exercising them. They involve the ability to master a technique which is taught and applied in a practice. Many of us have the capacity to play chess but there are enormous differences in how well we exercise this capacity, for we vary on the range of conceptual resources available to us. Our ability is a purely practical question, conceptually indissociable from our background and training. This differs from a disposition which determines an action, determinism being but a norm of description of the phenomena studied in mechanics and in computer programmes.

Abilities are related to understanding. We may be able to verify the correctness of an action although not understand it. We may know our depression is unreasonable and not a normal response to a situation, yet not understand it. Understanding is manifest in an array of circumstances, not just one. We may think we understand in a therapeutic session, but cease to do so when we get out into the public world. Understanding is not a particular mental state but a capacity to be clear about the circumstances under which we make the ascription that we understand.

Memory

Memory is a complex concept about which much has been written. We tend to think of memory as showing us the past. But if memory shows us the past, how does it show us that it is the past?

> It does *not* show us the past. Any more that our senses show us the present.
>
> Nor can it be said to communicate the past to us. For even supposing that memory were an audible voice that spoke to us – how could we understand it? If it tells us e.g. 'Yesterday the weather was fine', how can I learn what 'yesterday' means? (*Z* ¶¶663–4)

We can remember many facts and skills encountered in the past, but we do not necessarily remember when or how we learnt them. We can remember our school days, but we can also remember that we are going to Spain in 3 months time. We can speak, calculate and find our way around the world, without actively remembering or recollecting how to do them.

Freud was interested in recollection, remembering or failing to remember dreams and past events, especially in childhood. These, he thought, give a clue as to the causes of neurosis. The psychoanalytic account of infancy, which is a crucial part of its theory and practice, is obtained from the analysis of what patients have remembered about it during the course of treatment. We must, therefore, examine its concept of remembering. Throughout his work Freud depended on his theory that all events are inscribed upon the memory. These events are registered in different 'mnemic systems'. The important one, from his point of view, is the unconscious where lie the memories that cannot be consciously recollected since they are repressed. All the events of infancy are recorded here but are repressed and so not under the control of the subject. Special techniques of psychoanalysis are needed to recover them.

The ideal goal of psychoanalysis is the eradication of infantile amnesia (Freud 1937). Free association and the analysis of dreams and symptoms are important in this task. The remembering, to be therapeutic, occurs in the transference where repetition of the past occurs in the presence of the analyst. The analyst, however, also reconstitutes part of childhood history even in the absence of any memory of it on the part of the patient. He does this in terms of his theory. This, Freud assures us, has a therapeutic effect! (Ibid.)

Freud was under the influence of a very ancient picture of the mind and of the nature of memory and recognition (Hacker 1996, pp. 480–512). He reduced the concept of memory to memory-image storage and retrieval. So there is an 'inner process' which is the supposed referent of the words 'I remember', which we report on when we state what we remember. This picture arises from the assumptions of mentalism, the doctrine that the causes of observable behaviour are inner mental states, or processes. This picture gives rise to the problem as to how we remember something that happened in the past when it no longer exists. The temptation is to assume that since the past does not now exist there must be a 'memory item', a mnemic trace, which tells us authentically what is past. This item is presumed to be stored in the mind or brain, unconsciously in the case of childhood memories. Damage to certain areas of the brain which results in memory loss seems to confirm this.

Another part of the confusion is that we picture time as a river. We see an event now and then wonder where the present goes when it becomes past. It must go somewhere! We imagine the present *is* and the past is elsewhere. But the present is *not*; since it is always becoming, it cannot be grasped. If we listen to a melody, the past, present and the future of it are imbricated. The melody has duration, it is a virtual whole: that is, it changes as it endures, and it is not made of parts. Time is not made of parts; a clock does not measure time but movements in time.

When we remember we do not have to have a present mental image. 'If someone asks me what I have been doing in the last two hours, I answer him straight off and don't read the answer from an experience I am having. And yet one says that I *remembered*, and this is a mental process' (*RPP1* ¶105). We can describe the past and no image or picture need come to mind; but we may go on to describe and elaborate on our memory and this may involve images and pictures. The language game of memory precedes any images; otherwise, we could not remember until we had the images. We can remember smells, tastes and feelings and these also are not reducible to images.

Recognition is close to memory. Once more we are easily deceived about its nature. We imagine that an act of recognition involves comparing two impressions with one another. Our memory preserves a picture of what has been seen before which we match with our present perception when we recognise. But this need not be so, as we would have to recognise that the old impression in our memory is an image of what we are actually seeing; otherwise, it would mean nothing to us. Also recognition does not always occur. Thus I do not actively recognise my house when I enter it, or recognise my wife when I have not seen her for a few days; but I do not fail to recognise either. Recognising is not an activity that takes place in our mind. We cannot order someone to recognise but we can ask them to try to do so. When they do, it is an achievement which takes no time – 'Now I recognise her'. In ordinary circumstances, say seeing my house, there is no achievement; so we do not speak of recognising it (Hacker 1996, pp. 503–8).

How do we know if a certain memory item tells us authentically what is past? It may contain a faithful picture of what is remembered but how do we know it is a picture of the past and not a fantasy? Could it not be a play of our imagination? Neither a picture, a photograph, nor a mental image can tell us by itself what it is a picture of. Pictures and photographs may have names and dates on them but mental images do not. If we remember something, we can only have a sense of the past when we know how to remember. For something to be a recollection we must know that what it represents happened in the past, for our only access to the sense of the past is via the recollection. So the concepts of 'past' and 'recollection' are internally related; we cannot have one without the other.

We can have a feeling of pastness and this is not necessarily connected with memory. Thus we speak of the feeling of 'long, long ago' which is embedded in a context of gestures and linguistic phrases. Many fairy stories start in this way. These gestures can be misunderstood but they are not the same as phrases like, 'I remember him', 'Now the memory of that football match comes back to me.' While Proust was a master at evoking the past, many accounts of the past read as if they were descriptions of an unfamiliar culture which could be contemporary. Psychoanalytic accounts of childhood and infancy rarely evoke them but describe them as if they were a primitive form of adulthood.

Memory is a capacity that human beings possess but its manifestations are hugely varied. It does not have to be understood as an inner process of remembering, which goes on in the peculiar medium of the mind independent of expressing a memory, forgetting one, remembering a dream, pretending to remember or repressing it. We learn to exercise this capacity as we learn to speak. We judge whether someone is remembering or repressing without having any knowledge of the state of their brain, or having to peer into their 'inner world'. Remembering involves complex language-games which relate to concepts of time, place, our sense of who we are and much else. Undoing a repressed memory is a different and more complicated language-game from remembering our daily activities (A good account of memory is in Schulte 1993, pp. 95–119).

Communication

The importance of the difference between dispositions and capacities can be illustrated by how we convey meaning to one another.

A common picture of communication between people is that words are vehicles for thoughts which contain meanings. When we speak, the words convey the thoughts and meanings to the other person. The hearer then translates the sounds of the words back into thoughts or concepts. This picture assumes that the meaning of an expression is something correlated with it: there is the word and with it is the meaning or concept. For communication to be successful the speaker and the hearer must attach the same meanings to the same word. This notion of thought transference, the telementation theory of communication, has a long history and was clearly described by Locke and assumed by Freud and Saussure, who influenced the psychoanalyst Lacan (Harris 1988, 1996). This notion of communication between people is criticised in many places by Wittgenstein. Thus:

> We regard understanding as the essential thing, and signs as something inessential. – But in that case, why have the signs at all? If you think that it is only so as to make ourselves understood by others, then you are very likely looking on the signs as a drug which is to produce in other people the same condition as my own. (*PG* ¶39)

The trouble is that the thought transference theory does not allow for truth or falsehood. If a speaker says, 'Dogs bark', then the hearer will agree if the speaker and the hearer attach the same meaning to the words; he understands the sentence; it is within the speech circuit; conditioning or a drug could have caused the agreement. But the speaker is stating a truth about dogs; so it is not just a question about agreement, but of truth. Dogs do bark. This is a contextualised statement; to understand its truth or falsehood we need to know the context in which it makes sense to say something is true or not. The speech circuit notion is mentalistic; we exchange something from one mind to another. We must drop this picture of the mind as an isolated substance present to itself, to see truth and falsehood as depending on our openness to a shared world which provides their criteria (Harris 1996, pp. 93–109).

> Misleading parallel: the expression of pain is a cry – the expression of a thought a proposition.
> As if the purpose of the proposition were to convey to one person how it is with another: only so to speak, in his thinking part and not in the stomach. (*PI* ¶317)

This misleading analogy exerts a pernicious influence on our thinking about expression, the conveying of thoughts and the nature of psychoanalytic interpretation. It is the belief that the content of the proposition is hidden in the mind and can be inferred only indirectly. This is a basic belief of psychoanalysis, that we can only infer consciousness and mental processes in other minds, that the 'real' thought, the unconscious one, needs interpretation.

Instead of theorising about the transference of thoughts and feelings from one mind to another it is better to turn to the work of developmental psychologists who actually study how children develop the concepts necessary for understanding people and their thoughts and emotions. Much of this work was provoked by the later writing of Wittgenstein (Chapman and Dixon 1987; Tomasello 1992; Hutto 2008).

It is necessary to distinguish intentional attitudes from propositional ones. During the first 2 years of life infants show impressive responsiveness to intention-in-action. Thus 2-month-old infants react negatively if face-to-face encounters with significant others are disrupted, for example, if the baby smiles and the mother is depressed and just looks away. Later they are able to take part in basic forms of joint attention. These abilities are non-conceptual, 'instinctive'. They do not depend on the capacity to represent the mental state of others; the baby does not need a theory of the mind. It is an attunement to other humans depending on gaze, gesture, facial expression, tone of voice and smells. It is similar to the attunement other mammals have to their mothers.

Propositional attitudes develop much later and go on developing for many years. This includes a capacity to characterise a state of mind, one's own and others. That is, to be able to recognise that others are angry, sad or thoughtful. To be able to give reasons for this and understand other people's reasons. Young children can respond to other people's desires but do not understand reasons for them. For reasons are not isolated thoughts, or desires but involve understanding the way propositional attitudes interrelate. It is not just seeing what someone wants but seeing a reason why they want it. It is the ability to understand that someone may want something that is out of sight and perhaps in the far future. Most importantly, it involves the capacity to imagine contrasting perspectives and so understand what it is to aim at truth. Thus young children cannot make the distinction between 'what they take to be the case' and 'what is the case'.

A critical factor in developing an understanding of truth is experience in participating in conversations and exercising imaginative capacities appropriately. Thus deaf children who lack signing partners in their homes are severely delayed, sometimes into late adolescence and can fare worse than individuals with extreme autism. No equivalent delays are exhibited by deaf children who have signing partners in their home. The opportunity or lack of it to engage in conversations has been the factor most strongly correlated with this discrepancy (Hutto 2008, pp. 137–8).

Advances in science depend on contrasting perspectives. Science requires the ability to recognise that people may have a different take on things than oneself. This is what developmental psychologists do when they converse with children while simultaneously observing how they respond to various tasks, and how they use language. Rather than following a theory of development, they describe. This is fully compatible with modern biology in which new visual technologies, especially confocal microscopy, enable biologists to observe the molecular motors that drive embryonic development. This is part of a long tradition in the life sciences in which direct description is granted priority over theories (Keller 2002). This contrasts with psychoanalysis, and cognitive therapy in which particular theories of the mind are identified with by the practitioner.

People having only one perspective that are unable to cope with changes in it have difficulty in placing their feelings and emotions in a context. They have difficulty with propositional attitudes and tend to think in a primitive causal fashion about their feelings and thoughts – 'that's to blame' – instead of being able to reflect on the context and their relation to others that enables propositional attitudes to develop. It is this primitive seeking for an immediate cause that psychoanalysts conceptualise as using mental mechanisms such as projection and introjection. These theorists, however, are as mechanical as the people they seek to understand. They assume that there is an entity, the mind, so there is an inner world and an outer one, and as such beliefs must be either 'inner' or 'outer', introjected or projected. The term 'projective identification' is used to describe the basis of all relationships between people by many Kleinians (Hinshelwood 1991, 'Projective Identification' is a good summary).

A brief case history may make this clearer. A man consulted me because when he shaved in the morning he felt his next door neighbour was focusing a laser beam on his head, which 'shrivelled' his brain. In conversation with him it became clear that he did not know his neighbour very well, but he said he was quite friendly and they would greet each other on passing. He had no idea why his neighbour was being so aggressive and had not brought up the matter with him. Significantly he had consulted his doctor. By talking to him and being 'gently' sceptical about laser beams and shrivelled brains he soon gave up the idea. It became clear that he had been trying to make sense of a feeling of depression. There was no mechanism of projection. We need to understand how he used words to make sense of his life, rather than imagine that his words were necessarily being used to refer to something. Putting his feelings in a context through conversation enabled him to acknowledge that his feeling of depression was his responsibility.

The theoretical attitude ignores the difference between speaking about minds or bodies and speaking to people. So the importance of context, timing and conversation in understanding is overlooked. It is driven by the picture that there is a fixed reality 'out-there' which can best be described in scientific language. So people are 'really' objects performing various functions which can be understood by an 'objective' scientist. In an ideal world, both Freud and Klein thought that prophylactic psychoanalysis would be as compulsory as going to school. It would introduce children early to the 'reality principle'. But the difficulties of human relationships are not abstract puzzles that call for a technical solution, nor are they best understood in terms of some overriding theory. They may involve deep disquiets which are person-relative. It is an essential part of the human condition to try to make sense of one's origins and of course one's parents are part of this. It is also part of this condition to be responsible for one's feelings and thoughts and not be at the mercy of mechanisms.

> In philosophy we do not draw conclusions. 'But it must be like this!' is not a philosophical proposition. Philosophy only states what everyone admits. (*PI* ¶599)

Cognitive therapy

Cognitive therapists have similar problems with theory:

> The Behaviourists were meticulous about avoiding speculation about what is going on in my mind or your mind or his or her or its mind. In effect, they championed the third person perspective, in which only facts garnered 'from the outside' count as data.... The idea at its simplest was that since you can never 'see directly' into people's minds, but have to take their word for it, any such facts as there are about mental events are not among the data of science, since they can never be properly verified by objective methods. This methodological scruple... is the ruling principle of all experimental psychology and neuroscience today (not just 'behaviourist' research). All science is constructed from the third person point of view. (Dennett 1991, pp. 70–1)

It is certainly true that we cannot *see directly* into people's minds but we do not see directly into our own minds either. As we do not *have* minds we cannot see into them, since there is not an external relation between 'we' and our minds. We can express and state our thoughts and feelings not because we were taught to observe and represent our minds but by holding conversations with people who are significant to us in childhood (Hutto 2008).

The understanding of action in terms of capacities rather than dispositions differs from the representational view of the mind shared by psychoanalysts and cognitive therapists. According to the latter, there are mechanisms in the mind which are mental processes causally interacting with mental representations so constituting propositional attitudes. Fodor, a distinguished opponent of what he calls the Wittgenstein/Ryle tradition which *has made a shambles from which philosophy has yet fully to recover* (Fodor 2003, p. 9) puts it as follows:

> I'm assuming, in the general spirit of Representational Theories of Mind, that the mental particular that's in your head on occasions when you think *dog* is a token of the concept type DOG, just as the word that's on your lips when you say 'dog' is a token of the word type 'dog'. In both cases, the tokens are concrete particulars and the types are abstracta. Likewise, the mental particular that's in your head when you think that (judge that) *dogs bark* is a token of the mental representation type DOGS BARK. (Fodor 2003, p. 13)

This is unconvincing. There are different uses and meanings to words. Take the word 'good'. Fodor presupposes there is a single type 'good' but it can have different meanings, a multiplicity of tokens – a good piece of chocolate, a good marriage, etc. A dictionary often works in this way. It assumes there are linguistic units that can be clearly identified from one another; there are particular items of an abstraction – the type. As Fodor puts it, when you say 'dog', this is a token of the abstract type 'dog'. But can we clearly identify words and meanings outside a particular context? When a child is learning to speak, it is often difficult to identify a word. Does 'mamma' name a person, ask for attention, express love or what? Is 'I dunno' 2, 3 or 4 words? What about inflected languages? Can we identify particular thoughts and meanings? How many are there on this page? Some would say there are none, but few would agree on a particular number. Mental particulars occur 'in your head' – but whereabouts? In the brain? Neuro-physiologists do not find any there. What would they look like? A particular must reside somewhere more concrete than a gesture towards one's head. And where are types? In an abstract realm, a Platonic heaven?

The representational view of the mind is basic to much cognitive behaviour therapy (CBT). Emotional disturbances are held to be caused by dysfunctional beliefs. Beliefs and automatic thoughts guide behaviour. At root there are underlying cognitive structures or schemata, called 'core beliefs', that form the basis of cognitive disturbance. These are mental events that patients can be trained to report and so can be altered. Even language learning is assumed to depend on our having a set of innate beliefs.

The concept of belief, however, is not that simple. It is assumed that beliefs can be represented in the mind, so can be a cause. But if someone says 'I believe that "p"', that does not imply that 'p' occurred in their mind. This would conflate a belief with having a belief. If asked whether I believe it will rain, I look out the window at the sky. I do not observe the contents of my mind. If I report what I believe I do not look into my mind for evidence as to the belief. However, if someone reports on my beliefs, he must seek evidence for his reports and whether it is sufficient evidence may be arguable. Someone may say 'I am worthless', but this may be an expression of what he feels about himself, which is not necessarily a belief which is true or false. He may be perfectly aware that others do not agree with him. 'I can't stand being rejected' says something about how I feel about rejection, but that does not make it a belief.

These confusions arise because therapists assume that only the third person point of view is valid in science. This is part of their myth of science which confuses how scientists go about their business with how they report their findings. A scientist does not have to be 'objective' about his theory or experiments; he may be enthusiastic about them. What he does have to do, if they are to enter the precincts of science, is to state them in propositions so that others can understand them. His observations and experiments must be able to be reduplicated by experts and his theories must be comprehensible to them. He must understand that because 'I think or believe that "p"' does not mean that p. Heisenberg, one of the great physicists of the twentieth century, wrote: 'Science is rooted in conversations.' Thus the conversations between Einstein and Bohr were crucial to the development of quantum mechanics. Each had a position, were very different temperamentally, did not like each other, but they had a creative dialogue over many years (Beller 1999). This seems to be difficult for psychotherapists who too readily assume that if they think that 'p' then p.

A person seeking therapy is in conflict and disorientated. They are knocking their heads against the limits of thought, trying to think and do what cannot be done, or doing what they believe cannot be done. By revealing themselves to some other person who they trust, they may come to see creative possibilities, differences and similarities they had not seen before. So they may realise that things *need not* be as they thought *must* be, or that things *may* be as they imagined *could not* be. So they may move on, not by being told what to do, or being interpreted in terms of a theory, but spontaneously.

Therapists and patients participate in creating their own insights. An understanding is developed *which consists in 'seeing connections'* (*PI* ¶122). Thus a patient may re-enact the conflicts and anxieties in the room with the therapist which he had to deal with in the past in his family. By becoming aware of the moment-to-moment changes in these struggles and linking them with what is going on between the therapist and the patient enables the experience of being understood. Different ways of speaking, new aspects of the past, repetitions, reminders, absurdities and humour all play their part. It is impossible to give a complete list of what is done, as therapists and patients differ in what they feel as relevant. At root, however, we enable the person to reorientate themselves so they can move on from their confusions and despair, and live their life more freely.

If one does not know speech, one has no way of knowing men. (Confucius, Analects 20.3)

6
Elucidation

In this chapter I will show how psychological theories prevent us from seeing the world aright. An important theme in Wittgenstein is his exploration of the harmony between the structure of the world and the way symbols symbolise. He shows that there is no all-comprehending set of rules for the construction of propositions in which symbols occur. Instead, we have to turn towards the concrete phenomena of language-in-use to clarify the shifting patterns of how symbols symbolise.

Theorists of psychotherapy have a very different approach as they view the world and people in it through the spectacles of theory. Their theories are empirical and are allegedly based on the observation of clinical data. They build them, however, on various models of the mind. These are empirical hypotheses, inferred but not observable as such.

A central problem of psychotherapy is how to have a natural, unconstrained relation to the world and other people. According to Freud, every neurosis forces the patient out of real life and alienates him from reality (1911, p. 218). To explain this he claimed that people who are neurotic or psychotic suffer from phantasies, which prevent the correct apprehension of reality. Correct apprehension meant correct according to his canons of the scientific method. Phantasies are rather like day-dreams; they are organised scenes which are bound to unconscious wishes, which, in turn, are repetitions from scenes in infancy and propelled by instinctual impulses. The psychoanalyst must unearth these phantasies, which lie behind the products of the unconscious, including dreams, day-dreams, slips of the tongue and neurotic symptoms.

Similarly CBT practitioners tend to identify with what they believe to be scientific rationality. Humans are portrayed as information seekers who construct models of reality as if they are amateur scientists.

In neurosis the cognitive models are incorrect, in that they do not fit the real world and techniques are devised to correct them.

Both forget that in any empirical theory the one who makes the theory is necessarily outside it. We human beings make theories for various purposes but *we* cannot be subsumed under them. Whenever there is a representation of the world in propositions, there is a subject who is in a position to say 'I think...' This applies as much to the patient as to the therapist. Everyone measures the world. To subsume a particular group of people under a theory is to impose a measure on them, to fail to recognise their humanity and to fail to have an unconstrained relation to them.

Basic to these empirical pictures of the mind–world relationship is the assumption that there is an *a-priori order* of the world which guarantees the harmony between thought, language and the world. It seems that there is a real external world that we perceive and that science describes, and in addition there is an inner world of instincts, inner representations, psychical processes and maladaptive cognitions, which may disturb the harmony between the real external world and the person living in it.

Our thought and language enable us to describe and act in accord with scientific reality as language is supposed to reflect its *a-priori* structure. Reality is assumed to be independent of those who think or talk about it, so the meaning of words must somehow be correlated with it. The inner and outer world are a set of facts to which statements about them must correspond. The question is then raised as to how our thoughts, language and reality must be constituted for it to be possible to represent or not both the external world and the inner one.

It is assumed there is a fit, an isomorphism, between the form of thought and language, and the way things in the world happen to be. I say 'Snow is white' and this sentence somehow corresponds to the fact that snow is white if and only if snow is white. Instincts, the pleasure principle and cognitions may, however, interfere with this perception and I may judge falsely. This is most likely to happen when we make judgements about ourselves and others.

In short, thinking is conceived as rule-bound information processing and manipulation of symbols, mirroring an autonomous, pre-existing reality; when we fail to think properly our thought does not match reality.

This information-processing picture of the relation between thought, language and the world does not make sense, although it is a belief that is basic to much psychiatry, psychoanalytic theorising and cognitive therapy. It is a functionalism that has thinking as irrelevant to what is thought. Action is seen to be the result of rational thought instead of being at its source. It is based on the confused notion that there are facts, 'external and internal reality', which serve as a standard against which we judge whether our propositions make sense.

This misconstrues how we actually talk. It conceals the role of the way we live in our descriptions. It forgets that any theory or scientific activity implies there is a user who is necessarily outside the theory, using language to describe, frame hypotheses and create theories. We make theories for various purposes; to identify with a theory results in our being used by it, acting as if it were true (Elder, 1994; McManus 2006, pp. 213–34).

It implies that our minds can be understood as an object of descriptive and referential terms. We can be told what our minds are in essence: a complicated information processor, or an activity driven by unconscious forces. Language is seen merely as a descriptive instrument and words are referring names. The expert knows what is really going on in our minds; he seems to have direct access to it. This craving for an expert, who has immediate access to our minds, abolishes the need for expression and undermines the heart of the talking cure. It confuses truth with truthfulness. It is a true statement to say that water is made from hydrogen and oxygen. We may say this but we may not be being truthful, in that we may not have the faintest idea as to what that statement really means.

The talking cure helps us to master the logic of thinking, feeling and desire by attending to the different ways symbols symbolise. Thus we may need the responsive attention of others to support the sense of our own experience. To listen to an expression of despair with a bored, all-knowing expression deprives the words of sense in a person who is unsure of herself. It is the involvement of others in our words that constitutes a condition of their meaningfulness, and which helps to bring order to our confusions.

The task of elucidation is to clarify our confusions. To understand its nature we must distinguish between psychology and logic. Psychology is an empirical science but logic is not. Believing, thinking, desiring, feeling, sensing and meaning something seem to be mental activities which we can experience; so we are tempted to think that psychology, as an empirical science, affords the key to understanding them. This is a mistake. What are essential to these activities are their uses, and the operations involved, that is, what we are doing when we desire or feel. It is the proper business of logic to describe these operations.

We can say that the contribution of psychology to the understanding of logical problems is 'just as much as the chemistry of wood contributes to the solution of chess problems. By this I mean that logic is concerned with the game and not with the "stuff" from which the pieces are manufactured' (*VW* p. 473).

An empirical science is concerned to increase our knowledge of things and events in the world. Thus the chemical analysis of something tells us of what it is composed. Chemicals are analysed until we get to atoms. These, in turn, are analysed by the physicist into sub-nuclear particles and so on. Theories are created to explain these discoveries. Similarly, psychologists categorise the mind in various ways, creating theories using these categories to explain their clinical 'findings'. Ultimately, it is hoped that psychical processes will be analysed into brain processes and then into chemical and physical ones.

In contrast to science, logical or grammatical elucidation does not increase our knowledge of things. I will use 'logical' to include what Wittgenstein sometimes calls 'grammatical' as what he means by 'grammar' is not its ordinary meaning and it is simpler to keep to one word. A logical elucidation is concerned with the way we operate with words and pictures, the forms of representation or conceptual structures that are integrated into human activity. Language includes gestures, obscene ones, pointing at something, mime, drawings and the use of samples such as colour – samples. Language in this sense is far bigger than what is described in dictionaries, phrase books and books on grammar. In these, it is abstracted from the hurly-burly of human activity. A logical elucidation is concerned with the weaving of language in human life (Baker 2004, pp. 52–72).

Elucidation is a practice that depends on no theory, dogma or technical language. It seeks to understand the requirements for any language to be meaningful, for logic penetrates all thought and talk enabling us to make sense. Its task is to clarify what has been said or thought, to make explicit the logical structure which is implicit in our sentences. It is necessary as we often lack perspicuity in our relation to our own words. We imagine there is a meaning when there is none, or it is confused. We are not truthful. We easily forget how meaning shifts as the context shifts. For example, a word in a theoretical context will shift its sense in a practical one. Thus the meaning of 'unconscious' as ordinarily used is very different from the Freudian 'unconscious' which is an entity with a structure within the mind. Sometimes there is nearly pure rule-following, in which the facts that give meaning to the rules are constant, as in much science and mathematics. Often the facts about what the rules require depend on 'normal circumstances' for their understanding (*OC* ¶27). Thus: 'Let's meet sometime soon'.

Elucidation depends on the recognition that attention to the way we use signs to symbolise clarifies how we create meaning. We cannot go outside language and the world in order to understand how language works in the way it does. If we try, we become dogmatic, as in Freud when he tells us *the* meaning of dreams. For sure he tells us the psychoanalytic meaning of dreams and to think that it is *the* meaning, he imagines that his way of representing things is the only valid way. Telling one's dreams and finding meaning in them is an activity that humans in nearly all cultures take part in and is done for all sorts of different reasons. Psychoanalysis is just one use. Freud never elucidates the meaning of meaning.

Elucidation leads to the recognition of the autonomy of language; language cannot be a system with an absolute foundation outside of it. Speaking and writing is a human activity used for purposes that interest we humans. There is no reason to suppose that other 'intelligent' beings in the universe would have any interest in it – they probably have better things to do. Elucidation, however, is more basic than any empirical science, since all sciences assume we can make sense. Without language and meaning there can be no science.

Linguistics describes languages but, as it is a science, it has to use language to describe the languages. It has developed a large technical vocabulary. Books on grammar, phonetics, semantics or neurolinguistics use language to describe the facts of language systems. They assume its communicative powers. 'However language is not defined for us as an arrangement fulfilling a definite purpose' (*Z* ¶322). We are concerned with studying the requirements for language as such to be meaningful. That cannot be done by using language in the usual way as every way of expressing these requirements presupposes them and makes use of them. A technical vocabulary, or any meta-language, is still a language that means something and is developed for a particular use. It cannot tell us what enables meaning. This only emerges with close attention to the way signs are used.

Elucidations, therefore, are generally indirect and often involve *reductio* type arguments, as they involve recognising faulty pictures of language to which we are attached. An example of this is the widespread belief that every meaningful word must correspond to an object. The most important and difficult task of elucidation is that it must avoid all dogmatism for this rarely has any therapeutic action other than that of suggestion (Kuusela 2008).

If one tried to advance *theses* in philosophy, it would never be possible to debate them, because everyone would agree to them. (*PI* ¶128)

The wrong conception which I want to object to ... is the following, that we can *discover* something wholly new. That is a mistake. The truth of the matter is that we have already got everything, and we have got it actually *present*; we need not wait for anything. We make our moves in the realm of the grammar of ordinary language, and this grammar is already there. Thus we have already got everything and need not wait for the future. (*WVC* p. 183)

Wittgenstein goes on to say that any thesis in philosophy must be clear and give rise to no dispute. Dispute arises only when things have not been expressed clearly enough because then there is

a feeling that something has now been asserted, and I do not yet know whether I should admit it or not. If, however, you make the grammar clear to yourself, if you proceed by very short steps in such a way that every single step becomes perfectly obvious and natural, no dispute whatsoever can arise .... The only correct method of doing philosophy consists in not saying anything and leaving it to another to make a claim. That is the method I now adhere to. What the other person is not able to do is to arrange the rules step by step and in the right order so that all questions are solved automatically. (*WVC* pp. 183–4)

Elucidations are basic to therapy. Possibilities to which we are blind are revealed, rather than facts of which we are ignorant are discovered. It is concerned with reminders and recollections about our natural history. Therapy takes the form of a dialogue between people in which both are addressing a problem that engages them. A problem causing suffering is someone's problem and another's problem is another problem. Depression, for example, takes a different form for every person involved, which makes elucidation essentially person-relative. Everything depends on the *free* acknowledgement of the people involved (Baker 2004, pp. 22–51, 205–22). All we can do is to raise questions and give reminders, which may reveal misleading analogies or captivating pictures that create illusions of reason.

I will use three approaches that help to elucidate confusions about the relation between language, thought and reality. First, there is attention to the way an infant learns its mother tongue, then language-games and the place of logic in making sense. It may be helpful at first to quote a remark in which Wittgenstein summarises the problem of the relation of thought, language and reality:

> The agreement, the harmony, of thought and reality consists in this: if I say falsely that something is *red*, even the *red* is what it isn't. And when I want to explain the word 'red' to someone, in the sentence 'That is not red', I do it by pointing to something red. (*PI* ¶429)

This enigmatic remark, containing two platitudes, dismantles the traditional dualistic account in which it is assumed there is an *a-priori* order of the world containing existing objects to be named, and acts of mind that are directed at these objects. Consciousness, it seems, is one thing and that of which we are conscious another thing. The remark also lays bare the hidden nonsense in such a picture of our relation to the world.

It shows that the meaning of *red* is not an object. There is no such thing as being red, independent of any particular understanding of it being so. The absence of *red* is what makes the proposition false, not the absence of satisfaction, or failure to match a mental representation with reality. It is a matter of the logic of our language that 'It is false that p = not-p'. In the ordinary use of *red*, nothing red needs to be present or pointed out, although, in one way or another, red objects do usually enter into the learning of the word *red*. I may explain what I mean by *red* by pointing to something red, thus using it as a sample. But I am not then forging a connection between language and reality but employing a red patch as an instrument to explain what I understand by red.

There is no 'gap' between language, thought and reality. It is a false picture which produces this 'gap'; it is not there when we speak. It depends on the assumption that there is a world which lies beyond language and exists independently of it, sometimes dubbed Reality. But how can we speak of it if *it* is 'beyond' language? To understand how a proposition refers to something we have to grasp the meaning and position of its words, the particular occasion of its use including the way it is uttered, and the pattern of relationships, which includes our own role as speakers or hearers. To know my name is to know that I am Peter but at the same time to know that I am called Peter.

Learning one's mother tongue

Freud considered the basic unit for the function of speech to be the 'word', which he thought was a combination put together from auditory, visual and kinaesthetic elements. He thought we learn to speak by associating 'a sound image of a word 'with a 'sense of the innervation of a word'. We learn the language of other people by endeavouring to make the sound-image produced by ourselves as like as possible to the one which gave rise to our speech innervation. Essentially we learn to speak, spell, read and write by association of various images. Words acquire their meaning by being linked to an 'object-presentation' which is a complex of associations made up of a complex of visual, acoustic, tactile, kinaesthetic and other presentations (Freud 1891). The psychic apparatus sets up a 'language machine' which mediates between the inner world and public expression.

Freud thought that sexuality was the link between language and the world. He based it on the hypothesis of the philologist Hans Sperber who speculated that speech originally was used for summoning the speaker's sexual partner, the rhythm of manual work aroused sexual interest and, as time went on, sexual meaning became attached to work and other activities. So, at root, all words have a sexual meaning (Freud 1916–17, p. 167).

This account of the origins of language can be fruitfully compared to the opening sections of *Philosophical Investigations* where Wittgenstein discusses and criticises an account Augustine gives on the origin of language. The latter is similar to Freud's in that both have a primitive idea of the way language functions, concentrating on the word. 'It is this: the individual words in language name objects – sentences are combinations of such names.' It is assumed: 'Every word has a meaning. This meaning is correlated with the word. It is the object for which the word stands' (*PI* ¶1). This picture of meaning is criticised by Wittgenstein as being senseless. Sense and meaning are practices that develop as we become initiated into language: meaning is not something that can be attached to words or to anything. Language and the world it speaks of are internally related; there is no need of an external relation such as sexuality to link them.

To clarify this, Wittgenstein reminds us how the way in which we learn our mother tongue differs from the way we learn a second language. Some of the facts that have been found by developmental psychologists can be of importance to therapy although they are not involved in the same task as therapists who are concerned with people who are out of touch with their *own* development.

When we learn a second language we mostly learn a collection of contingent facts about signs; we learn which signs can be combined to create the symbols used to express what is expressed in one's mother tongue. We can ask questions like, 'What is this called'? 'How do you say this?' 'How do you pronounce this word'? 'What does this character stand for'? 'How do you tell the time'? We learn which concepts are expressed by which words in the foreign tongue. In short, we already understand what words and meaning are, but we want to know how to express them in a new language.

In learning a second language we tend to translate from it to our own, especially if we have a written piece to translate. At first we usually do a literal translation; we seek referential equivalence between the two languages, depending on dictionary meaning and our knowledge of grammar, hence the temptation to concentrate on the word. This may be enough for reports on facts and simple requests but it misses out on the expressive use of language which is far more difficult to translate as it requires an intimate knowledge of both languages. A child learning its mother tongue, however, first uses expressive language; only much later is it able to use the language-game of literalness. Non-literate people learn a foreign language in a similar way.

Initiation into our mother tongue is not a simple matter of teaching and learning, for the infant cannot know what it has to learn. It is not the same as learning to do something, such as learning a vocabulary, a grammar or a technique. For an infant can have no concept of language and so cannot want to learn it. It is in no position to decide what language to learn. We cannot say the word 'language' without language. There is no name for a name – every word presupposes other words. Language has no word for the definition of its own being. It is senseless to say 'Language exists'; it would need a metalanguage for that to make sense and a meta-meta-language to understand that. Language is not an object that we can stand back from and use; nevertheless, we can decide what to say when we speak.

Language is not an object but is that which gives us access to objects. We can describe in general terms what it is like to learn a particular language but not to use language in the first place, because to do this we would have to be able to think what it was like to have no language at all, that is, to think what it would be like not to think.

Like most mammals an infant has to join in the life of its species in order to survive. Infants differ from other mammals, however, in that from about 1 year onwards they have the ability to understand the intentional actions of others. She is bathed in speech and conversation from the people around her, and as she is human she has the possibility of joining in, which she is keen to do. In time she has to understand how to tell people things, what it makes sense to say, rather than merely repeating what is said. Learning to speak is not just to learn to react to signals, to utter sentences or react to orders. It is to understand what people are saying, which involves joining in with them not mechanically but spontaneously. It requires particular people, who are familiar, to whom it responds as an authority. She, however, is in no position to decide who understands human activities and language; she must follow her initiation blindly. It is only much later in her life that she may be able to look back and see her initiation was perverted in some ways.

> When do we say a person has learned an expression like 'I have a pain'? He must behave like an ordinary human being. If a child gave expressions of pain, when the cause of pain was absent: or of delight, when this cause of pain was present; this is a child we cannot teach. (Suppose we really taught him to use the word 'pain', but we did not take him to the doctor, etc.) If we want to teach a child a psychological word, he must behave like a normal being: even if, because of courage, he represses the expression of pain.... The frame of reference to which we fasten these words is ordinary human behaviour. (*LPP* pp. 158–9)

Children learn to speak not by mapping words onto perceptual experience but by trying to understand and take part in the adult's activities. It cannot be given explicit instructions as to how to speak. Thus mother pushes the child into the car saying 'Let's go!' or struggles with the child saying 'Let me wipe your face!' She treats the child as a human being so it picks up simple language-games. It is understanding the intentions of the adult in various contexts that is important. The child is involved in various events composed of actions and roles and it seeks to make sense of them and respond to them. It does not learn grammatical rules but responds to situations created by adults and learns grammar when it goes to school.

Since an infant is part of the human world, there is no need for a desperate search launched by a subject to get in touch with an 'outer' world or 'reality'; this is a phantasy of psychoanalysts. Infants, like ordinary adults, live in the world, not in an inner or outer one. The infant, however, has no concept of a subject, or of an inner or outer world. The world that the infant is part of is not the world we can describe using propositions. It cannot represent things in the world in the propositions of language for these do not exist for it. At first she can only give voice. As Wittgenstein wrote:

> Anyone who listens to a child's crying with understanding will know that psychic forces, terrible forces, sleep within it, different from anything commonly assumed. Profound rage & pain & lust for destruction. (*CV* p. 4)

The infant's cry, like the wolf's howl, the lion's roar and the mouse's squeak, is not articulated; nature is speaking, not human language. The cry says nothing but it shows. We may interpret it but there are no words, names and grammar to guide us in our understanding. We describe the infant's behaviour in terms of natural law – instincts, reflexes and so on.

Around the age of 1 an infant will begin to articulate. Its expressive behaviour begins to be articulate; it does not merely cry if hurt but can say it is and later justify its protests. It begins to learn what things and actions to pick out which make sense to adults. It starts to understand living beings that follow rules. Then it can partake in that form of life which depends on obeying, disobeying, making up and dealing with exceptions to rules. Our form of life is not fixed, it changes. Rules are not rigid; we have to learn to judge them rightly. 'Not only rules, but also examples are needed for establishing a practice. Our rules leave loopholes open, and the practice has to speak for itself' (*OC* ¶139).

Primates such as bonobo apes are very close to us and we have many pre-linguistic gestures and sounds in common with them. Nevertheless, they cannot use language to mean, to convey information or to symbolise. Their gestures are almost exclusively to regulate grooming, play, fighting, sex and travel, rather than directing the attention of others to outside things and events. Their gestures and vocalisations are for imperative purposes, to affect the behaviour of others directly, rather than share information or attention in a rule-following way (Tomasello 2003).

In human infants, gestures such as 'requests' for wanting something (open hand extended, fretting or mutual gaze) or requests to be lifted up (arms overhead, fretting or mutual gaze) gradually develop into the rule-following of an adult speaker's request.

The infant's gesture of 'request' is not the same as an adult's, for she can have no concept of requesting an object. An adult can answer if asked: 'Is that what you want?' An infant cannot; it has to learn the language-games of wanting and requesting from its interactions with adults. An adult can recognise her behaviour as an intended instance of a request, and can say what it is she is doing. A request is not just a conventionalised pattern of behaviour but involves recognition that it is a particular kind of communicative act which is part of a cultural practice and which the child can learn to participate in (Tomasello 2003, Taylor and Shanker 2003).

This way of understanding the development of language takes into account the upright posture and the hands in the development of human language; these developments greatly increase the variety of gestures that can develop. Some chimpanzee gestures are common to us; thus sibling rivalry and mother–child cooperative behaviour, with all their accompanying gestures, are important features of both.

It is often assumed that pointing at things and being told their name is basic to language learning as it appears to link language with things in the world. This is a mistake. We can define many things by pointing, for example, proper names, names of colours, names of numbers, names of animals and plants and names of directions. But suppose if we say 'This is called west' while pointing at the setting sun, there is no guarantee that such a definition will be taken in the way it is wanted. I point west at the setting sun and the learner thinks it is the sun that is called west. There is no way of pinning down the meanings of the words we define in this way.

If we point to something, say a cat, and say **that** is what the word 'cat' means, the infant must already know what pointing involves, in order to understand what a cat is. For the bearer of a name is not the same as the meaning of one. We can talk about a cat without one being present. If, for example, we point to a cake and say 'This is delicious', the child must already know what sort of thing a cake is to understand what we have said. If we define something, say an acute angle, we show the child angles and then pointing to an acute one, tell him ones like this are less than 90 degrees; in other words, angles must be recognised by the child before they can be defined. In short, merely pointing at things, without any other practice in the use of words, cannot constitute learning one's first language.

An important feature of the early learning of language is its concreteness, particularity and idiosyncrasy. 'There is individuality and contextedness everywhere, signs of broad-based rules nowhere. T did begin bringing order and systematicity to her language during her 2nd year of life, but it was a gradual, constructive process. It did not resemble in any way the instantaneous and irrevocable setting of parameters' (Tomasello 1992, pp. 264–5).

The structure of reality cannot be understood as necessarily mirrored in language. We cannot ground propositions with sense in any intrinsic structure of an independent reality. The meaning of a word is not something in the world that is correlated with it. Understanding meaning cannot be separated from the fact that we have to be initiated into language. Instead of looking into the mind, or studying words, to understand how we make or fail to make sense, we need to understand the child's initiation into language wherein it comes to master sense making through the use of signs.

The ancient Greek Pyrrhonian sceptics, who were concerned to cure 'the conceit and rashness of the Dogmatists', were well aware of this. Thus Sextus argued that basic ways of living, human forms of life, cannot be taught or learned. The way of teaching can be neither by evidence or by argument; there can be no experts in it and theories are redundant (Sextus 1994, Book 3, pp. 29–30).

Play

Being initiated into language is closely connected with playing. If a small child is playing, it is not trying to do anything beyond the game. It is not looking for fame, or success, nor is it following a prior set of rules. It is simply engaged in the game and allowing chance to play its part in the way the game may turn out. It is not merely imitating what adults are doing nor finding or following a set of rules.

A psychoanalyst who has emphasised the importance of play is Winnicott (1971b). He made many acute observations about the importance of play and its difficulty in disturbed children. He discussed the importance of what he called the transitional object in infants. Thus infants will often put their thumb in their mouth and then a bit of cloth or blanket along with their fingers. This may then become precious to the infant especially at the time of going to sleep or when it seeks comfort. He thought this transitional object to be an important mediator between what is objectively perceived and what is subjectively conceived.

Unfortunately, Winnicott's observations are vitiated by his theoretical convictions. He thought that the infant's relationship to the world has to be explained. The infant had to make a journey from subjectivity to objectivity (Ibid., p. 6). So there is an intermediate area between the two that is necessary for the initiation of the relationship between the child and the world. This is made possible by mothering in the early stages of development (Ibid., p. 13). Transitional objects are part of this intermediate area. Winnicott imagined that at an early stage the infant conceives the idea of something capable of meeting its needs that arise from instinctual tension. So there is a problem of the relationship between what it subjectively conceives and what is objectively perceived. Conceptions are subjective and perceptions are objective so how do the two meet?

This is a pseudo problem created by misunderstanding our initiation into language. It assumes that the relation between us, other people and the world is an external one rather than being an internal relationship. We cannot get outside ourselves, our language and practices to observe our selves and the world and then wonder how they become related. We are in the world and cannot be separated from it. There can be no 'I' or 'we' that it makes sense to separate from the world we live in. There is not an external relationship between a mother and her baby, or 'I' and the world. Winnicott, like Freud and other psychoanalysts, is a mentalist assuming that meaning and concepts are subjective and so constituted by mental occurrences in the mind. They believe there is an inner subjective world of meanings which are somehow connected with subjective states and these are prior to the use of language. The infant has to make a journey from the purely subjective to objectivity.

From conception the infant is in the world as the mother's uterus is as much part of the world as the room I am sitting in. Since the unborn baby has no language, it cannot conceptualise the uterus; it cannot think that it is confined in something, whereas we can think and perceive that we are in a room and perhaps confined to it. The infant is in the world both when in the uterus and after birth responding to it but unable to conceptualise. It makes no sense to say that the infant conceives an idea of something to relieve an instinctual tension. This is a purely theoretical notion, a picture, which is projected onto infants. It is to imagine they have an inner private language, but no psychoanalyst has demonstrated how this is possible and Wittgenstein has shown it is senseless (*PI* ¶¶243–486).

The phenomenon of the transitional object occurs as the infant has not developed the concepts of objectivity: the transitional object is neither without nor within; these concepts have no meaning for it. The infant does not have to grow to accept external reality as there is no external reality for it to accept; it is already in the world but has not got the concepts of inner and outer. The transitional object is best understood as part of an early language-game. Later by talking and interacting with people and objects it may learn to develop the concepts of objectivity. This is a subtle business and many have a poor grasp of it. The ability to distinguish between what we think and feel and what others do is rarely perfect.

Coming to have things to say and finding a place in the human world is a huge task as it requires the development of an orientation to the world through language. Language is not just a tool which we find useful to learn but is a mode of action, a way of doing things, and is integral for our development as persons in the human world. There is an internal relation between the acquisition of language and becoming who we are. Our entire linguistic practices imbue our words with life and enable us to be lively (Tomasello 1999).

Language-games

Wittgenstein suggested that a helpful way of thinking about language is to use the notion of language-game. 'I shall call the whole, consisting of language and the actions into which it is woven, a "language-game"' (*PI* ¶7).

> If we want to study the problems of truth and falsehood, of the agreement and disagreement of propositions with reality, of the nature of assertion, assumption, and question, we shall with great advantage look at primitive forms of language in which these forms of thinking appear without the confusing background of highly complicated processes of thought. (*BB* p. 17)

A language-game is an object of comparison (*PI* ¶¶130–1). It specifies the connection between spoken words, actions and situations, which need not be spoken. Once specified, a game can be compared with another bit of talk to show the way it connects with further actions and situations. To describe a language-game is to depict one of the ways people move in space and time. So describing a language-game can throw light on false pictures of human action. Thus the picture of an inner world gives a misleading description of how we act. We do not, for example, look into our inner minds to decide what we intend to do (*RPP1* ¶548).

These *primitive forms of language* (*Sprachspiel*, speech or language-play) remind us that the early development of language involves play. The to-and-fro movement of much play is not tied to a goal; we cannot put into words any specific point to it. Think of kicking a ball against a wall. The aim perhaps is to hit the wall, but it is fun even if we miss. Play is spontaneous and its ease does not refer to the absence of effort but to the absence of strain: if we resist the temptation to think in terms of a specific goal, we need not demand to win. Being initiated into language is purposeless to the child as it can have no concept of a language to learn if it has no language.

Language-games are a way of using signs with which the child begins to create words, sentences and, so, meaning. It is a feature of our natural history. There is no explanation for this ability but of course it needs a human brain.

> It is sometimes said that animals do not talk because they lack the mental capacity. And that means: 'they do not think, and that is why they do not talk'. But – they simply do not talk. Or to put it better: they do not use language – if we except the most primitive forms of language. – Commanding, questioning, storytelling, chatting, are as much a part of our natural history as walking, eating, drinking, playing. (*PI* ¶25)

The notion of language-game emphasises that speaking, like a game, is a practice. We learn meaning first by learning how to use words in particular situations, not by isolating them and associating them with an object, as we do in looking up a meaning in a dictionary. Similarly, we can learn to play a game by watching it and then taking part, not by learning rules. In some games rules are essential, as in chess; sometimes the rules are loose as in playing ball on the beach. It is the same with language; compare mathematics with chatting. Some words have strict rules for their use; others such as 'boo' and 'oops' do not. Onomatopoeic words are governed by sound.

Rules can help to determine what makes sense and what does not. It may make sense to say 'I see a cat'; it does not make sense in the same way to say 'I see a thought'. The phenomena of language are related to one another in many different ways. The analogy of game is used as there are all sorts of activities we call games – board games, ball games, solitaire, Olympic games or the game of war. Some involve skill and some not, some are competitive, some amusing, some dangerous and so on. There is no fixed property common to all but they have a family resemblance.

> You must bear in mind that the language-game is, so to say, something unpredictable. I mean: it is not based on grounds. It is not reasonable (or unreasonable).
> It is there – like our life. (*OC* ¶559)

The notion of language-games can be compared to the formula style that has been identified in early oral poetry, especially of Homer (Parry 1971). Early oral epics are constructed from a corpus of phrases for different characters and actions which the poet weaves together. There are standard phrases that are used to describe a god or goddess, a hero, the launching of a ship, the way a hero arms for battle, and standard phrases for the way death is described, for speeches of report, challenge, boast and counter-boast, rebuke and encouragement. The point is that the language, action and context are woven together.

Items in the human world and language meet through language-games. This can be seen clearly in ancient languages where we have a record of early writing: in ancient Egyptian the sign for 'a god' is a flag and the sign for 'perfect' is a heart and windpipe. When these signs are combined they form a sentence which means 'the perfect god' (cf. *Tract.* 4.016). Items in the world such as the human body and its parts, mammals, birds, fishes, reptiles, insects, vegetation, parts of ships, furniture and clothing are signs which when combined in particular ways in a sentence become symbols which depict the facts they describe. Human vocal sounds are used similarly in speech.

When we are first initiated into language we are primarily concerned with expression. This is rooted in our natural responses and activities such as smiles, expressions of pain, hunger, thirst and discomfort. A human child is naturally responsive to human speech; within a week or so it can differentiate between its mother's language and a foreign one. When the child gets older and more sophisticated, it will respond in increasingly subtle ways to gesture, music, colour and taste. Language develops in accord with these responses – meaning develops in the stream of life. A nursery rhyme means nothing to an infant, may delight an older child and may have little interest for an adult.

The distribution of meaning of a particular language-game happens according to variations that are intrinsic to the objects themselves. It is not a matter of pure concepts throwing a net of identities over 'reality' to generate possible experience. There is no 'higher' regulating mechanism. It is not identities but meaning and significance that help to create language-games. Words do not get their meanings from extra-linguistic elements; rather their meanings are created from within language-games. Thus the concepts around potty training vary greatly in families; in some it has slight significance and in others it is a serious matter and the child will use the concepts accordingly. Only later in life it may learn to criticise and modify these concepts.

Language-games are necessary to articulate judgements such as true or false. These develop much later than the expressive use of language. The words 'is true' only makes sense because human beings make judgements, dispute and verify assertions. The language-game allows us to see the symbols in the signs, that is, whether the sentence makes sense. There is an internal relation between the truth of a statement and the language-game which is its home. We cannot see truth because it is not an object; we may see something is true but we do not see truth. 'Is true' does not state a relation between a proposition and a fact or between a proposition and a set of beliefs. It is not independent of use.

> Really 'The proposition is either true or false' only means that it must be possible to decide for or against it. But this does not say what the ground for such a decision is like. (*OC* ¶200)

There is no new information gained if we ask whether a statement which we say is true agrees with reality or the facts. For the concept of truth cannot be explained without reference to the language-game of calling statements true.

> Well if everything speaks for a hypothesis and nothing speaks against it – is it certainly true? One may designate it as such. – But does it agree with reality with the facts? – With this question, you are already going round in a circle. (*OC* ¶191)

The correct use of 'is true' depends on agreement in a community on the conventions, rules and criteria, whereby we apply these words. We recognise its objectivity by our awareness that 'I think or believe that p' or 'People say that p', and p do not entail each other. What we or the community take to be true is not necessarily what is true. Thus, 'I think or believe that Pythagoras's theorem is true' is merely a statement about my psychology. 'Everyone believes Pythagoras's theorem' is merely a statement about the beliefs of a particular community. Its objective truth is revealed when the proof is understood; then we can be truthful.

Objective truth, as it can only be stated in a language-game, depends ultimately on trust:

> I really want to say that a language-game is only possible if one trusts something (I did not say 'can trust something'). (*OC* ¶509)

Delusions

The clinical importance of these distinctions can be illustrated by considering a statement made by someone in therapy who insisted that 'My thoughts are in the drawer of your desk.' This accusation was repeated many times with much anger for many months. Now it has the conventional form of a statement of facts such as 'My purse is in the drawer of your desk.' But in ordinary English usage thoughts are not objects that can be in desks, although in psychoanalysis it is assumed they can be in minds. So the statement appears to be nonsense, a false belief, a delusion in psychiatric terms.

But this is to move too fast and not to trust the patient's use of words. She doggedly repeated this 'delusion' until the therapist ceased to try to explain or interpret it. As I have indicated, and as has been argued by Frege and Wittgenstein in great detail, a word does not have meaning in isolation; only as it occurs in a sentence and context does it have logical properties and so can mean something. What a word means depends on how it is used in the sentence, and the meaning of a sentence depends on the context in which it is used. We cannot assume that words always have been assigned their usual logical role. There are not two heterogeneous items: 'My thoughts' and 'are in the drawer of your desk' for which we know the meaning and so they should not have been joined together in the sentence, because that contravenes the laws of logic. Logic is not a set of general laws which rule sense.

A speaker is always in a context even if he is by himself. The idea that there can be an isolated speaker or sentence with meaning is nonsense. We are always in a context even if we are floating alone in a spacecraft. If we imagine an isolated sentence or word, then we tend to take as the meanings of words, mental pictures or acts of an individual mind (Frege 1950, p. 10).

This is what is done in psychiatry and psychoanalysis when they label sentences as delusional. They have an abstract, literalist view of language, a confused notion of logic which fails to trust the way the patient uses language, and ignores that the way we live and have been brought up plays a part in the use and meaning of words. They split the notion of truth from *speaking* truthfully. Instead of making clear what is thought or said by the patient, they assume that language is always referential. So if the patient's words do not refer to a 'real' object then it is delusional. However, the patient may be using words in an unusual way, and it would be dogmatic to say they *must* use words conventionally. Psychoanalytic and psychiatric experts have an external relation to the patient; so they try to correct his brain or his mental apparatus or his words and thoughts as in cognitive therapy. They do not allow the patient to show what he says.

> You say to me: 'You understand this expression, don't you? Well then – I am using it in the sense you are familiar with. – As if the sense were an atmosphere accompanying the word, which is carried with it into every kind of application. (*PI* ¶117)

For much psychiatry and psychoanalysis the only rules in town are the rules for the statements of science and 'common sense'. If we understand that language is not ruled by rules, then we are not bound by a particular set of rules that a certain group of people value. We can make sense of statements such as 'My thoughts are in the drawer of your desk.' Briefly, her mother was a professional expert on how to bring up children. She had fixed rules throughout the day as to how children ought to behave. Everything, including play, was elaborately planned by her. Her child had to fit exactly into her theoretical scheme. So she grew up not recognising that she had a mind of her own.

Given this upbringing, it made sense that this woman accused the therapist of keeping her mind in a drawer. She had no concept of the possibility of a meeting of minds without one trying to obliterate the other. It was important that the therapist respected the woman's fixed belief and did not, like her mother, try and impose 'reality' on it. The woman was speaking truthfully when she had the courage to insist that her mind was in the therapist's drawer. To explain it as a delusion, a false belief, is to confuse truth with speaking truthfully. This leads to treating her brain chemically or her mind psychoanalytically, or her thoughts by cognitive techniques; this also assumes there is a real meaning which the experts know. These would be another way of obliterating her mind. It was only by allowing her language to show what she said that she was enabled to enjoy a meeting of minds with her therapist.

Statements of fact and truth are part of a language-game and their meaning depends ultimately on trust. Meaning is not an act of an individual mind or mental picture. Neither is logic a set of rules that must be applied to language nor is logical syntax concerned with the proscription of combinations of signs or symbols. Rather, it enables the signs we use, when we give voice to our thoughts and feelings, to symbolize. Can we assume that the language-game of truth was being used when she said 'My thoughts are in the drawer of your desk' and that she was deluded – out of touch with 'reality'? Or was her language in perfectly logical order but was unusual in its meaning and needed clarifying?

> But if you follow other rules than those of chess you are *playing another game*; and if you follow grammatical rules other than

such-and-such ones, that does not mean you say something wrong, no, you are speaking of something else. (*Z* ¶320)

The rules of grammar are not the source of necessity. They are autonomous in that they are used to describe ways we humans may represent the world (*PI* ¶¶371–3). Language does not mirror any essence of the world; Wittgenstein is very careful not to become dogmatic about the essence of essences (Kuusela 2008, pp. 184–214). We cannot get outside of language and describe the world as it 'really' is. Language is not accountable by reference to any particular reality. It is a contingent fact that we speak and act as we do, a fact which depends on our human needs and interests.

> Why don't I call the rules of cooking arbitrary; and why am I tempted to call the rules of grammar arbitrary? Because 'cooking' is defined by its end, whereas speaking a language isn't. Therefore the use of language is autonomous in a certain sense in which cooking and washing aren't. For anyone guided by other than the correct rules when he cooks, cooks badly; but anyone guided by rules other than those for chess plays *a different game*, and anyone guided by grammatical rules other than such and such doesn't say anything that is false, but is talking about something else. (*BT* p. 187)

In neurosis and psychosis there is a failure to make sense of some area of life. This failure is not a question of truth or falsehood: the person is not making a mistake, she is not out of touch with some independent reality, and in need of some technique to cure her. As grammar is autonomous, signs as such do not make sense and meaning does not determine how they are used correctly. We give signs meaning in our use of them and so adopt standards of correctness. These standards are not necessarily followed in neurosis or psychosis. The individual cannot make sense of something or things that have happened to her and so she comes to use words in an unusual way, especially when in therapy. Areas of language, or even language itself, may become 'dead' or meaningless, as in severe depression. The sufferer requires an initiation, a participation, on the part of the therapist, rather in the way caretakers and a child participate by engaging in events wherein the child develops language. This involves close attention and responsiveness to the particularity of the person and the concreteness of the situation, rather than applying general concepts and rules of procedure.

Neither psychoanalysis nor CBT recognises the autonomy of grammar. Psychoanalysis has developed a particular logic and grammar of the unconscious which depends on Freud's metaphysical beliefs (Elder 1994). CBT assumes that the third person point of view is the only scientifically correct one, so autonomy is removed from the individual who must follow what most people assume. Both practices tend to claim to be the best possible treatment for neurosis, to be the 'real' cure.

The autonomy of grammar means that there can be no final grammar or logic of the mind or anything else. Grammatical rules are not statements about the correct practice of language but are tools for description. If this were not so, it would destroy the creativity of language and human freedom as we would be bound by certain meanings. Language is 'beyond' us, and it is not answerable to any particular group of people; we cannot control it as a whole, although we can control parts of it, and make up new bits, as in computer languages.

Logic

Wittgenstein's investigations were centred as much on logic and mathematics as on psychology. His discussions took place against the background of his investigations of language, concept formation and the idealizing assumptions that are widespread about meaning and truth. For him, as for Kant, his interest in logic was part of his quest for self-understanding and self-knowledge, rather than adding to a special branch of knowledge aimed at impersonal truth. Logical investigations would disentangle metaphysical confusion and lead to clarity, authenticity of expression and an improved mode of life.

> An investigation is possible in connection with mathematics which is entirely analogous to our investigation of psychology. It is just as little a *mathematical* investigation as the other is a psychological one. It will *not* contain calculations, so it is not for example logistic. (*PI* ¶¶2, 14)

Wittgenstein was Russell's student and protégé and a friend of Frege, the great logician. They tried to prove the continuity between arithmetic and logic. This failed, but the concepts and insights developed by them in the course of this programme widened into making more precise the subject matter of logic. They created mathematical logic, which is basic to the development of computer science. This has been applied to cognitive science and CBT, for example, in making computer models of aspects of behaviour and even in actively using computers to perform therapy.

Wittgenstein's investigations were initially provoked by the problems of mathematical logic at the end of the nineteenth century, above all, by the paradoxes of set theory, of which Russell's paradox is the most famous. This paradox shows that if we talk about the class of all classes that are not members of themselves, we fall into a contradiction. A way of putting it is to consider the Sicilian barber. He shaves only and all those in his village who do not shave themselves. Does he shave himself? If he does, then he does not *only* shave those who do not shave themselves. If he does not, then he does not shave *all* those who do not shave themselves (Whitehead and Russell 1910, Vol. 1, p. 40).

The problem is that the class of all classes appears to be a denoting concept, that is, one whose job it is to point to something which a proposition is about. Thus if we say 'Snow is white,' we can point to the whiteness of the snow and can talk about the class of all white things. But the paradox shows that the class of all classes that do not belong to themselves is a denoting concept which does not denote anything. It is a contradiction. It follows that there is no logical ground for the postulation of classes. They are not logically necessary entities and so truths about them are at best contingent.

Wittgenstein came to see the relevance of confusions about the nature of classes, not only for logic and mathematics, but for understanding psychological language. He realised that the study of notions such as mind, the inner and the outer world, self, understanding, desire, thought and feeling was essential for understanding the nature of language and the place of logic and so necessity in our life. His investigations on logic are subtle and there is a large literature of commentary (e.g. Baker 1988; McGinn 2006; Potter 2009). I can only provide a sketch of them.

Following Frege, he rejected the 'psychologizing' of logic. According to this theory, a necessary truth is a proposition about mental entities. Thus the law of non-contradiction would state the incompatibility of the mental state of believing that p with the mental state of believing that not-p. Thus interpreted it would be a law of thought. Psychology would tell us how we *must* think. We would be subject to empirical laws of thought. There are simply facts of the matter about which of our propositions makes sense. Psychoanalysis, cognitive therapy and most psychiatry take this as a truth and devise ways to correct our thinking. They evaluate the standards as to what makes sense and what is irrational.

This vision, however, removes any responsibility that we might have in the range of our beliefs and the way we talk. It assumes empirical facts, such as the unconscious, cognitive mechanisms and brain structures dictate which aspects of objects are worth describing; and what ought to be considered before acting. Neither the nature of necessity nor the meaning of meaning is analysed, and the importance of aspect perception is passed over (McManus 2006, pp. 227–9).

The sciences depend on our being able to make sense. To see how this is done we must understand the place of logic in our lives. We tend to think that logic is a set of true propositions about the world that can be established *a-priori* and are universally true. What can be truer than the syllogism: Socrates is a man, all men are mortal and, therefore, Socrates is mortal? Or the statement: If A = B and B = C, then A = C?

Wittgenstein's basic insight into logic is that its propositions are radically different from all others. They are not theorems of a special science describing relations among entities in a special logical realm. They are independent of everything to do with intuition or acquaintance.

> There is not any question at all here of some correspondence between what is said and reality; rather is logic *antecedent* to any correspondence; in the same sense, that is, as that in which the establishment of a method of measurement is *antecedent* to the correctness or incorrectness of a statement of length. (*RFM* ¶¶1, 155)

Logic has no content, it is not about anything; nevertheless, it is involved in reasoning about anything whatever. So its status is of a totally different kind than any science but is essential to all science and reasoning. This includes psychotherapy, as it involves helping people who are 'unreasonable' or who have 'lost' their reason.

As Wittgenstein wrote: 'The 'experience' which we need to understand logic is not that such and such is the case, but that something *is*; but that is *no* experience. Logic precedes every experience – that something is so. It is before the How, not before the What' (*TLP Ogden* ¶5.552).

Light on the place of logic in drawing a limit to thought, truth and falsity can be gained from considering tautologies and contradictions. A tautology such as 'Either it is raining or it is not raining' does not say anything about the world but states what is necessary; we do not need to look out of the window to see if it is true or not as we would if we were to say 'Either it is raining or it is snowing.' Similarly, a contradiction such as 'It is raining and it is not raining' is senseless since it does not tell us anything about the world; it is not compatible with any situation. These sentences are senseless but not nonsensical. Their sense is given in the logical properties of the symbols alone. They *show* the formal, logical properties of language and of the world (*TLP* ¶6.12). The space inhabited by language is between the two extremes of tautology and contradiction: the space of possibility. Everything that happens in the world is contingent; the only necessity is logical necessity (*TLP* ¶6.124).

Tautologies are always true, whereas each of the two members of the alternative are contingent; they could possibly be or not be. Contradictions, on the other hand, are always false, but again its two members are contingent so they could be true or false. They are propositions which constitute the limit of language and are fixed by the totality of propositions that can be true or false.

There are certain fundamental logical words. These include 'and', 'or', 'not', 'if ... then' or 'every'; they have their symbolic substitutes in technical logic. These words do not name anything, they stand for nothing, but they are fundamental to how reality is represented in language. A clear understanding of their use shows us how it is possible to say something determinate about things in the world. They do not represent real relations between things but express formal relations between propositions. They do not make a substantive contribution to the sense of the propositions in which they occur but determine what facts are of like sense and what of opposite sense.

Logical operations in themselves are tautologies for they say nothing about the world but provide the form of a proof. Take a basic logical proposition such as the modus ponens. If we are given the fact that p implies q and then given p we want to know why it follows that q. Suppose a student says 'I don't see why it follows.' All we can do is to repeat 'Look! *if p* and $p \rightarrow q$, surely, *then q*.' We cannot produce any further fact or argument to persuade him. It is a rule and we cannot get behind it. The signs speak for themselves but we have to see them in the right way. The argument is valid because it is a tautology: given the premises, the conclusion must follow. Logical truths are based on meanings whereas non-logical ones are determined by facts.

The validity of a logical inference is internal to the senses of the propositions involved in the inference. It differs from a causal inference, which needs a law that connects one situation to another, for example, in the natural sciences we seek the laws of nature. In the case of logical inference the relation from one proposition to another is justified by the propositional symbols themselves. We derive one sentence from another according to a rule (*RFM* p. 39). These rules of transition do not depend on anything external to the system of representation to which the propositions belong. Thus if we understand the meaning of 2, 3 and addition we see that $2 + 3 = 5$. We do not need to look at 'reality' to find the evidence for this, as we would in making a causal inference. If the propositions in the inference are understood, we see that the inference is valid. A course in elementary logic would not help; we must have been initiated into the use of language before we can benefit from any course on logic. It cannot govern its use. Logical necessity is part of our natural history; we humans can recognise internal relations, other mammals cannot.

Wittgenstein argued that descriptive sentences are meaningful by virtue of their depicting a situation. As they are sentences they have a structure made of names combined in a determinate way. Thus 'John loves Jill' does not mean the same as 'Jill loves John.' It is this structure that enables them to picture contingent situations. They are essentially true or false, right or wrong, and it is only because of this that they can make significant claims about things. They show how things might stand and when we assert them we say they stand just as it shows them to be standing. I say 'John loves Jill' and you decide if the sentence is true or false by what you know of them. The sentence opens a space of possibility which is either realised or not. So descriptive sentences can only be true or false if we understand them independently of knowing whether they are true. They are contingent as is the empirical reality they describe. Necessity does not apply to them. We use them to identify what is the case and what is not. If we are in a position to confirm that something does exist then we can say it is true; if we cannot then it is false or perhaps a true belief on our part. These sentences show what they say, but cannot say what they show.

We are concerned with what is said or done through uttering words or sentences in various circumstances. The place of logic shows itself in *how* expressions are used with sense; this is essential to their meaning *what* they do. When language represents states of affairs, logic is immanent in our expressions.

What corresponds to a particular thought is not something we can grasp independently of the sentence in which the thought is expressed. It is impossible to describe the fact that corresponds to a descriptive sentence without simply repeating it (*CV* p. 13). Thus I say 'There is a vase on the table.' Now, how can I describe the fact that corresponds to that sentence other than simply repeating it? This shows the limit of language. 'We cannot express through language what expresses itself in language' (*TLP* ¶4.121).

> If a Frenchman says: 'It is raining' in French and an Englishman also says it in English, it is not that something happens in both minds which is the real sense of 'it is raining'. We imagine something like *imagery*, which is the international language. Whereas in fact:
>
> 1. Thinking (or imagery) is not an accompaniment of the words as they are spoken or heard;
> 2. The sense – the thought 'It's raining' – is not even the words *with* the accompaniment of some sort of imagery.
> 3. It *is* the thought 'It's raining' only within the English language. (*LC* p. 30)

A thought is not a contextless, self-interpreting, ghostly entity in the mind which makes sense independently of language use.

We can elucidate the sense of an expression by providing equivalent signs. We cannot, however, express in the form of a proposition with sense what the use of signs presupposes, namely, a mastery of their logical-syntactical employment. A term cannot refer to something and at the same time refer to the fact that it refers to it. The name of a name is not a name. If one were to name a name we would no longer be able to distinguish between word and thing, concept and object. It is because 'rose' is not the name of the name 'rose' that in uttering 'rose' the rose can appear.

If I say 'The book is red' then it is contingent that the particular sounds or shapes of the sentence are correlated with a particular object, for a different language would sound and look different. But that a particular name is correlated with a particular object in the sentence is necessary if we are to have a language.

Differentiating between logical propositions and ordinary empirical ones is vital in psychotherapy but they are often confused. Thus most psychoanalysts and CBT practitioners assume the uniformity of propositions. Their scientism and psychologism lead them to this. Reality as described by science is the only true reality; there is an *a-priori* structure of the world which science describes. The specific features of a person's language must be reduced to the 'neutral' descriptive language of science. Thus expressions of love may be reduced to 'attachment', or the sexual instinct, for these lend themselves more easily to empirical explanations. Freud's mythology of strict psychical determinism is made because he conflates causal inferences with logical ones (*TLP* ¶¶5.136–5.1362). In understanding a particular person the homogeneity of their propositions cannot be assumed; they make logical inferences as well as causal ones. The syntax and vocabulary of science is crafted for the needs of science. Ordinary language between people is usually addressed to a particular person. It is the specific features of a person's language that correspond to its untranslatable expressions. There is no necessity for all language to be reduced to the rules of scientific language.

Propositions have many uses – descriptions, sentences in fiction, dream reports, natural laws, theorems in mathematics, etc. We can say of them that they make sense or not, are true, false or uncertain and we can collect evidence for or against them. The nature of the evidence will depend on the particular use of the propositions. The evidence and truth of a dream report is different from the report of the structure of a molecule and both differ from the report of a feeling. Logical propositions are not like that. They are tautologies and therefore necessary and neither true nor false because they convey no information about the world or mind.

There are many theories in psychotherapy. A theory represents the conditions of sense; it shows us what symbols signify to the theorist. It reveals the way the theorist wants us to look at the facts, the concepts that are important to him and how particular words and expressions are to be used to make sense; his picture or model of therapy – for example, that it depends on a causal model. It shows us a way of making sense of our experience and has a particular application.

Wittgenstein's understanding of logic, however, refutes the belief that there can be a picture of reality that is necessarily true. Different theories have different uses or ways of thinking through and conducting therapy but no theory *must* be true (*PI* ¶¶422–7). To see through theories we have to attend to how symbols symbolise. We have to distinguish between propositions that are being used to say how things are and propositions that draw attention to how the expressions of our language are being used. We need to see that what is essential to symbols symbolising in the way they do cannot be expressed in propositions that can be compared with reality for truth or falsehood. We cannot stand outside reality to see how symbols *must* symbolise. There is no pure essence of representation. This distinction is rarely made by therapists. Theories, observations and inferences are telescoped into describing how things are. Hence the dogmatism of the various schools.

Concepts and objects

> Philosophical investigations: conceptual investigations. The essential thing about metaphysics: it obliterates the distinction between factual and conceptual investigation. (*Z* ¶459)

The confusion between concepts and objects is endemic to psychoanalysis, CBT and neurosis. Perhaps this is most clearly seen in such notions as that there is an internal world containing internal objects and that thinking occurs in our heads or brains.

If we fail to distinguish concepts from objects we fail to make sense, although we may appear to do so. The differentiation between them is a way of talking about logical articulations and so what makes sense. Concepts are the expression of our interest and direct it (*PI* ¶570). They can be divided into material and formal concepts. Material concepts tell us that an object is of such and such a sort. Thus in the sentences 'Venus is a planet,' 'I am frightened' and 'She is called Joan,' the concepts are 'is a planet', 'am frightened' and 'is called Joan'. Concepts are incomplete; they do not tell us anything by themselves as they are locations within a sentence that they can take up. They must be connected in a sentence by logical syntax to have a meaning. So concepts are not objects. Contrast 'Venus' which we can point to with 'is a planet'. As concepts are connected they cannot meaningfully be referred to outside the context of a sentence, as that would imply that they were objects. Thus a horse is an object, we can point to it, but the concept of a horse is not, as in the sentence 'Dobin is a horse.'

A formal concept, on the other hand, concerns a mode of signification, whereby a symbol signifies or represents what it does. It is descriptive of a way of symbolising (*TLP* ¶4.126; McGinn 2006, pp. 183–91). For example, facts, minds and numbers are formal concepts. You cannot point to them or define them by means of a proposition. You could point to me sitting in a chair and say that is a fact but you are pointing to me sitting in the chair, not to the fact. Formal concepts mark possibilities for the combination of symbols. Thus it makes sense to say 'My mind is blank' but not 'My mind is eight.' A formal concept is the mark of an internal relation between propositions belonging to the same space. It is represented in language by mean of a whole class of propositions.

Formal concepts characterise how symbols symbolise, not what they signify. So a formal concept like 'object' must be conceived as part of a coordinate system that allows us to express, rather than constituting a determinate position within that framework (McGinn 2006, p. 183). Thus there are similarities between how we talk about objects, primary colours or quantities and other formal concepts. Formal concepts function as principles of judgement within the relevant forms of life; so they cannot be demonstrated as they must be presupposed or denied in the demonstration itself. We cannot infer from the existence of chairs, bacteria, etc. to the existence of physical objects for example.

Take a formal concept such as 'physical object'. Now chairs, bacteria, stars and much else are physical objects. A physical object is a formal concept; it is not a 'something'. The question arises as to whether it exists? Obviously chairs, etc. exist but do physical objects? Is the sentence 'There are physical objects' an empirical statement for which we could have evidence? What would this evidence look like? We can only speak of evidence if there is the logical space for being wrong. Does it make sense to doubt whether physical objects exist or not? Could we be mistaken about it?

> 'A is a physical object' is a piece of information which we can give only to someone who doesn't yet understand either what 'A' means, or what 'physical object' means. Thus it is instruction in the use of words, and 'physical object' is a logical concept. (Like colour, quantity, ...). And that is why no such proposition as 'There are physical objects' can be formulated.
>
> Yet we encounter such unsuccessful shots at every turn. (*OC* ¶36)

Formal concepts are essential to language embedded practices. The child first participates in various practices following rules blindly. It does not grasp general principles and then act appropriately; rather it learns the rules by playing, by engaging in practices where it learns to make practical judgements about how it should or should not respond to the demands placed upon it. Thus by interacting with dolls, chairs, bottles or spoons, it will gradually learn to confer order on these activities and so catch the drift (*PI* ¶210) of what it is to be an object. By counting things, measuring shapes and distances it will come to understand the rules governing quantity. By seeing how people behave and act it will come to understand the formal concept 'mind'. By responding to words and sentences appropriately it will come to understand their meaning. The general facts of nature and human capacities create the form of life of the individual.

As has been said, confusions between concepts and objects are endemic in psychoanalysis and in neurosis. One confusion it leads to is the nature of the inner and outer world. The distinction between them is endemic to psychological theorising. Psychologists tend to take opposing camps. Psychoanalysts and their offshoots emphasise the inner world – the unconscious. Behaviourists and many cognitive therapists emphasise the outer world. To Wittgenstein: 'The world and life are one' (*TLP* ¶5.621) and much of his work was to show this. The problem is a very old one. Thus Heraclitus in about 500 BC wrote:

> Although the account (logos) is shared, most men live as though their thinking were a private possession. (Heraclitus 1979, Fragment 3)

The psychoanalytic position is well summed up in Hinshelwood's dictionary:

> Freud's momentous starting point was to take seriously what neurotic and psychotic patients said to him, and he started with the assumption that they were conveying something comprehensible that was real for themselves. Internal or psychic reality is the conviction of the reality of the psychic world that exists unconsciously and is felt inside the person.
>
> Klein elaborated this with the theory of internal objects; she made a discovery that created a revolutionary addition to the model of the mind, namely that we do not live in one world, but in two – that we live in an internal world which is as real a place to live as the outside world....Psychic reality could be treated in a concrete way. (Hinshelwood 1991, p. 330)
>
> The experience that the subject has of an object inside himself gives him a sense of existence and identity. Our relations with objects comprise what we are. (Ibid., p. 68)

It is certainly important to take seriously what patients say but can we assume that they are not confused? May it not be that a source of their confusion is precisely because they feel that their mind and sense of existence and identity is inside them and that that comprises what they are? Are they not suffering from 'a kind of general disease of thinking which always looks for (and finds) what would be called a mental state from which all our acts spring as from a reservoir' (*BB* p. 143)

What is meant by reality? Psychical reality, it is claimed, is a discovery; it is in the mind and contains processes and objects that have been mapped by psychoanalysts on the basis of their clinical experience. But do these processes exist or are they merely explanatory? Thus in physics there is a clear difference between a theoretical entity used to explain phenomena and discovering whether it exists. The Higgs boson, for example, is a theoretical entity, a concept at present, and has not yet been proved to exist and if it cannot be shown to exist the theory that posits its existence may have to be changed. How do psychoanalysts prove that internal objects exist and are not merely posited by them to explain certain phenomena? Freud thought that the death instinct and the various forces and particles of physics were all the same kind of mythology (Freud 1932, p. 211). Where is the objective evidence that the death instinct exists?

A formal concept, as a part of what symbols are, cannot meaningfully be set down alongside the proposition that this concept serves to characterise, as if they were on the same level. By way of example: A patient was sent to me because he kept trying to hang himself. He told me that he felt he was a ghost but if he hanged himself and died it would prove he was not a ghost since ghosts do not die.

This man imagined he did not have a living body. But does it make sense to say or think 'I have a body'? Who is one informing? Is it an empirical matter as to whether I have or do not have a body? How do I set about proving it? Both 'I have a body' and 'I do not have a body' as statements are nonsense as the body is being used here as a formal concept. Our bodies function as a principle of judgement so that we can use material concepts about it – it is ugly, old or beautiful. But as it is a principle of judgement it is not on the same level as the concepts which are used to make judgements.

> What finds its reflection in language, language cannot represent.
>
> What expresses *itself* in language, *we* cannot express by means of language.
>
> Propositions *show* the logical form of reality.
>
> They display it. (*TLP* ¶4.121)

Many psychoanalysts and cognitive therapists fall into a similar confusion. They tell us that we have a psychical apparatus, internal objects and mental mechanisms; if they are Jungians, archetypes; and if they are cognitive therapists, mental particulars in our heads. These, they assume, are empirical objects and mechanisms obtained by close observation of clinical data. Certainly there are fathers, mothers and children who have all sorts of relations to one another and certainly the family is basic to human life. But what does it mean that there is an archetypal father and mother in the internal world and that our relationships are caused by them? Are these mental particulars? Children have fears and nightmares, think archaically, may become preoccupied with the inside of their own and mother's body and have archaic causal explanations for their anxieties. But does that mean that there are internal objects causing this?

A child is learning how to use language, the way symbols symbolise. Instead of realising that formal concepts are part of what symbols are, that they are part of the coordinate system that enables the child to express things, it uses them to determine positions within that system. Thus it posits things as something to blame, a primitive notion of cause. To that end it creates good and bad objects; but 'good' and 'bad' are concepts, not objects. There is a deep tendency in children and in many adults to create something to blame when they have a primitive idea of how language functions. This idea persists in those who imagine there are objects in the inner world.

Children learn *in time* who to call their mother and father and to make sense of the relationships in their family. There is no need to posit internal objects that cause them to behave in certain ways. It is a confusion to imagine that there must be something in their inner world that *makes* them do what they do. This is to join in the confusion between cause and reason. Children learn the appropriate rules for action in the context in which they live. It is when they feel anxious that they may try to cross bridges before they've got to them and so feel that something makes them act.

Thought

Confusions between concepts and objects can be further illustrated in confusions about thought. One is the widespread belief that we think with our heads. If people in Western society are asked where they think they often point to their heads. Now teachers sometimes say 'Use your head' which roughly means attend more closely, and we all know that we must have a brain to think. But is thinking a process in the head? Or is this belief a symptom of dissociated thinking in which we imagine that thoughts are ghostly entities in the head, in the inner world, dissociated from language use?

One of the most dangerous of ideas for a philosopher is, oddly enough, that we think with our heads or in our heads.

The idea of thinking as a process in the head, in a completely enclosed space, gives him something occult.

Is thinking a specific *organic* process of the mind, so to speak – as it were chewing and digesting in the mind? Can we replace it by an inorganic process that fulfils the same end, as it were use a prosthetic apparatus for thinking? How should we have to imagine a prosthetic organ of thought? (*Z* ¶¶605–7)

Of course Freud did – the psychic apparatus is a prosthetic organ of thought.

Thinking does not take place anywhere inside the mind or brain although it is a necessary condition of thought that we have human brains. It is people who think and report or express thoughts. The thinker will be somewhere when he thinks, in his bath perhaps, and that is where he thought. Of course to report a thought requires very complicated processes occurring in the brain but these are not the same as the report of a thought. 'The question "Where does thinking take place?" always implies the mental image of a mechanical process taking place in an enclosed space, very similar to the *processes* in an adding machine' (*BT* p. 173).

Thus a patient, when he consulted me, felt he had to think. This gave him a terrible headache and he would describe it as if a machine in his head was going round so fast that it overheated. Less dramatically, many people feel they have to frown and exert themselves to think. But to think we need to be 'clear-headed', no exertion is needed but attention; there is no sense of activity in the head unless we identify with representations of ourselves.

Thinking is a very varied concept. It is interchangeable with belief, imagine, mean and calculate. It is not a definite mental process that occurs privately in our mind. We can 'have a thought', a thought can occur to us, it can cross our mind, we can confess one, we can keep it to ourselves, tell someone what we think, express one, be tortured by them, have our head full of them, be thoughtful and so on. It is totally misleading to impose unity on this diversity; it leads to elevating one aspect of thinking to a defining principle of all thought. Instead of forcing it into the Procrustean bed of theory, it requires careful attention to the use of language in the particular situations in which the concept is used (*PI* ¶¶316–62).

When we think, especially when we do sums 'in our head', we may gesture towards our head. Similarly, we may gesture towards our heart when we express love. But it does not follow that when we do this that we are pointing to peculiar processes going on in our head or our heart. It is not bits of us that think or love but *we* think and *we* love.

> Kissing the picture of one's beloved. That is *obviously not* based on the belief that it will have some specific effect on the object which the picture represents. It aims at satisfaction and achieves it. Or rather: it *aims* at nothing at all; we just behave this way and then we feel satisfied. (*PO* p. 123)

It is the neurotic as well as the psychoanalytic and cognitive theorist who imagine, when they think about thinking, that it must be a process occurring in an enclosed space – in the head or mind. They imagine that gestures must have a purpose such as pointing at something. In classical psychoanalysis the patient must lie on the couch and report his thoughts and feelings. Gesture is frowned upon and interpreted as acting out. But if somebody walks around the room, say gesturing his dissatisfaction, are the gestures aiming at anything other than expressing his dissatisfaction?

The psychoanalytic and cognitive position is that thought is the activity of a mechanism which, if it is working correctly, produces truth or reality. Thought is essentially divorced from language and gesture. So in much CBT various techniques are used to correct the mechanism when it is producing 'incorrect thoughts' as in depression. In psychoanalysis thought is driven:

Thus: 'Thought is after all nothing but a substitute for a hallucinatory wish; and it is self-evident that dreams must be wish-fulfilments, since nothing but a wish can set our mental apparatus at work' (Freud 1900, p. 567).

Wishes, for psychoanalysis, are the force that turns the wheels of the mental apparatus. But does this make sense? I can sit in a chair on a cold winter's day and wish I were at the seaside in summer but not move from my chair. Is there an external relation between a desire and its fulfilment so that desire could be a force that brings about its fulfilment? This would make us robots as it would destroy the internal relation between desire and its expression. If I want an apple, it is an apple I want and I may have to move to get it. I might change my mind and become confused about what I want. There is no ghostly force in my wanting that brings about its fulfilment.

Thinking is not an activity of the mind, as speaking is of the mouth. When we talk about the activity of the mind all we are doing is using a mental image and probably forgetting that the mind is not an entity and thinking is not a process.

> A thought is essentially what is expressed by a proposition, in which context 'expressed' does not mean 'brought about'. A cold is brought about, but not expressed, by a cold bath.
>   One doesn't have a thought and *apart from it* language. – So it's not that one has the signs for someone else, but only a mute thought for oneself. A gaseous or ethereal thought, as it were, as opposed to visible, audible symbols. (*BT* p. 175)

Logic enables us to express the possibility of how things might be. It is given as we make judgements about the world, when we have a language that we use to say how things are. 'Logic is interested in reality. And thus in sentences ONLY in so far as they are *pictures* of reality' (*NB* p. 9). Understanding the place of logic enables us to keep meaning apart from describing things in the world, how things stand for propositions to be true. For logic is concerned with what it makes sense to say and with what is senseless. It clarifies the difference between our representations and we who make and use them.

The visual room

An important confusion about the inner world, consciousness and phantasy is that we have them. It is assumed that we possess consciousness and an inner world containing various objects and processes and that my inner world belongs to me and is separate from yours. These inner experiences are supposed to be unique to the person who has them. Laing, who was trained as a psychoanalyst, put this belief well:

> I see you and you see me. I experience you, and you experience me. I see your behaviour. You see my behaviour. But I do not and never have and never will see your *experience* of me. Just as you cannot 'see' my experience of you.... Your experience of me is not inside you and my experience of you is not inside me, but *your experience of me is invisible to me and my experience of you is invisible to you.*
>   ...Social phenomenology is the science of my own and others' *experience*. It is concerned with the relation between my experience of you and your experience of me.

...Since your and their experience is invisible to me as mine is to you and them, I seek to make evident to the others, through their experience of my behaviour, what I infer of your experience, through my experience of your behaviour.

...The relation of experience to behaviour is not that of inner to outer. My experience is not inside my head. My experience of this room is out there in the room. (Laing 1967, pp. 15–18)

This popular nonsense occurs when psychology replaces logic resulting in a confusion between concepts and facts. For example, when we see a person it is odd to say that we experience them, or for that matter that we do not. We do not use the concept of experience that way. But if we met a man with two heads, we might go home and say we had quite an experience. Wittgenstein tries to loosen the hold of this picture of experience and our understanding of others by discussing the concept of the 'visual room' (*PI* ¶¶398–402).

Suppose someone is sitting in a room. If he is self-conscious, he is aware that he has a certain perspective on the room which differs from someone who is sitting opposite him. The visual impression or experience of the room will differ between the two. Wittgenstein calls this the visual room, in contrast to the room in which they both are sitting. Now we are tempted to say that as each person is only aware of his own impressions, the immediate content of his experience, then each is eternally shut out from the others' experience. As Laing wrote: 'I cannot experience your experience. You cannot experience my experience' (1967, p. 16).

Wittgenstein's reply is: 'I understand you. You want to look about you and say: "At any rate only I have got THIS" ' (*PI* ¶398). In other words, the person imagines he has *got* something private and unique to him that is the immediate content of his experience; it is as if he could point into his inner world and say '*This* is what I see.' But what is this possession that he has got? The visual room?

He continues:

Couldn't I ask: In what sense have you *got* what you are talking about and saying that only you have got it? Do you possess it? You do not even *see* it. Don't you really have to say that no one has got it? And indeed it's clear: if you logically exclude other people's having something, it loses its sense to say that you have it. (*PI* ¶398)

I have a perspective on the room which I might be able to draw. I can give you the drawing but I cannot give you my perspective and you cannot take it away from me other than pushing me away and sitting on my seat. But then of course I have another perspective and now you have yours which is the same as mine was. A perspective cannot be detached from the act of experiencing it, in contrast to the actual room which we both can see but which exists separately from anyone's seeing it.

The visual room is not an object that I can have or own; it does not exist on its own and cannot be anywhere, either in my head or in my mind. If we claim that it is an object for consciousness, then we can slip into confusion. For an object, as usually understood, exists when no one perceives it. An object for consciousness, on the other hand, is internally related to consciousness as they necessarily occur together. It makes no sense to say 'I am seeing an apple but no-one is seeing it.' The visual room is a new concept which we may develop when we learn the language of self-consciousness. It is a change in the way we organise our experience. It is a point of view and not a new fact or object. Laing was right when he said that my experience is not inside my head, but he was wrong to say it is *out there in the room*. Experience is not an object that is anywhere.

If we possess our experience, minds and consciousness, then further confusions arise. Projection, introjection, identification and projective identification are all terms that describe processes that are widely believed by psychoanalysts to actually occur in the mind. Freud states:

> The most striking characteristic of symptom-formation in paranoia is the process which deserves the name *projection*. An internal perception is suppressed, and, instead, its content, after undergoing a certain degree of distortion, enters consciousness in the form of an external perception. In delusions of persecution the distortion consists in a transformation of affect; what should have been felt internally as love is perceived externally as hate. (Freud 1911b, p. 3)

This account assumes that there are separate object-like minds and 'egos' and that some of their contents may be passed over into the 'external' world or into other minds. We are not told of the nature of the 'space' across which thoughts and feelings pass.

We can perceive people eating things and spitting them out; these are facts. But taking things into *ourselves* and keeping them out is metaphorical language with a very different logic. To go back to the visual room, supposing 'A' is sitting in one chair and 'B' in another chair opposite. 'A' sees a mouse, as it is within his perspective; 'B' cannot see it from where he is sitting. Suppose they both believe that the visual room is an entity that each of them has and they alone know what is in it, and neither remembers that they both are actually in the same room. Then when 'A' says he sees the mouse, 'B' will imagine that 'A' is introjecting something. But if 'B' says he sees a mouse and there is no mouse for 'A' to see, then 'A' will think 'B' is projecting. In other words, because neither of them moves and each thinks his visual room is an entity which he alone possesses and knows what is in it, then they will be forced to think in terms of optics, the science from which Freud derived the terms, rather than thinking of the way we speak when we are in a room together. Thus, 'I see a mouse, come and have a look.'

This way of conceptualising may fix the psychoanalyst as well as the paranoid; both are under the spell of a fixed picture of experience. The psychoanalyst puts himself and his patient physically in a fixed position. The patient lies on a couch with the psychoanalyst behind him, observing. It is against the rules for the patient to observe the analyst and if he attempts to, it is analysed. This may confirm to both parties that they each *have* consciousness and an inner world. The paranoid person allegedly projects his difficulties outwards and the psychoanalyst projects his image of the mind onto the patient. They both have lost their grip on the shared world.

We need to understand the use to which words are being put when people 'project', 'introject' and 'identify'. For a large class of cases the meaning of a word is its use in the language (*PI* ¶43). When people 'project' they are using words to express a particular picture they are attached to. They are not trying to correlate words in a mistaken way with 'external reality' but may well 'see' the hatred in people's faces or 'see' that everyone in the bus is talking about them. The person who says he is being poisoned is expressing what he feels. He is unable to have a free and trusting relation with those he feels are poisoning him. The one who introjects is not taking anything into him but is expressing his inability to free himself from others and express his own thoughts.

Similarly, psychoanalysts who employ the concepts of projection are expressing their attachment to their belief that the 'real' world can ideally be described in scientific language and that the main function of language is to refer. They assume that the language-games of the physical sciences are more fundamental than any other but give no reason why this is so. The descriptions of science, of course, are of great importance, but scientific knowledge depends on a particular use of language and particular types of evidence. But scientists were children once.

> The child, I should like to say, learns to react in such-and-such a way; and in so reacting it doesn't know anything. Knowing only begins at a later level.
> A child must learn the use of colour words before it can ask for the name of a colour. (*OC* ¶¶538, 548)

Language is far richer than the particular language-games of the physical sciences.

The tyranny of systems of expression can only be broken by effecting a change of aspect. We must free ourselves from the thrall of the ideal by acknowledging it as an image that possesses us and which gives rise to a misleading aspect.

> The aspects of things that are most important for us are hidden because of their simplicity and familiarity. (One is unable to notice something – because it is always before one's eyes). The real foundations of his enquiry do not strike a man at all. Unless *that* fact has at some time struck him. – And this means: we fail to be struck by what, once seen, is most striking and most powerful. (*PI* ¶129)

For example, a student was asked to see someone who was paranoid. The patient had received a lot of treatment and felt that therapists were trying to steal her mind. For some weeks she would come into the room and just search it, as she thought it was bugged; in psychoanalytic terms she was projecting her suspicions into the room. Instead of interpreting this, after a bit the student joined in and searched too. Soon the patient began to see the ludicrousness of the situation and they both began to laugh. There was a change of aspect and so a meeting between them became possible.

7
Back to the Rough Ground

I will now discuss the talking cure in its relation to mental disorder to highlight differences between an empirical approach and an elucidatory one. Freud, Jung and the cognitive therapists were psychologists whose quest was the essential structure of the mind and the causes of neurosis and psychosis. In the early twentieth century Freud and Jung formed an enthusiastic partnership to further 'the cause'. Freud wrote, 'Nothing can befall our cause as long as the understanding between you and me remains unclouded' (McGuire 1974, 212 F, October 1910). Jung wrote, 'Anyone who knows your science has veritably eaten of the tree of paradise and become clairvoyant' (Ibid., 28 J, May 1907).

Jung, especially, held that psychology constituted the fundamental discipline on which all sciences should be based, as it grasped the subjective factor which underlay them (Shamdasani 2003, p. 15). This belief enabled them to make massive generalisations not only about neurosis and psychosis but about civilisation, religion, art and 'primitive' people. They ignored the work of Frege (1984), Husserl (1900, Vol. 1) and many other thinkers, including Wittgenstein (*TLP* ¶4.1121), who pointed out that psychologism, the belief that psychology was the basis of logic and so all sciences, did not make sense.

Ironically, because the various schools of psychoanalysis misunderstand the nature of subjectivity, they are ruled by it. The relationship between Freud and Jung moved from unjustified optimism and idealization to mutual rejection and denigration of each other's theories and persons. Members of the various schools are usually unable to detach themselves from their founders, idealizing and identifying with their theories.

Freud believed that knowledge is passed on from father to son. He explained the rivalry between him and his ex-disciples by his oral theory of the relationship between father and son. The son ends up either as a *slave*, inheriting by imitation, or as an *impudent puppy*, inheriting by biting and trying to swallow the theories. This is the history of most of his disciples. It was a father–son relationship in which the disciple is taught to imagine himself and the encounter with the patient in the way Freud did (Breger 2000; Davies 2009, pp. 98–123). Freud thought theories are a possession which are passed on, like an inheritance. If this were so, rational judgement between various theories would be impossible, and there would be no truth. A theory in science is for use in a particular situation; there are complicated criteria as to its usefulness, and it is not to be identified with and possessed.

Freud was fond of the metaphor of depth; it was his 'discovery' of the unconscious causes and sexual origins of mental disorder that were crucial. Jung appealed to the heights, he wrote:

> Were I a philosopher, I should continue in this Platonic strain and say: Somewhere, in a 'place beyond the skies', there is a prototype or primordial image of the mother that is pre-existent and supraordinate to all phenomena in which the 'maternal', in the broadest sense of the term, is manifest. (Jung 1938–54 *CW* Vol. 9, Part 1, 75)

Both were visionaries and sought the sublime and the ideal; for one it was in the heights and for the other in the depths. For both it was in the mind. Neither recognised that theories are created by human beings within a historical context; they depend on a background of concepts and presuppositions that are often unacknowledged. They are not produced by some 'subjective factor' in the mind. The user is necessarily 'outside' the representations of the theory; this enables him to use it. If he identifies with it, he is then subject to it; he cannot think freely.

Freud, Jung and most analysts surrendered to enthusiasm. This, Locke tells us, is 'founded neither on reason nor divine revelation, but rising from the conceits of a warmed or overweening brain, works yet, where it once gets footing, more powerfully on the persuasions and actions of men than either of those two, or both together' (Locke 1706, Book 4, Chapter 19, Section 7). Locke, who was a physician as well as a philosopher, pointed out, in his perceptive chapter on enthusiasm, that it tends to occur in men with a melancholy disposition or who are conceited. Such people have a corrupt judgement because they tyrannise over their own minds, allowing beliefs to be imposed on them; so they, in turn, dictate to others. They do not allow truth to show itself freely through the deliverances of language (Ibid., Book 4, Chapter 19, Section 2).

Wittgenstein can help us get back to the rough ground of human life. The heights and depths may then interact with one another on the ground, which is not an independent realm. It is there we struggle with the temptations of height – of ideas – and the seductions of depth – of passions. We strive after the sublime or the depths when we are confused about our relation to language; then there are false appearances which we strain to reach. Instead of moving with what is under our noses on the ground, we are subject to an urge to penetrate appearances to grasp the cause or the essence of everything empirical. Or the magic of language leads us to be seduced by violent passions and destructive sacrifices. These delusional urges lead to the proliferation of ideas, theories and dogmas, insisting things must be thus-and-so. The ideal, however, is better understood as an object of comparison; the comparison of ideal with what actually happens can throw light on the latter.

We do not need *to learn anything new* in our investigations but 'to *understand* something that is already in plain view. For *this* is what we seem in some sense not to understand' (*PI* ¶89).

Human misery, confusion and despair are transhistorical and cross-cultural but are expressed and responded to according to the culture and the place of the person within it. In modern Western culture, people assume that a role of the human sciences is to explain and cure confusion and despair. So the various forms of misery are classified according to what appears to be naturally occurring categories. But are there essences of misery to be expressed in categories? Are neurosis and psychosis, for example, naturally occurring categories, transcultural, which describe fixed conditions? Is a technical language here better than the ordinary one, developed over many centuries, for describing and expressing the various forms of misery? Is the latter too coarse and material?

The clinical framework

It may be helpful to look briefly at the framework within which contemporary clinicians in psychiatry and psychotherapy work. On the whole, they use a disease-centred model. The term 'neurosis' was coined in the eighteenth century to describe people who were diagnosed by physicians as having a functional disorder unaccompanied by detectable organic changes in the body. There was enormous success in finding the physical causes of many illnesses in the nineteenth century. Freud followed this pattern and claimed to discover the psychological causes of functional disorder, that is, changes in the mind of these people.

Concepts such as mental health and what is mentally normal and abnormal arose. It was assumed that 'psychological' problems such as troublesome behaviour, emotions and beliefs conform to a theoretical framework in which behaviour and emotions are outward symptoms of an internal dysfunction. The causes were unconscious: the disease was caused either by a disorder of the brain or by unconscious processes in the mind or by maladaptive cognitive processes. They certainly needed an expert to cure them.

This is problematic as 'minds' and their causal mechanisms do not exist in a pathologist's bottle. We can isolate a causal micro-organism but we cannot isolate a mental process. Ordinarily we are fairly familiar with our own minds and those of others; we do not refer to experts to tell us what is going on in them. Some 'minds' we can get along with but others can be extremely troublesome, sometimes to their 'owners' and sometimes to other people. So what is the normal mind and who decides it and on what grounds? What is the relation of these 'minds' to human action?

Freud and other mental health professionals, for example, took the conventional view that homosexuality was abnormal, although many people then and since do not consider it so. Freud, however, 'discovered' abnormalities in the unconscious of homosexuals which explained their behaviour in psychoanalytic terms, and other psychoanalysts confirmed these. One of his more bizarre 'findings' was that homosexuals were more afraid of castration than heterosexuals; they had a 'castration complex' – Freud was a genius at concocting catchy scientific-sounding phrases (Freud 1905). This was proclaimed as if it was an empirical fact, but no empirical studies were done as evidence for it and it is difficult to conceive of one that would be ethical. It was a rationalisation that enabled Freud to 'explain' homosexuality in his terms. An example of confusing the empirical with the conceptual, unclarity about the concept of normality, and showing the dangers of theoretical talk in psychotherapy, rationalisation is a process that psychoanalysts claim to diagnose, not indulge in.

Diagnostic concepts tend to be based neither on freely talking to people, careful attention to the difficult concept of normality, nor on considering precisely what one is doing when one makes a diagnosis. Diagnosis of physical complaints is different from complaints about one's mind or the way one lives. Few of us know what goes on inside our bodies so we sometimes need an expert to tell us. But what is the inside of our minds? Nevertheless, diagnosis is important. Clinicians and committees have their special interests and theories to pursue. A diagnosis is often welcomed by people. Record keeping, financial management and access to services depend on them. They are useful in solving problems of responsibility: 'I can't help what I do, it is my unconscious'; 'I am not weak-willed but I've got substance abuse disorder'; 'My child is happy, he is always watching television, but he has attention deficit disorder.' They are useful in distracting attention from the harmful consequences of some social and political policies. They allow 'normal' people to locate irrationality in others and not question their own concept of reason.

Diagnosis has its down side. Many people are confused about their life; they may not be able to make sense of what has happened to them, especially events in their childhood and after severe trauma. Some consult mental health professionals. A diagnosis such as schizophrenia, obsessional behaviour disorder, etc. may reassure but does not help in making sense of a life. Classifying people does not necessarily lead to understanding them. Diagnosis may dismiss significant aspects of experience and the person may become trapped in a negative framework – 'that schizo', 'she's just neurotic' – and so they naturally turn to drugs for help. (A good critical account of the complexities of diagnosis and the disease-centred approach is given in Bracken and Thomas 2005; Moncrieff 2008.)

The talking 'cure'

> If you come here to help me, then you are wasting your time. But if you come here because your liberation is bound up with mine, then let us begin. (Australian Aboriginal Woman in Cohen and Timini 2008, p. 275)

What is called a 'neurosis' or 'psychosis' is a confused practice, a way of living that creates misery to oneself and maybe others. It is not an entity or set of processes in the brain or mind that have become abnormal. If a person says 'I have cancer' or 'I have an infectious disease,' then this makes sense as the individual may be said to have or possess these conditions; roughly they are understood by medicine as pathological entities or processes in the body. But if they are encouraged to believe 'I have a phobia' or 'I have paranoia' etc., then they readily fall into confusion. For these are not entities that are anywhere. It encourages the primitive response to something that we have but do not like, to look for a cause, something to blame, and try to get rid of it (*PO* p. 373).

Is a neurosis or psychosis 'a something' that we can get rid of? Does knowing the cause of something necessarily lead to understanding?

If someone is in despair because their child has died, does knowing the cause relieve the suffering? Is there a fixed effect following a fixed cause in conditions such as despair? Is this a satisfactory explanation for human beings in whom historical understanding, the significance of some events and the insignificance of others, is so important? Or do we need to look at what is already there with a different framework?

The problems which attention to the nature of talking seeks to relieve are not hidden, in the way empirical facts may be, which can be disclosed by careful observation, experimentation and theory. We want to understand something that we, in a sense, already know, something that is evident if we attend. What is it to become anxious, depressed despairing? How is it that we often act thoughtlessly, greedily, enviously and arrogantly? Does a theory which explains this help us, or do we need to attend more closely at what we do or fail to do? Do people who lead fairly fruitful lives have a better theory about the mind than those who are neurotic?

The temptation is to think we must see through the ordinary use of language to find a real meaning which needs a special language, as if something hidden needs to be brought to light. But in general there is no such thing as a meaning, a sense, which lies behind what we express. Rather we respond appropriately or not to what people say; if we do not understand what they mean we ask them to clarify, a dialogue may ensue. It is only activity that gives life to sense or language. We need descriptions of our use of language and reminders of how expressions are used. It is not theory that we need, but understanding, to break the spell which binds us to certain forms of language.

The difficulty is that psychoanalysis, CBT and much psychiatry build on the confusions of the society in which they were conceived. One of its 'foolish superstitions' (*PO* p. 129) is scientism, the belief that scientific explanations are the only ones that really count, for it is science that reveals the 'real' world. In science we rightly create theories and look for causes; there are rules of evidence and procedure which scientists follow and the results obtained are scientifically true. But there is more to human life than science. There are lots of things we do quite successfully without following scientific methods. Above all, as we have said, science depends on our ability to represent; if we are to test or apply our representations then there is necessarily an agent who does not come within them. Superstitions, such as scientism, result when this is not understood.

If we are to get some clarity about human misery then we need to question the face value of language:

Human beings are deeply imbedded in philosophical, i.e. grammatical confusions. And freeing them from these presupposes extricating them from the immensely diverse associations they are caught up in. One must, as it were, regroup their entire language. – But of course this language developed as it did because human beings had – and have – the tendency to think *in this way*. Therefore extricating them only works with those who live in an instinctive state of dissatisfaction with language. Not with those who, following all their instincts, live with *the very* herd that has created this language as its proper expression. (*BT* p. 311)

A way of looking at facts in a fresh way is discussed by Wittgenstein in terms of aspect perception and aspect – blindness (*PI* ¶¶2, 11). 'I contemplate a face, and then suddenly notice its likeness to another. I *see* that it has not changed; and yet I see it differently. I call this experience "noticing an aspect" ' (*PI* p. 165). This is important in psychotherapy.

Ordinarily we spontaneously see things and may describe them. We see things and employ the words to describe them seamlessly, without having to interpret them. Faces, chairs, trees and so on are seen as themselves, without any awareness that it is one of several options. Thus we could see a face as a mask, or a person as an automaton, but ordinarily we do not. We easily see one aspect of ourselves and others – 'I am unlovable', 'I am a failure', 'It's all a rat race'. Pointing out new aspects can be a way of breaking the mould of our customary thinking.

Free association is a traditional way of breaking this mould. Chance and randomness are important elements of human culture. In many cultures there is a tradition of casting lots, coins, or yarrow sticks in China, as a means of accessing wisdom. Free association is a way of doing this with words. Chance evokes aspects of reality that had been hidden. To see the two aspects of the duck–rabbit one has to allow chance to work.

Randomness and order are two complementary ideas. They are present in the world simultaneously. Randomness is a feature of quantum mechanics and plays a crucial role in the theory of evolution. It is also a primordial source of mathematics; thus chaos theory and complexity theory are important branches of mathematics. But Freud's metaphysical beliefs in determinism blocked any insight into chance; he has no place for the incalculable. Free associations, he thought, were determined by unconscious forces which his technique unearthed; psychoanalytic interpretations are rule bound in that all forces must come from the unconscious. One can understand his theories and the authoritarianism of psychoanalysis as a defence against the place of chance in human life; all is ordered according to the theory, the practice is rule bound as laid down by the authorities of psychoanalysis (Davies 2009 gives many contemporary examples).

Nevertheless, Freud was a master at seeing aspects. Thus under his tutorship I see a person rubbing his nose and then suddenly see it as masturbating; I see a woman's genitals and then I see them as if she was castrated. Thousand's of examples could be given from the writing of psychoanalysts. Unfortunately, one of its features is that instead of pointing out aspects when necessary, it assumes they are 'real' and must exist in the unconscious. So our ordinary way with things is downplayed. Noses are 'really' penises, our partner is 'really' our mother or father and so on. The unconscious meaning is the real one. This is dogmatic. We are under the influence of the pneumatic theory of thought. That is, we assume that behind our understanding and meaning there must be a structure, the unconscious, that we can only glimpse with the help of an expert, but on which we depend for our thoughts and utterances to make sense.

There is a similarity to some medieval theologians who sought 'typological parallels'. There are Biblical passages which bear some resemblance to each other. Thus the Crucifixion is supposed to have been prefigured in the hoisting by Moses of the brazen serpent, the elevation above the earth being the basis of the comparison. Biblical scholars can find hundreds of such parallels. These combinations, although to the outsider appear artificial, result in the creation of a network of dependant replicas, far removed from the paths of ordinary experience. But they can be taken as proof of the truth of Christianity. It becomes a closed and self-justifying system, inaccessible to reason. The believer, when suitably trained in establishing these relationships, will be rewarded by finding these replicas wherever he looks for them.

Freud claims to show us the products of the unconscious, not only in neurotic lives, but in art, religion and 'primitive' people. Thus he had no need to learn a 'primitive' language, let alone speak to a tribal person to find out how they make sense of their lives; he knows that they are merely subject to unconscious forces that he has 'discovered'. Analysts, like many medieval theologians, become enthroned as interpreters of similarities that are hidden from the uninitiated. They operate by separating what seems to be significant to them, from the hurly-burly of ordinary life. They can transform the entire world of their knowledge into a vast exhibition of replicas dependent on their beliefs. Psychoanalytic tenets are taken as axiomatic. Devices are used to manage doubt and dissent. What is wanted is identification with the particular school of psychoanalysis. Thought is kept within tightly defined boundaries. The methodical skills needed to test disciplinary claims are not taught.

> A *picture* held us captive. And we could not get outside it, for it lay in our language and language seemed to repeat it to us inexorably. (*PI* ¶115)

One picture of the mind prevalent among therapists is that it is an entity external to language but designated by it. This is a seventeenth-century Lockean conception of the mind and language, in which language is understood merely as an instrument of communication. It is assumed we understand the world through ideas in the mind and require language to communicate them. We imagine our mind is an entity and that language can describe it objectively.

Instead we must see that the mind is constituted by our use of psychological concepts. There are very many notions of 'mind' if we look at history or different cultures and these people could make good sense of their lives. Without language there is no understanding. We learn concepts of desire, belief, hope or despair in our initiation into language. A dog can express its desire for a bone or for sex but we have concepts and so can feign desire, demand it, use it and express it in innumerable different ways according to our culture and mastery of language.

The picture of the mind, as containing real contents which can be described, is repeated inexorably in psychoanalysis and CBT. However, the reference of words is not to be understood in the mind's grasp of the things it thinks about. We can only think about things by having words, but the content of the words, their meaning and so the possibility of their truth or falsehood depend on the occasion on which they are said. Thoughts are open to interpretation. It is the practice of speaking that enables us to name and think about things. It is our initiation into language that is primary. Thought does not precede language but language precedes thought. A child must have a considerable mastery of language before it can understand the concept of thinking about something. Our ability to describe cannot be characterised independently of the ability to symbolise. Understanding is not a mental state that underlies use but is a primitive ability of human being.

> One of the most important tasks is to express all thought processes so true to character that the reader says, 'Yes, that's exactly the way I meant it.' To make a tracing of the physiognomy of every error. (*BT* p. 303)

We tend to model conceptualisation on vision, on pictures and diagrams rather than propositions. We then project these pictures, seeing the picture rather than truth (*PI* ¶295). Ideas and concepts are imagined to be mental images, like mental photographs. But photographs and images need interpretation, they require a method of projection to be understood, whereas the meaning of a sentence depends on the use we make of the symbols that constitute it. Words are deeds, to speak is to do something: it is the language-game that is fundamental. We learn the rules of the game by playing it (*OC* ¶95). Thus it is necessary to attend to the use of words within the context of practice, for that is what makes them true or false rather than the experiences and images we may have when using them. When we say something and mean it there does not have to be some mental process going on, for example, in the unconscious, that guarantees and determines once and for all the meaning of the symbols, or that guarantees that what we think we mean is not what we really mean but that the real meaning is in the unconscious. For a large class of cases the meaning of words is their use, which is woven into the tapestry of human life (Baker and Hacker 2005, Part 1, pp. 129–58).

Understanding meaning is not grasping some entity which is *the* meaning; this is a referential confusion. There is a difference between what words mean and what is said in them on occasion. A sentence does not express a thought on its own but is usable in many different circumstances for expressing a true thought. Thus we may say to someone 'You are envious.' This is a meaningful sentence. But it will not express a true thought to the person addressed if they are unable or unwilling to hear and judge the truth or falsehood in that remark. Meaning does not connect to truth directly as it cannot fix truth without taking into account the standards by which the words did what truth demands (Travis 2008).

The notion of meaning is connected with understanding, which is an ability to use and understand language in the countless different circumstances of use. To understand someone's utterance involves understanding how it is to be taken; it is not just a matter of seeing whether certain rules have been followed or broken. It is a practical skill which humans are able to learn. Thus if a dog is trained to salivate at the sound of a bell, it does not mean that it understands the concept of mealtime. But we are capable of learning to hear the physiognomy of meaning in the sound of a bell. We 'get it' where the 'it' can be anything – a joke, dream or a subtle mathematical argument.

In a formal system, such as mathematics, where there is general agreement over the interpretation of symbols and rules, agreement is got by strict training and drill. Those who do not calculate as the others do are quickly rapped on the knuckles. This agreement is a contingent fact about human behaviour. It is not a necessary fact about the symbols and rules that imposes itself on helpless humans.

> Just as the words 'I am here' have a meaning only in certain contexts, and not when I say them to someone who is sitting in front of me and sees me clearly, – and not because they are superfluous, but because their meaning is not *determined* by the situation, yet stands in need of such determination. (*OC* ¶348)

Many words have a 'soul' or 'face' that expresses the kind of use that constitutes their meaning. This Wittgenstein called 'the experience of meaning' and is at the basis of the direct way that a word is connected with its meaning. Thus words like 'danger', 'love', 'sex' and 'consumer' all have an immediate meaning to a contemporary English speaker. That is, they have more than the epistemic sense of technical words such as 'hippocampus', 'quaternion' or 'projective identification'; these words do, however, have a 'scientific' sound and look.

In understanding the fine aspects of meaning Wittgenstein often turned to musical allusion (e.g. *PI* ¶¶527–31). Hearing music is partly conceptual. Someone who is musically educated does not merely hear notes but hears themes, melodies, harmonic function and progression, rhythm, structure and, perhaps, history – 'It's nineteenth century'. These involve the ability to notice certain differences and have the appropriate experiences. Music is not paraphrasable as we cannot explain without remainder what it means. Beating time to the music, talking about it in appropriate ways and recognising the rightness of the way it goes indicate our understanding. We do not observe the mind of the listener and infer its internal state and mechanisms. Indeed, we can even perceive if a pupil is merely copying a master; we can hear if his phrasing is his or an imitation.

> There is a strongly musical element in verbal language. (A sigh, the intonation of voice in a question, in an announcement, in longing; all the innumerable gestures made with the voice). (*Z* ¶161)
>
> But you do speak of *understanding* music. You understand it, surely, *while* you hear it! Ought we to say this is an experience which accompanies the hearing? (*Z* ¶159)

The modulation of the voice, facial expression and gestures all contribute to the meaning of the sentences we say; they are not psychological processes that accompany it (*LW1* ¶¶366–83). They are objective features of meaning and must be distinguished from feelings as psychological processes or experiences that may accompany our use of words. Thus the rhythm with which one speaks or reads is a structure, a 'something else' that enables the whole to be more than the sum of its parts.

> Sometimes a sentence can be understood only if it is read at the *right tempo*. My sentences are all to be read *slowly*. (*CV* p. 65)

Meanings are not in the head or in the unconscious but are anchored by language in the physical environment and in social practice. Sense, on the other hand, can be independent of the existence of objects or states of affairs in the world or in the mind. This is clear in nonsense verse which is not the absence of sense but the presence of an important kind of sense. Nonsense is not the same as gibberish. Nonsense is a sense that is released from its bond to syntax, meaning and clear reference but is sensual in the rhythm and sounds of the words. Some psychotic speech has sense but no meaning, yet is not gibberish. Significantly, it is easy to write gibberish, fairly easy to compose nonsense verse, but very difficult to make it memorable.

> 'Twas brillig, and the slithy toves
> Did gyre and gimble in the wabe:
> All mimsy were the borogoves,
> And the mome raths outgrabe.
>
> (Carroll 1970, p. 191).

Slips of the tongue

One of Freud's most fruitful insights was to see the importance of slips of the tongue and their similarity to symptoms in neurosis. Seeing a slip of the tongue *as* a miniature neurosis is an example of aspect perception. It may be helpful to consider an example from the point of view of the talking 'cure'. At an initial interview a young man gave an account of his childhood, which was a variant of the 'wicked stepmother' theme. When he finished he turned to me and said, 'I suppose it was all *inviteable*.' I repeated: 'Inviteable??' He looked very embarrassed and after stuttering variations on this said: 'I meant inevitable.' 'Inviteable' is not an English word but a slip of the tongue. For the man did not say, to explain himself: 'To coin a new word inviteable' but said something he did not mean to say.

Freud as a psychologist and empiricist looked for the explanations and the causes of the phenomenon. He constructed a theoretical representation of the mind in which there was an inner world, the unconscious, where the causes lay. Using his method, a slip of the tongue could reveal its cause, the 'real meaning' which lay in the unconscious.

But, as we have said, meaning something cannot be reduced to *the* meaning. There is a relationship between what is said and what is meant but they are not the same. Meaning something is different from and not reducible to saying or writing it. They are not two parallel processes in which one occurs in the 'external world' – the speaking – and the other in the 'inner world' – the meaning. As we ordinarily read a text or listen to someone speaking, we catch on to what they are saying without there having to be an inner procession of meanings occurring in the mind. We listen to the play of language within the context which gives it meaning. Contrast 'Pass the mustard please,' said at an English lunch of beef, to it being said when on a camel crossing the Sahara when the food has run out.

> The meaning of a word is not the experience one has in hearing or saying it, and the sense of a sentence is not a complex of such experiences. – (How do the meanings of the individual words make up the sense of a sentence 'I still haven't seen him yet'?) The sentence is composed of the words, and that is enough. (*PI* p. 155)

Occasionally we have what Wittgenstein calls a meaning experience (*Bedeutungserlebnisse*). This is what happens when we make a slip of the tongue, forget a word or make any other parapraxis. In these moments the question of meaning springs up. We ask 'What does it mean?', 'What has happened?' The question 'What do you mean?' is very different from the question 'What was going on when you spoke?' The former is a riddle rather than an empirical problem that needs a solution. It contrasts with cases of ignorance, in which we do not know the answer to a question. If I am asked to name the different types of quark I would simply say I have forgotten, which is not surprising as I am not a particle physicist. But if, as a doctor, I could not remember the number of chambers to the human heart, that would be a meaning experience which would call for understanding.

Understanding what a person says depends on the sentences used. These are made of words which are not just signs but symbols because

they are used with sense and so endowed with meaning (*TLP* ¶3.32).
If we do not understand we can ask for other sentences that explain or
paraphrase what was said. Understanding a meaning experience, however, is different because we do not know what is meant by it; it is a
happening and not a cognitive matter. If asked, 'Do you really mean
that?' is not a request for a paraphrase but rather a question as to
whether the speaker is serious, or whether he really understands the full
implications of what he has said. This is what interests us in parapraxes
and neurotic symptoms.

It is a question here of expression rather than knowledge. What is
seeking expression in a parapraxis? What is it trying to make manifest? An expression is never merely a sign that points to something else,
something in the mind or the unconscious. Rather what is expressed is
itself present in the expression.

We must clarify the muddled 'thought' expressed by the word 'inviteable'. It is an example of the sign/symbol confusion which philosophy
is full of (*TLP* ¶3.324). A sign is the part of a symbol that is perceptible
by the senses and as such is arbitrary. When signs are strung together
in a particular way they become logical units with a meaning and are
symbols; they are articulated in such a way that they express a set of
possible facts. Now the words 'invite' and 'inevitable' can be strung
together with other words to make sense. Thus, 'It is inevitable that I
will die'; 'I invite you to a party.' But 'invite' and 'inevitable' belong to
very different logical categories. 'Inevitable' involves deep notions such
as fate and destiny, the relation between freedom and necessity and the
inevitability of suffering, whereas 'invite' does not.

Ironically, when he said 'inviteable' truthfulness spoke, in that it
showed he was trying to live as if the inevitable could be invited – a confused relationship between freedom and necessity, a compulsive attempt
to live a life without suffering. He was saying something that cannot be
meaningfully said as he was trying to live something that cannot be
lived. 'Invitable' is an example of cross-category equivocation which is
the result of allowing different occurrences of the same sign to symbolise
items of different logical categories. Examples from newspaper headlines
are: 'British Push Bottles Up German Rear', 'Crowds rushing to See Pope
Trample 6 to Death' (Conant 2002, p. 415). 'Incest More Common than
Thought in America' and 'Home Secretary to Act on Video Nasties' are
two from the *Guardian* – thanks to Mike Harding.

The dissolution of the problem amounts to a confession of having
been misled by the sign/symbol confusion and a conversion to a new
conception of things (*BT* pp. 302–3). To clarify we must engage in the

dialectical relation between the already expressed – 'inviteable' – and the not yet expressed, to recover the expressible. The not yet expressed is ultimately an expression; however; it is not an object co-existing with the expressed, such as a complex in the unconscious, as Freud's subjectivist conception of expression would have it. This appeal to the unconscious takes away our responsibility to make sense. It is nihilistic in that it separates freedom from necessity, suffering from living. Making sense is done by moving within language, roughly by free associating and expressing what we feel. Rather than looking for a cause, we allow language to speak as it is the breath, blood and soul of human existence.

> A main source of our failure to understand is that we do not *command a clear view* of the use of our words. – Our grammar is lacking in this sort of perspicuity. A perspicuous representation produces just that understanding which consists in 'seeing connections'. Hence the importance of finding and inventing *intermediate cases*. (*PI* ¶122)

In the talking 'cure' we speak freely. In doing so we make various attempts at meaning; in time a new way of looking at things may develop. Over many months he began to find the logical space between the categories expressed by 'invite' and 'inevitable'. He had deeply resented that much in the world was independent of his will; so compulsively lived as if it both was and was not. He was double-minded and so in conflict: ' "But *this* isn't how it is!" – we say. "Yet *this* is how it has to *be*" ' (*PI* ¶112).

Ordinarily it makes sense to be compelled to act in some way by people, although we may resent it. But to be compulsive is to compel oneself, which is nonsensical. It reveals a confusion between logical necessity and the contingencies of the empirical world. The compulsive is projecting logical necessity onto the empirical and so is living in a constrained relation to the world. This leads to despair.

Free association, saying what comes to mind, is not a rule-bound method to follow in order to get a particular result. We are concerned with riddles which require elucidating rather than finding causes of some disorder. The logical syntax of language determines meaning when compatible meanings have been assigned to words. An illogical thought, such as 'inviteable', is not a thought (*TLP* ¶3.03) but a riddle. A significant proposition consists of symbols, but 'inviteable' combines incompatible categories. The young man could only express himself in riddles as he was under a spell.

His confusions were not about something, about a specific subject matter, but the way to live a life, for example, what to take responsibility for and what not, the place of necessity rather than compulsiveness. This was expressed in his inability to use the appropriate symbols. There is no way of spelling this out in propositions describing the contents of the unconscious. This would be the application of a method. A riddle is not an empirical mistake subject to experiment and inference but an expression of sign/symbol confusion.

Dreams

This confusion can be illustrated in Freud's theory of dreams. His most 'momentous' discovery was to find *the* meaning of dreams. Rather than showing the issue at stake in understanding meaning, in *The Interpretation of Dreams* he uses a method to find *the* meaning of dreams:

> Our first step... teaches us that what we must take as our object of attention is not the dream as a whole but the separate portions of its content. If I say to the patient who is still a novice: 'What occurs to you in connection with this dream?', as a rule his mental horizon becomes a blank. If, however, I put the dream before him cut up into pieces, he will give me a series of associations to each piece, which might be described as the 'background thoughts' of that particular part of the dream. (Freud 1900, pp. 103–4)

He does much the same process in analysing parapraxes and neurotic symptoms. Using this method he claims to have discovered *the* meaning of dreams, slips of the tongue and neurotic symptoms.

In technical matters it is often helpful to break down the problem into parts, solve each part and then put the parts together. But understanding the meaning of an expression is not a technical problem. If it were, the meaning would depend on the technique rather than the person who expresses. Frege wrote: 'I do not begin with concepts and put them together to form a thought or judgement; I come by the parts of a thought by analyzing the thought' (Frege 1979, p. 253). Here he opposes a common view of thought, which Freud accepts unquestionably, namely, that if we take hold of its independently thinkable components and then put them together to form a coherent whole, we can find its meaning. This belief comes from the tendency to look at mere isolated words or phrases to understand their meaning, rather than at the sentence as a whole as it is used. To determine the meaning of a word we must discover what contribution it makes to the sentence in which it figures. Words are not isolated objects that have fixed meanings. It is the propositional whole that has primacy over its parts.

> We ought always to keep before our eyes a complete proposition. Only in a proposition have the words really a meaning. It may be that mental pictures float before us all the while, but these need not correspond to the logical elements in the judgement. It is enough if the proposition as a whole has a sense; it is this that confers on the parts also their content. (Frege 1950, p. 71)

Freud's method takes words out of their context which forced him to look for their meaning in the realm of the psychological. Frege in 1884 (1950 Introduction) pointed out this consequence. Freud's discovery actually was to lay down the rules for the *psychoanalytic* meaning of dreams. It explains meaning in terms of the psychological accompaniments of the spoken words such as the associations or the mental acts with which we utter them. It fails to distinguish the meaning experience from the sense of a sentence.

Freud has a theory of dreams which he believed stated their essence. *The secret of Dreams was revealed to him* on 24 July 1895 (Masson 1985, Letter to Fleiss 12 June 1900). Notice the romantic language! The dream work is their essence and this is driven by wish fulfilment; at root a dream is the fulfilment of a wish (Freud 1900, Chapter 6).

This is a hypothesis depending on a particular picture of the mind, wishing and dreaming to which Freud was wedded. It implies that when we say 'I dreamt last night that...' we are describing a dream we had. The logic of describing a dream, however, is very different from describing a picture which we can possess (Boss 1977). There can be no dream which is separate from its description; we cannot look at and possess a dream, we remember it. We say what we have dreamt, we express it; this may be helped by talking to someone, but telling a dream is not the same as describing something. As we tell the dream it can evolve out of itself. To imagine dreams as pictures from which we can read off a description and make an interpretation is to employ the simile of a physical picture. But this makes no sense. Who perceives these pictures? Freud gave the psychoanalytic criteria for the meaning of dreams ignoring their logic.

Freud assumes that a dream arises from sensory images and unconscious wishes; thus the source of dreams is in the mind or brain. It is difficult to see how this makes sense. Suppose someone reports that they dreamed last night they were in Russia. What is the evidence that this is a true report of something that happened? There may have been physical signs such as eye movements that they were dreaming but there could be none that they dreamed they were in Russia. It is senseless to argue that perhaps they were in Ukraine. Furthermore, there is no final report of a dream: a person reporting one may remember more of it, change bits of it and so on. The criteria for the truth of a report of a dream are different from the criteria for the description of processes in the mind or mental apparatus.

A dream is a lifeless string of signs, according to Freud, and it needs a wish to set it in motion and interpretation to find its meaning. But this is curious. Many dreams are vivid and full of life on telling, and may express what is troubling a person. But Freud pictures the wish as an inner process that somehow causes meaning. Wittgenstein wrote: 'Ever and again comes the thought that what we see of a sign is only the outside of something within, in which the real operations of sense and meaning go on' (*Z* ¶140). Dreams are far from being dead signs pointing to some inner process. They vary between jumbled images whose connection is obscure to a clear picture of some dream event. Like any story or picture they lend themselves to various interpretations.

Freud (1900, p. 312) noted that logical words do not occur in dreams, or in hallucinations. But when we describe a dream, or hallucination, then we use these words, because to say anything determinate, such as 'I had a dream last night,' requires logical words. Freud thought that the incapacity of dreams to express logical words was due to the nature of the psychical material out of which dreams are made. However, there is no such thing as psychical material. Dreams are images and not a notational system which codifies a natural language. An image that does not represent sounds cannot express the different meanings of sentences like 'A cat is on the mat', 'A cat was on the mat', 'A cat might have been on the mat', or 'A cat ought to be on the mat'. Furthermore, images cannot express logical categories, such as modality and negation: 'A cat is not on the mat', 'A cat does not exist'. Neither dreams nor free associations are true or false in themselves. But they may provoke thought and this involves logic and so truth. Freud's most important discovery, that he discovered *the* meaning of dreams, is nonsense.

A dream or hallucination may be full of meaning to the experiencer. We make further sense of them by remembering and describing them to someone, perhaps free-associating and linking them with events in our life. Reporting one's dreams is a language-game that is taught, not formally of course, but in the activity of living. In this game it makes no sense to ask if the dreamer really had the images they reported during the night; whether his memory deceived him or not is beside the point. This contrasts with other occasions in which it is of great importance to check whether a memory is correct and there are ways of doing so. Dreams and their meaning figure in 'the weave of our life'. There is a distinction between 'being the meaning of' and 'determining the meaning of'. A picture of a person may help us to determine the meaning of a picture but the meaning of a dream is the way it is used, its place in our life. If asked 'What is a dream really?' surely the right answer is: 'Don't you know? Have you never dreamt?' Different people and cultures would elaborate differently (A good historical account of the understanding of dreams in Western culture is Shamdasani 2003, pp. 100–61).

The logic of illusion

Let us look at the logic of illusion. An illusion is not a false hypothesis; it is not subject to experiment and verification. If you treat it as one then what you infer from it is not a contradiction, but an incoherence. We cannot say what it is we cannot think; if we try to, it will only be a form of words, a nonsense. But this nonsense is not gibberish; it may be difficult to see as it involves using signs without sense to express 'thoughts'.

An example may make this clearer. For thousands of years mathematicians tried to trisect an angle with straight-edge and compass yet failed, although intuitively they imagined it to be possible. A striking achievement of nineteenth-century algebra was to prove that it is impossible. How could mathematicians have thought something that is nonsense? How are we to understand this?

The proof showed that they were 'thinking' something which is actually unthinkable. They were in the grip of a picture and so took nonsense for sense. They assumed that as we can easily bisect an angle with straight-edge and compass there must be a similar expression, 'trisect' one. They had a picture of bisecting an angle and assumed that trisecting it would fit the same picture. The proof showed that those who were searching for a trisection construction did not fully understand what they were trying to do; they were incoherent without realising it. They appeared to be asking meaningfully about the possibility of doing something but actually they were using signs that were without sense; they were trying to do something that is logically impossible. This shows that there can be no systematic account that can distinguish a sentence with real meaning from one that does not fully express a thought, desire or intention. We can give no general account of how to keep one's uses of language within the bounds of sense (Floyd 2000). Incoherence is always possible.

The proof brought about a change in our conception of things; it was a critical intervention, an action. It required reflection on the frame of the original question and so a reframing of it. There was no method of solution. However, careful attention to the different use of the signs in bisecting and trisecting an angle led to a shift in the way we see things, to a new picture. But this shift cannot be seen until it has happened. It is like the problem set by the king in the fairy tale who told the princess to come neither naked nor dressed, and she came wearing a fish net. The king was then forced to accept that she was neither naked nor dressed although he did not know beforehand that that would be the solution (*AWL* p. 185).

Suppose a child is frightened of a rather sinister-looking cupboard; he goes by it giving it a wide berth and perhaps saying some magical words. He is in the grip of a picture that there is a bogy in the cupboard. How can we cure the child of this illusion? Suppose we tell him, factually, that there is no bogy in the cupboard. This is usually of no help as it is merely a solution; the child may think that there is no bogy but perhaps a vampire or some other unnameable monster, or perhaps the bogies are elsewhere. We have used an internal negation which merely eliminates the object of negation. In other words, we have implied the child is simply mistaken, that it has made an error; we have taken the child to have an empirical problem.

We need to shift the framework within which the child is living when it pictures the bogy in the cupboard. We need an external negation. That is, instead of keeping the framework and looking *beneath* the surface for a cause of the child's anxiety, we need to rearrange what already lies open to view so that it becomes surveyable (*PI* ¶92). An external negation does not imply anything positive. It involves no implication or theory regarding the existence or non-existence of bogies. But we may take the child by the hand, gently encourage it to open the cupboard, have a good look and see the dust and cobwebs so that all is surveyable and open to view, the child feels there is 'nothing' there. This is the negation of the negation of non-being.

We are held captive by an illusion. In neurosis the whole weight is put on a picture which cannot be replaced by another. This can be illustrated by someone who hears Romeo say 'Juliet is the sun' and does not understand it; it appears absurd. This failure to understand would not be remedied by pointing at Juliet and then at the sun and saying Juliet is like that. We need to show aspects of Juliet which Romeo and our confused listener would find meaningful in comparing her to the sun.

What is important is the use of neurotic language in life. It is an attempt to make sense of a life rather than an inability to correctly refer to scientific reality. We must shift the way things are seen. Beliefs make no sense independently of the practice in which they are embedded. Propositions appear to stand in an internal relation to the possible state of affairs which they present; but 'reality' does not have 'elements' independent of a particular language-game. Language-games do not depend on the linking of words to objects but on our life together in the world; this involves agreement in judgements about the world and each other, and in definitions. Ultimately, the relation between a proposition and state of affairs is made by the language-game. This relation can only be shown, to state it is to fall into nonsense.

Consciousness

Confusions in understanding illusion can be illustrated by Freud's notion of consciousness. Psychoanalysis is deeply Cartesian. Descartes meditated by himself and 'found' that the fact of consciousness is the foundation on which knowledge must build. Freud built on this, believing consciousness is a fact of individual experience open to immediate intuition, 'a fact without parallel, which defies all explanation or description' (Freud 1940, p. 172); to Freud, consciousness is 'only that of a sense-organ for the perception of psychical qualities' (Freud 1900, p. 615). It enables us to be immediately aware of our own states of mind; we have to infer that other people have it. Put in ordinary language, consciousness is magical, defying all explanation. That Freud built his theories on such an esoteric notion as consciousness shows how far he was from the rough ground of ordinary living.

According to him, consciousness is self-contained but has gaps in it. The unconscious 'is necessary because the data of consciousness have a very large number of gaps in them; both in healthy and in sick people psychical acts often occur which can only be explained by presupposing other acts, of which, nevertheless, consciousness affords no evidence' (Freud 1915a, p. 168). We infer the unconscious because consciousness has gaps, so we know of 'the existence of psychical acts which lack consciousness' (Ibid., p. 172).

Wittgenstein, who was more interested in the use of language than in solitary introspection, asked: 'What can it mean to speak of "turning my attention on to my own consciousness"? This is surely the queerest thing there could be!' (*PI* ¶412). He pointed out that we do not speak as if we observe or perceive our own consciousness. With what would we perceive it? With our consciousness? What particular point or object do we attend to?

> Do I observe myself, then, and perceive that I am seeing or conscious? And why talk about observation at all? Why not simply say 'I perceive I am conscious'? – But what are the words 'I perceive' for here? – why not say 'I am conscious?' – But don't the words 'I perceive' here show that I am attending to my consciousness? – which is ordinarily not the case. – If so, then the sentence 'I perceive I am conscious' does not say I am conscious, but that my attention was disposed in such-and-such a way.
>   But isn't it a particular experience that occasions my saying 'I am conscious again'? *What* experience? In what situation do we say it?
>   Is my having consciousness a fact of experience? (*PI* ¶¶417–18)

> Imagine an unconscious man (anaesthetized, say) were to say 'I am conscious' – should we say 'He ought to know'?
>   And if someone talked in his sleep and said 'I am asleep' – should we say 'He's quite right'?
>   Is someone speaking untruth if he says to me 'I am not conscious'? (And truth, if he says it while unconscious?) And suppose a parrot says 'I don't understand a word' 'or a gramophone: 'I am only a machine'? (*Z* ¶396)

I do not have evidence that I am conscious in the way that I can produce evidence that I have money in my pocket. We do not have privileged access to our consciousness and can see if we are or are not conscious; 'I am not sure if I am conscious or not' is surely nonsense if I understand English. We may feel groggy, dazed or half-asleep, but if we are aware of these states we are conscious. The statement 'I am conscious' is not an empirical one but may be a signal on coming round from an anaesthetic; it could just as well be replaced by asking for a cup of tea. I cannot become conscious of my regaining consciousness in the way that I may be conscious of someone else regaining it. My own consciousness is not an object of possible experience but is a precondition of any experience I may have. I cannot know I am conscious but I must be conscious to say I know something. I may dream that I am conscious and, say, flying through the air and that I decide to go some place, but that does not mean either that I am conscious, or that I decided anything, or that I am flying.

> 'Nothing is so certain as that I possess consciousness'. In that case, why shouldn't I let the matter rest? This certainty is like a mighty force whose point of application does not move, and so no work is accomplished by it. (*Z* ¶402)

This 'mighty force' drives psychoanalytic theory and much cognitive neuroscience, but it can do no work other than allow it to support a house of cards. According to Freud, our awareness of our own consciousness is more certain than the presence of other people in the world; we know we are conscious but only can infer the presence of others. This belief opens the door to psychoanalytic interpretations of the unconscious, as if other people are mere inferences, who we can only understand by interpreting them. In much neuroscience consciousness is believed to be a property of the brain, so research is directed at how neural processes produce it (Bennett et al. 2007 is a lively discussion between cognitive neuroscientists and a philosopher on this matter).

However, because we are unable to doubt we are conscious does not mean that it is an item of knowledge. In fact it shows it is not, as empirical knowledge can always be doubted. The word 'consciousness' only began to be used in its modern sense in the seventeenth century. Were people unaware of such an important 'fact' before then? Suppose I am told 'Perceive your consciousness' and I say 'I can't' while someone else says they can. What is the difference, other than words, between these two? The confusions about consciousness is illustrated by the fact that some scientists claim that the nature of consciousness is unknown and one of the greatest puzzles facing mankind; others, including Freud, claim that everyone knows what it is but it is the unconscious that is important (Bennett and Hacker 2003, pp. 293–322; Bennett et al. 2007). Both parties seek to explain it, one by turning to the unconscious, the other by researching neural processes.

Therapy however is a practice: 'We want to walk: so we need friction. Back to the rough ground!' (*PI* ¶107). Wittgenstein thought from within the bustle of human life:

> Consciousness in another's face. Look into someone else's face, and see the consciousness in it, and a particular *shade* of consciousness. You see on it, in it, joy, indifference, interest, excitement, torpor and so on. The light in other people's faces.

> Do you look into *yourself* in order to recognise the fury in *his* face? It is there as clearly as in your own breast. (*Z* ¶220)

We do not see consciousness on the face as we see spots and neither do we infer it.

We see people are conscious from their behaviour, speech and the way they express themselves, as we see other mammals are conscious. We do not infer it from their bodily movements. We may have the thought 'I am conscious' and say it to oneself thinking it makes us aware of our own states of mind. But this is nonsense. What is the 'it' that we observe and the 'who' that observes? The sentence is not a thought but perhaps a reassuring noise, reminding us that we exist, for it says nothing. Consciousness is neither a something nor a nothing and cannot make us aware of any state of mind. But if we respond to the world and people in various ways we can be said to be conscious.

The internal world with its unconscious forces is the arena for a Freudian story but it is not where we live our lives, act with conviction and enjoy the conviviality of human life (Moyal-Sharrock 2007, pp. 211–35).

> If I see someone writhing with pain with evident cause I do not think, all the same his feelings are hidden from me. (*LW2* ¶22)

We do not usually infer that a person is in pain, as Freud would have it; we see and respond to the *person* in pain.

Certainty

An important question is what is it for a sequence of actions and sentences to carry conviction? What enables us to be aware we are walking on the rough ground rather than swinging in the air attached to our illusions? What gives thought footing, a metaphor used by Charles Travis? As any therapist knows, neither logical nor empirical proof necessarily produces conviction in neurosis; nor will a child be convinced by empirical evidence that there is no bogy. A theory depends on assumptions and inferences and may not carry conviction because it depends on particular assumptions which are not shared. The use of reductio arguments can show that a thought once entertainable as true is shown to be nonsense, but this may not produce conviction; we do not live by arguments.

Wittgenstein pointed out that there are certain sentences which are peculiar in that they look like empirical propositions but are not treated as such. Thus suppose someone, in ordinary circumstances, holds up their hand and says 'This is my hand,' or says or thinks 'I have a body,' 'I have a mind' or 'There are other people in the world besides me'; these sentences are empirical yet, unlike ordinary empirical propositions, they cannot sensibly be doubted. They are not falsifiable empirical sentences depending on observation but ordinarily stand fast. For example, if someone were to argue that he does not have a body then it sounds absurd, as our natural familiarity with our bodies is more certain than any argument could be. Any evidence for or against it is no more convincing than the statement itself. This certainty is not of the order of knowing; we do not discover we have a body or a mind, or that we are human beings; they are immune to mistake, a flawless know-how.

We cannot turn on and investigate the credentials of these statements from a standpoint independently of the way of responding we acquired on learning to speak. We are mammals and have the basic responses of mammals on which our human responses are built. There is no evidence that other mammals and babies know they have a body. We use our hands and bodies and respond to people long before we can talk and refer to bodies and minds. We show our certainty in the way we act and speak.

> My life shows that I know or am certain that there is a chair over there, or a door, and so on. – I tell a friend e.g. 'Take that chair over there', 'Shut the door', etc. etc. (*OC* ¶7)

These *hinge* propositions are not certain in the abstract, but constitute our form of life. They express what we do, the facts of our living (*RPP1* ¶630). All language-games depend on them. In an abstract argument with some idealists, it might make sense to say 'Well, after all we do have bodies'; but it would not make sense to declare 'I have a body and a mind' in the way we might say 'I have £10 in my pocket'. Propositions that stand fast are the starting points of patterns of inference and description. They are a condition of their possibility; they do not articulate objects of sense but the bounds of sense. They are natural for us humans. In psychosis, however, they may not stand fast. People may say 'I do not exist', 'I have not been born' or 'I am a were-wolf'. The form of life of these people is alien to most of us, and it is difficult to find our way with them.

Our conception of what is humanly possible and sensible is poised on these propositions. They stake out the logical grounds that determine sense. Our sureness is logical, enacted and ineffable; it goes without saying. We do not assume these propositions or even take them for granted; we do not have to be informed of them before we can act; they are not foundational in the sense of being logically prior to any action. Psychological concepts are indeterminate; their objective uncertainty is not due to any epistemic shortcoming. Rather they are basic in act (*LW1* ¶¶887–8; Moyal-Sharrock 2007).

> Giving grounds, however, justifying the evidence, comes to an end; – but the end is not certain propositions striking us immediately as true, i.e. it is not a kind of *seeing* on our part; it is our *acting*, which lies at the bottom of the language-game. (*OC* ¶204)

> I want to regard man here as an animal; as a primitive being to which one grants instinct and ratiocination. As a creature in a primitive state. Any logic good enough for a primitive means of communication needs no apology from us. Language did not emerge from some kind of ratiocination. (*OC* ¶475)

This understanding of the place of sureness in ordinary human life contrasts with that of psychoanalysis which is based on theories and is algorithmic and rule-based, claiming certainty. Freud had a dogmatic blue-print of the mind and built up from this. He clearly stated his position in his address delivered in the Goethe house at Frankfurt in 1930:

> My life's work has been directed to a single aim. I have observed the most subtle disturbances of mental function in healthy and sick people and have sought to infer – or, if you prefer it, to guess – from signs of this kind how the apparatus which serves these functions is constructed and what concurrent and mutually opposing forces are at work in it. (Freud 1930a, p. 467)

Ironically, his position was the opposite of Goethe's, who detested the idea of a hidden reality beneath phenomena, to be inferred by a theory. Wittgenstein was close to Goethe; both considered meaning to be inseparable from context enabling a sentence to express thoughts. Both resisted the falsifications of a unifying theory and embraced particularity and multiplicity. Thus Faust says: 'In many hued reflection we have life.' Wittgenstein considered the following lines from Goethe as a motto for the *Philosophical Investigations*:

I have heard this reiterated for sixty years –
And cursed at it, on the quiet.
I tell myself a thousand times:
Nature gives everything amply and gladly,
She has neither core
Nor husk,
She is everything at once.
Just ask yourself,
Whether you are core or husk.

(Baker and Hacker 2005, pp. 30–1)

Theories are hypotheses; they seek to explain phenomena and there must be evidence for or against the inferences involved. But to infer and make a theory or explanation is an action and for that we must exist. The sureness with which we act is based on our existence and that is not cognitive. It is surely nonsense to think or say 'I know I exist'. People who think or say this are usually out of touch with their source of action, their animal being.

A phobia

A professional woman consulted me as she had a phobia for spiders. The word 'spider' sent shivers down her spine and whenever she returned home after work she had to take a torch and examine her whole flat for spiders before she could settle down. She had been in psychoanalysis for 3 years, which she felt had helped her, but her phobia remained, in spite of the analyst's many interpretations of its symbolism. She had also tried CBT which had not helped much, she said. She knew more about spiders than I did and was perfectly familiar with the fact that statistically she was very unlikely ever to come across a poisonous spider in England. But when she 'thought' about spiders, or when she returned to her flat, she behaved nonsensically with regard to them.

For some months she spoke mostly about her childhood, and how she felt she had to protect her mother, who was a persistent 'worrier'. One day she asked me whether she could scream in the session. I replied that the only rules I had given her were the times we would meet, the fee she must pay and the number of days notice to cancel a session. For a number of sessions she tried to get me either to give her permission to scream or to forbid it. I did neither as it was important for her to find her own desire rather than obey rules blindly. Then for a few sessions she decided, spontaneously, to give some blood-curdling screams during the session. I merely covered my ears. After the scream there was a strong sense of anti-climax – nothing happened, there was no meaning experience and the house did not fall down! After a month or so, the phobia greatly improved and soon she was completely free of it. In our discussions she was clear that the episode of screaming was crucial in helping her come to her senses.

This woman could not think spiders, especially on returning home. She would try to put sentences together containing the word 'spider' in their logical relationship with other sentences in our language to make sense and judge whether they were true or not. Her thoughts, however, were a blur; she was subject to the sign/symbol confusion. She was unable to make judgements about spiders when she returned to her flat; as 'spider' was not a symbol to her but a concatenation of signs, she did not have the logical space in which a judgement can be made. Her thoughts about spiders were not in a logical relationship to other thoughts with the possibility of being true or false. Instead, the sign 'spider' had associations and feelings tied to it; it was a meaning experience for her. She was helpless and anxious and so subject to her associations to 'spider' in accordance with the natural laws described by psychology which she was compelled to follow (Diamond 2000, pp. 149–73).

Her fear of spiders was not an empirical fear such as 'I would be frightened if I found a live cobra in my bedroom.' This conveys a truth that could be empirically verified. It makes sense; cobras are dangerous to those unused to them. It would be untrue to say that she believed that spiders in England are common and dangerous; she knew they were not. But when she returned to her flat she was under the illusion of meaning something when she 'thought' of spiders. A senseless thought is one to which no sense has been given; it is not one which has no sense because of the sense that it already has been given. She was trying to solve a problem where no problem exists. She was bewitched by language and so was anxious as she had lost her footing in meaning.

> Not funk but funk conquered is what is worthy of admiration & makes life worth having been lived. Courage, not cleverness; not even inspiration, is the grain of mustard that grows up to be a great tree. To the extent there is courage, there is connection with life & death. (*CV* pp. 43–4)

We need to reach beneath the fog of empirical psychology to make explicit that there is no purely conceptual answer to her problem, only the appearance of one, so no wonder she was anxious. We encourage the person to speak and express themselves and attend to what they are doing. It is the activity of speaking in the presence of a person who responds appropriately that allows new ways of expression, and new aspects to develop.

Her problem can be understood as a version of Moore's paradox (Moore 1993, pp. 171–212). He pointed out that it would be absurd for someone to say 'I believe that "p" but it is not the case that "p" '. Our patient knows that it is not the case that harmful spiders are likely to be found wild in England; she knows this on the basis of ordinary experience as well as looking up the facts in scientific books. But her actions show that she actually believes that it is the case when she returns to her flat. Now a psychoanalyst would be likely to say that unconsciously she does believe that dangerous spiders are around. He would be likely to tell her this, so she would now say or think, 'I unconsciously believe that dangerous spiders might be around my flat.' But if she said this, she would not be speaking truthfully but merely be following the authority of the analyst. Furthermore, his 'evidence' for her unconscious belief is merely theoretical, it fits psychoanalytic theory and it is a belief, not knowledge.

She can only have knowledge of what is going on when she can *express* and so acknowledge her feelings and thoughts about spiders within a context which respects her anxieties. She is not mistaken about her knowledge of spiders but is self-deceived; she merely believes but is unable to judge the likelihood of finding spiders in her flat (Finkelstein 2003, pp. 117–19).

When we talk to someone we may discover she has certain beliefs. But we do not discover our own beliefs; we have them. There is a difference between how we discover what someone else believes and from how we know what we believe.

> I say of someone else 'He seems to believe ….' And other people say it of me. Now, why do I never say it of myself, not even when others *rightly* say it of me?? Do I myself not see and hear myself, then? – That can be said.
>
> If I listened to the words of my mouth, I might say that someone else was speaking out of my mouth. (*PI* ¶¶2, 10)

Freud imagines this when he speaks of the unconscious. Unconscious talk is as if another person were speaking through one's own mouth (Freud 1915a, pp. 171–2).

Often we think we know what it is we are trying to say but when we say 'it' we realise that we are talking nonsense. Yet we feel compelled to express ourselves in an infelicitous manner. Commonly we mention an object when what is needed are concepts and new aspects, as in our case of a phobia. This is vividly seen in couple therapy. It may start in simple causal terms: 'The problem is my wife, she drinks too much and mostly refuses to have sex with me.' But with time people cease to get satisfaction from naming the other as some sort of causal object and move to concepts. There is the beginning of a meeting of minds.

One vital point is: 'Don't for heaven's sake, be afraid of talking nonsense! Only don't fail to pay attention to your nonsense' (*CV* p. 64). We determine the limits of language from within. The person is invited to talk and mostly he talks nonsense. He feels compelled to do so as he is trying to express 'thoughts' that cannot be thought as they involve a confusion of categories. In our case, the confusion is between the ordinary meaning of 'spider' and the category of spider as a symbol of evil. We do not contradict nonsense and try to replace it by some notion of normality we may hold. This would be to determine the limits of language from without. The person has not violated fixed criteria for the use of words, and she has no difficulty in speaking; rather she cannot establish criteria for their use in a particular context. So dogmas and theories are not overwhelmed by 'better' ones that we are committed to. Rather by being subject to strain, they collapse under their own weight.

> If in life we are surrounded by death, so too in the health of our understanding by madness. (*CV* p. 50)

It is only by talking nonsense and seeing how our expressions misfire that we can be led to see how and why they misfire and so come to understand each other (Conant 2002, pp. 386–92). Someone coming for psychotherapy is in despair; they know something is 'wrong' but are unclear as to what it is. So they have a degree of clarity as they are aware 'something' is wrong. If the therapist, however, takes an observer's point of view, assuming an external relation to the patient's problem, and that he is objective and so can give a diagnosis and correct treatment for the condition, then he implies that he, the therapist, is correct. He thereby assumes that the patient has lost all touch with her truth; but this is not so as the patient and her problem have an internal relation to one another whereas the therapist assumes an external relation to the problem. So it is imperative in the talking cure to work with the patient's understanding of her problem and not to assume that the therapist's objective view is the sane one. Our phobic patient had to express her fears, learning the language-game of expressing fear, rather than using spiders as a cause of her anxieties (Canfield 2007, p. 15).

> Men are so inevitably mad that not to be mad would be to give a mad twist to madness. (Pascal, Pensées, ¶412)

Elucidation is dialectical in that we cannot know in advance what is and what is not nonsense. But the activity of speaking and attending to our nonsense may lead to the 'liberating word' (Ostrow 2002, pp. 125–35).

The first and third person

There is much confusion in psychotherapy because of misunderstanding the difference between the language we use when talking about other people's thoughts, feelings and sensations and our own. The source of our knowledge of the world around us is perception. We look, hear, smell and touch. We perceive objects, states of affairs and events, and can describe them in words, perhaps drawings, and sometimes set them to music. Our descriptions can be true or false, accurate or clumsy. Other people can perceive the same things if suitably placed and may agree with or correct our descriptions. We can use instruments to observe more closely what we perceive. Technology and the physical sciences have developed instruments and modes of description that enormously extend our knowledge of the world we perceive.

We also perceive other people in the world and can observe their behaviour and describe it, usually using the third person singular or plural, 'He sees ...', 'she wishes ...', 'they all think ...', 'he is in great pain,' 'she intends to ...', etc. Or we may use 'that' clauses: 'I see that he is angry.'

> The psychological verbs to see, to believe, to think, to wish, do not signify phenomena (appearances). But psychology observes the phenomena *of* seeing, believing, thinking, wishing. (*Z* ¶471)

We can point to someone who looks sad, who is thinking he should take a holiday, who feels his toe is tickling, but we cannot point to the sadness, the thought or the feeling. Our psychological concepts are neither perceived nor have the certainty that named objects have. If I say my toe tickles I might be kidding, but we usually trust each other to be truthful in ordinary circumstances. Under special circumstances we may have good reason to be suspicious, for example, if someone has a motive to deceive us. If we find that we have been grossly misled by what a person says about his thoughts, feelings, and sensations, we do not usually feel we have gone crazy, as may be in the case of our ordinary perception of objects, but that we are a bad judge of character or that person is a skilful liar.

> It is only in normal cases that the use of a word is clearly prescribed; we know, are in no doubt, what to say in this or that case. The more abnormal the case, the more doubtful it becomes what we are to say – if there were for instance no characteristic expression of pain, of fear, of joy; if rule became exception and exception rule; or if both became phenomena of roughly equal frequency – this would make our normal language-games lose their point. (*PI* ¶142)

Infants cannot pretend to have feelings and sensations as they have not learned the concepts of pretence. We may not know why an infant is in pain but that it is in pain is usually certain. Pretence requires us to have mastered such concepts as pain, pleasure and pretence and this occurs later in a child's life. The ability to talk about our thoughts, feelings and sensations, and whether they are genuine or not, only makes sense when we are confronted with a living human being who understands us. When a child talks to her dolls she pretends they are human and this is parasitic on her talk with humans who do understand her. Thus if the child says her doll is ill it does not mean that she thinks it is alive. On the contrary, if the mother thinks the child is ill then logically it must be alive.

First-person awareness and discourse cannot be understood the way third person is. We do not perceive our own thoughts, feelings, emotions and intentions. My acknowledging that I am angry, in despair or thinking of Christmas is a very different language-game from knowing someone else is. I do not look into my mind or observe my behaviour and conclude that I am angry, whereas I may observe that someone else is angry, from their behaviour and situation.

If self-knowledge is construed as the presence of an inner object in front of a subject, an inner perception, then the linguistic dimension of thought is concealed. It is language that gives access to the relation of the subject to itself, not inner perception. But we easily imagine that we can represent inner objects and processes, making them present to oneself, in the sense of an inner picture. But this confuses the sensuous – actually seeing a picture – to a relationship that is logical – the way we talk of our own intentions, feelings and thoughts. There is no fool-proof way of recovering an object of my thought from what I think about it. For a thought of a particular object – say a chair – requires both fit, the object has to be as it is thought of being, and it must also have a causal role, the chair props me up whether I think of it or not. But we can give no account of what it is for a thought to be directed at a particular internal object and how to distinguish its causal role from our thought of it.

To understand a sentence such as 'I am envious' is not to represent an object 'envy' which we have been told we have, but to understand its expression. We articulate it by saying 'I am envious', behaving appropriately. Thus when someone tells me with a smile that he has been told by his analyst that he is very envious but that it is unconscious, then it is clear that he does not understand envy as to be envious is painful and leads to despair. We recognise envy in ourselves when we are *in* it and this is expressed by sentences and gestures. It is recognition and acknowledgement, truthfulness, that is important here, not reporting other people's observations, however true they appear.

It can be helpful to recall how we are taught to recognise things and processes, in contrast to how we learn to recognise our own thoughts, feelings and sensations. After a basic initiation into speaking we can point to things in order to name them for the child now understands the gesture of pointing. We can say 'This is a teddy bear and that is a fox' pointing at the creatures or at pictures. When we have learned the criteria which tell us what the object is, we are, in normal circumstances, certain what it is. For example, if someone entered the room and told me I was not sitting on a chair but was on the floor, I would be seriously disturbed, if I was sure he was serious. If others agreed with him, I could only conclude that I was crazy or perhaps they were.

Can we point to our own thoughts, feelings and sensations? How do we learn the difference between an ache in our toe and a tickle? The thought that we should take a holiday and the feeling that we must? Our liking for some people and our love of someone? Are these objective facts in the same sense as my sitting on a chair is a fact? Do we teach children to recognise their thoughts, sensations and feelings by looking into their minds and observing what is there? Or do they learn by interacting with people, expressing what they feel and think, have others respond and value what they have expressed? Is it valid to look into a person's mind, see what they are 'really' thinking or feeling and then tell them via some interpretation? Is the descriptive, factual, uninvolved knowledge of another's mind truthful?

In the act of expression we may use psychological words. Expressive concepts such as 'I am sad' or 'I am thinking of him' do not describe things or contents such as sadness or thoughts for there is no logical distinction here between a word and what it designates or between a psychological concept and the 'mental thing'. Contrast beings that had no concept of sadness with ones who had no concept of bacteria. In the latter we would say that for them bacteria do not exist. But we would not conclude there were no bacteria in their world. In the case of sadness, however, if people had no concept of it, we would not say that sadness exists in their world but is unnoticed. We would have to say that there is no sadness in their world. Many psychological words such as sadness, happiness, grief, joy and lying do not refer to any kind of objective object or process, but they do refer to *someone* who is sad, etc. (Finkelstein 2003; Chauvier 2007).

Language is deceptive. We can say 'I have a dog' or 'I have a liver' and we can also say 'I have a thought' and 'I have a feeling.' Dogs and livers are things we can possess or loose and find again, but our own thoughts and feelings are not things or processes. We cannot possess but we may express them or say we have them. Expression here is not like expressing toothpaste from a tube in which the toothpaste is in the tube and merely has to be squeezed out. Rather desires, beliefs and thoughts are expressive of that of which they are the concept; they do not designate these acts or behaviours but constitute instances of desire or thought. Squeezing toothpaste is a description of something moving from inside to outside. But the concepts of desire, belief and thought are instances of themselves when expressed. They do not just occur in sentences that are attributive but are a range of expressive behaviour and experience that are part of our lives and not narrowly intellectual attributions that fail to take seriously our way of being human.

> 'I noticed that he was out of humour.' Is this a report about his behaviour or his state of mind? ('The sky looks threatening': is this about the present or the future?) Both; not side by side, however, but about the one *via* the other. (*PI, PPF* ¶29)

> 'I can only guess at someone else's feelings' – does that really make sense when you see him badly wounded, for instance, and in dreadful pain? (*LW1* ¶964)

Expressions are used to describe as well as express. For example, I may go to a doctor and say I have a pain in my leg – a description. But I may wince and cry out, 'It hurts,' when he touches a certain spot – an expression. We can observe that other people are in pain, or having emotions, thoughts and intentions. The truth of these observations depends on criteria which may be obvious, for example, a person loosing their temper, or may be subtle, for example, 'Does he really love me?' Our own expressions on the other hand do not depend on criteria but truthfulness; it does not make sense to ask someone for evidence that they are sad or in pain although they may justify it. 'Of course I am sad because . . . ' But if he says 'I am sad because my wife left the room for five minutes,' then we might not understand him.

There is a difference between a report or representation of a state of mind and an expression:

> When someone says 'I hope he'll come' – is this a report about his state of mind, or a manifestation of his hope? I may, for example, say it to myself. And surely I am not giving myself a report. It may be a sigh; but it need not. If I tell someone 'I can't keep my mind on my work today; I keep on thinking of his coming' – this will be called a description of my state of mind. (*PI* ¶585)

When we think about feelings, thoughts, emotions and desires, it seems natural to imagine that they are things or processes that could be hidden. For we can hide them, may prefer not to speak about them and pretend to have one or other of them when we do not. If they are hidden it is easy to assume that they must be hidden in some place in the mind, hence the notion of the unconscious and an inner world. Material things can be hidden and it makes sense to ask where they are hidden. But are thoughts and feelings things we can say are present or not in some space? We can talk of a place in our mind but this does not mean it is a place in space.

Misunderstanding the difference between the first- and third-person use of language leads to our reifying the inner world:

> The 'inner' is a delusion. That is: the whole complex of ideas alluded to by this word is like a painted curtain drawn in front of the scene of the actual word use. (*LW2* p. 84)

The picture is clear but not the application:

> We would like to project everything into his inner. We would like to say that *that's* what it is all about.
>
> But in this way we evade the difficulty of describing the *field* of the sentence. (Ibid., p. 82)

For example:

> I am for instance convinced that my friend was glad to see me. But now, in philosophizing, I say to myself that it could after all be otherwise; maybe he was just pretending. But then I immediately say to myself that, even if he himself were to admit this, I wouldn't be at all certain that he isn't mistaken in thinking he knows himself. Thus there is an indeterminacy in the entire game.
>
> One could say: In a game in which the rules are indeterminate one *cannot* know who has won and who has lost. (Ibid., p. 86)

Does an expression necessarily stand between the other's experience and me? We often see people who we recognise are pleased, unhappy or afraid, without their saying anything.

> 'We *see* emotion'. – As opposed to what? We do not see facial contortions and make inferences from them (like a doctor framing a diagnosis) to joy, grief, and boredom. We describe a face immediately as sad, radiant, bored, even when we are unable to give any other description to the features. – Grief, one would like to say, is personified in the face. (Z ¶225)

The confusions generated by the picture of the inner world can be illustrated by the Freudian and Kleinian belief that there is a death instinct that is opposed to the life instinct in the inner world and that the struggle between the two accounts for neurosis and psychosis (Hinshelwood 1991, pp. 266–70). The death instinct manifests as rage and aggression towards the self and other internal objects that are felt to be bad. Klein thought there is an innate entity in the mind of the infant, primary envy, which is related to the death instinct.

But death is not an entity. Death alone is proof of life for life is essentially contingent. To be alive means we are mortal. To deny death is not to live fully. Death is not destructive as it is not a thing or an experience. Rage, aggression and envy are signs of life.

> So too at death the world does not alter, but comes to an end.
>
> Death is not an event in life: we do not live to experience death. (*TLP* ¶¶6.431–6.4311)

If there is innate primary envy in all infants, then the body is effectively conceived as an insentient thing within which there is envy and other processes. We have a picture of envy and other instincts as occurring in the inner world conceptually unconnected with the infant's body. Supposing the infant turned to stone, then according to this picture, envy and the rest could carry on (*PI* ¶283). We are bewitched by the picture of the body as a thing and envy as a private process occurring in it; the body and envy exist like two bubbles side by side, a dualism that is endemic to psychoanalysis.

> Look at a stone and imagine it having sensations. – One says to oneself: How could one so much as get the idea of ascribing a *sensation* to a *thing?* One might as well ascribe it to a number! – And now look at a wriggling fly and at once these difficulties vanish and pain seems able to get a foothold here, where before everything was, so to speak, too smooth for it. (*PI* ¶284)

A face can light up with pleasure but not with envy; it can be radiant with joy but not with envy, malice and bitterness; we can be green with envy but not with pleasure. Can we be sure that the infant attacks the breast out of envy if he has not got the concepts? If an adult is envious it is a fallacy to infer that he must have been envious of the breast. If he claims to remember it, when seeing an analyst, then this evidence is worthless, as memory is unreliable and suggestion is powerful; both the analyst and the patient are subject to the powerful mythology of causality.

The picture of envy as an entity that is inferred to exist in the inner world is encouraged by nominalising sentences and assuming this grammatical transformation does not change the meaning. Thus, 'He is envious' describes a phenomenon for which there are criteria. But if we nominalise and say 'He has envy,' then envy becomes set off by itself as a real content and established as a condition that exists somewhere – perhaps in the unconscious. This sleight of hand is endemic in psychoanalytic theorising.

> Only of a living human being and what resembles (behaves like) a living being can one say: it has sensations; it sees; is blind; hears; is deaf; is conscious or unconscious. (*PI* ¶281)

Instead of playing with grammar, we need to distinguish between a creature that is at home with concepts and one that is less so. Only of what behaves like a human being who has been initiated into language can one say that it is envious. Right judgement of other people's emotions and thoughts is not from theoretical propositions to others but from whole to whole.

> Think of the recognition of *facial expressions*. Or the description of facial expressions – which does not consist in giving the measurements of the face! Think, too, how one can imitate a man's face without seeing one's own in a mirror. (*PI* ¶285)

The nominalising use of language leads to the assumption that internal objects cause our actions; this distortion of grammar leads to the belief that the normativity of language, our ability to see differences and similarities, and so see patterns of use and reach agreement in the practices of using words, is merely a superficial phenomenon. We think we know what we mean when we speak but, according to these theorists, we often do not. The attempt to dig below the normative practices of speaking a language leads to deep confusions. For the intentionality of language disintegrates, it no longer makes sense to be asked what *we* mean when we speak; our responsibility for what we say and think is covered over and handed to experts. It is the language machine, the mental apparatus, internal objects and cognitive structures that churn out the 'real' meaning of what we say. The source of these normative assumptions lies with the experts.

Most psychological concepts are grounded in the forms of expression of the living body of humans and mammals. Many expressions of anger, fear, pleasure, pain, comforting, intending and sex are shared by mammals and us. Just approach a monkey in the wild and see it baring its teeth! But we conceptualise and so can vary and enrich our range of expression as is most notable with sexual behaviour. This, in humans, is very far from being solely instinctive behaviour; the huge variety of ways of courtship and expressions of love between people and within different cultures contrasts markedly with other mammals.

The expressive human body is not a thing that can be pinned down with certainty; the indeterminacy of the logic of the inner is crucial to being human; if it were not and obeyed mechanical rules then we would be automata and not human. Ordinary language, novels, plays, films and poetry recognise this indeterminacy; judging the expressions of others is a skill requiring experience.

Insight

The concept of insight plays a central role in classical psychoanalysis as well as in its divergent branches, in psychodynamic therapy and in the psychiatry of psychosis. Roughly it is the condition that occurs when the client acquires an emotionally charged and action-guiding knowledge of their disorder, its causes and meaning. The definitions of it are as divergent as they are prolific even in orthodox psychoanalysis. There is little congruence between the different schools even in the issue of the contents of the client's insights (a good general survey in Jopling 2008, pp. 31–106). But that insight into the causes of the disorder is important is a dogma of nearly all schools. Most believe that this puts the person into touch with an 'inner' or 'core' or 'real' self or 'inner child', and that this is highly desirable.

There are confusions about insight because of confusions between meaning and truth. We may understand the meaning of a statement such as 'You have an Oedipus Complex,' but how these words are to be taken in order to be true requires grasping what truth is under the particular circumstances in which they are spoken. Who and what fixes the standards for judging the given words? The meaning of insight tends to embody the theoretical position of the particular school of therapy. Thus in psychoanalysis, insight into the unconscious causes and meaning of the neurosis is considered essential. Dissensions from orthodoxy are assumed to be caused by 'losses of insight', the causes of which are unconscious to the dissenter. Such *ad hominem* dismissals of dissenters are the rule in psychoanalysis and continue to this day (Davies 2009, pp. 124–45). This deflecting of doubt and clinging to certainty goes with the tendency to identify with the words of the one who 'knows' – Freud, Klein, etc. The meaning of their words is understood but the disciples are unable to distance themselves from the words of the master to judge what truth demands. Freud believed that identification is the means by which the human subject is constituted, in which case there would be no truth about the subject (Freud 1921).

It is significant that the term 'insight' became popular in the English-speaking world; Freud did not use the term. He wrote of strengthening the ego, *Wo Es war, soll Ich werden*, which is usually translated as *where id was, there ego shall be* (Freud 1933, p. 80). Analysis enables the analysand 'to transform what has become unconscious and repressed into preconscious material and thus return it once more to the possession of his ego' (Freud 1940, p. 415). Freud is assuming that truth is simply a possession of the ego, completely ignoring the place of language, other people and understanding in judging truth.

It is usually assumed that interpretations or some other procedure that the school fancies lead to insight and cure. But the possibility of the placebo effect is rarely seriously considered (Jopling 2008). Plato knew 'the cure of the soul has to be effected by the use of certain charms, and these charms are fair words' (Plato 1987). Hippocrates wrote, 'sometimes simply in virtue of the patient's faith in the physician that a cure is effected' (Hippocrates Regimen, 2).

What are the criteria for the truth of an insight? As has been pointed out, third person statements have criteria as to their truth. There are criteria as to whether someone is angry, sad, surprised, desiring or thinking. These are not always clear, and it can be difficult to discern if they are feigning pain, for example; discerning the nature of someone else's desires and thoughts can be impossibly difficult. In the case of intentions and wishes, we can usually see from the person's behaviour whether they are talking truthfully or not.

Self-deception, however, is altogether unlike the failure to recognise a third-person expression. I may be mistaken about a third-person expression, but familiarity with the person helps; their culture is important, thus the expression of anger in another culture is not equivalent to ours. Self-deception is not a mistake but a confusion. It is not a matter of ignorance, that one does not know certain truths about oneself – one's developmental history, personality structure, unconscious motivations and other psychological facts – but that one is not truthful.

A statement is not the primary locus of truth but is grounded in the truthfulness of expression. We can express our intentions, desires, feelings and thoughts as well as state them (Finkelstein 2003). A common form of self-deception is the inability to mourn for a loss. When we mourn we express our sadness. But it is common in Western societies to be discouraged from the expression of mourning; this can lead to self-deception and suffering in the form of depression. The individual may state they are sad because of a loss, know they are, but be unable to express it and become depressed.

The relation between human suffering and self-deception is important. Suffering from self-deception can be treated by giving drugs, or some plausible explanation, perhaps in terms of a theory or story, or finding a 'cause' and then 'extracting' it through talking, hypnosis, etc. But these treatments can conceal the truthfulness of expression and lead to deeper suffering in the form of despair.

Insight can be compared with a crucial term in Wittgenstein's method, *Übersicht* (*PI* ¶122; Baker 2004, pp. 290–2). An 'overview' consists in seeing connections and new aspects of a problem. It involves a reorientation as to what counts as understanding the problem; it is not an increase in knowledge and so cannot be conveyed in statements. For an *Übersicht* the problem must belong to a particular person; what is an illuminating aspect to one may not be to another. So it is not an insight that depends on a theory of causes of a particular condition which can be stated as a general truth. It is not directly transferable from one to another so it is not theoretical understanding. It involves a free and spontaneous exercise of imagination and requires truthfulness and courage as it undoes self-deception.

Transference

The practical importance of confusions about the inner world can be illustrated in the notion of transference love. The concept almost defines psychoanalytic treatment and is a good example of the dogmatism that haunts it. For it is claimed that transference-based therapies are the best. There is no evidence for this and it is difficult to see how there could be. The precise definition of transference-based therapy is combated as is the precise definition of 'cure' in psychotherapy.

Some understanding is best obtained by an example. An American woman came to me for the treatment of depression. She was the daughter of a successful psychoanalyst. She said he had a liberal, independent and critical mind and considered he knew everything about women and children and managed the household in a liberal way. However, she felt unloved as a child and was frightened of her father. She said she was never a child but a demonstration model. Her mother was considered a failure by her father and died in her fifties, worn out and sad. In her teens she was sent to a famous psychoanalyst for analysis which was successful as she knew how she was expected to behave as an analysand. She married a clever and successful Englishman with whom she had children.

After a month or so, she became increasingly angry with me. She said she hated English men, especially ones with an 'Oxbridge' accent. She especially hated blond English men, which I am, and was contemptuous of me as she thought I was sexless and snobbish, particularly towards Americans. In other words, she was expressing anger and contempt towards me.

This did not make much sense. Most obviously, why did she come to see me regularly twice a week? I work in central London and there are hundreds of analysts and therapists within a mile or so, some of them would be American, and lots would neither be blond nor have an 'Oxbridge' accent. Why did she not go to one of them? Furthermore, I had never discussed Americans with her. She was making sweeping generalisations, which would be unusual as she was a well-educated woman. I was not fulfiling the criteria of a person she was justified in being furious with. I had merely become a signal to her, like a red rag to a bull. Her behaviour towards me is an example of 'transference'.

It is generally acknowledged that transference is the terrain on which psychoanalytic treatment is played out. Freud thought that patients transfer unconscious ideas regarding parental figures onto the analyst. These may be affectionate feeling that is, positive transference, or hostile ones that is, negative transference. It is assumed these have their source in the patient's relation to their parents. These components are related to the Oedipus Complex – a boy's love for his mother and fear of his father and the other way round in girls. During treatment the patient repeats his infantile conflicts within the transference. So his pathological behaviour comes to be re-orientated around his relationship to the analyst. This is transference love, which enables the analyst to interpret what is going on because the patient's hidden erotic impulses are made immediate and manifest.

Psychoanalysis understands transference as a discovery and as such an objective truth. However, the theoretical concept of transference is confused due to false analogies and a language myth (Harris 2009). It assumes that there is a speech circuit that involves the transfer of the speaker's thoughts and feelings across to the hearer. As described by Money-Kyrle: during a normal analysis 'there is a fairly rapid oscillation between introjection and projection. As the patient speaks, the analyst will, as it were, become introjectively identified with him, and having understood him inside, will reproject him and interpret' (Money-Kyrle 1956). So understanding people consists of cycles of introjective and projective identifications, and interpretations. We take meaning into our minds, digest it as best we can and then project it out again into some other mind. Meaning is thought of as some kind of entity which we can take into ourselves, introjection, and then discharge it, by projection, into other people.

This is a muddle. In transference the person is not introjecting a thought or projecting one; thoughts and meanings are not entities in the mind or head that can be transferred. But they are using language in an unusual way. When they refer to the analyst they are not referring to an objective person, but using language in the therapeutic task of trying to make sense of certain relationships in their past. It is that that has to be respected rather than interpreted. Furthermore, transference love is not love; in love we respect the other, in transference 'love' we do not.

The woman had a fixed picture about men with whom she had a close relationship, probably related to her experience with her father. The language she used about me reflected this. The meaning of an expression is determined by the practice of employing it, by the application made of it. When she spoke to me she did not speak to me as I understand myself. There was no meeting of minds. However, she was working through, trying to make sense of, her confused relation to her father. She had no concept of the possibility of an intimate relation to a man other than what she had to her father. She had never been able to express truthfully her feelings for him; there had not been a meeting of minds. He knew all about love, he was an expert, but it was a picture of love that captivated him. He could talk about it using propositions but not express it truthfully.

How is she to be helped to move from her particular use of language to talk to me? She was expressing anger and contempt but was oblivious to what it showed. She confused meaning what she said with what her words meant, in the particular context of speaking to me. The focus for me, therefore, was not so much on what she said but on what it showed. We had to move from showing to saying and this can only be done indirectly. Thus if I were to say 'You are projecting your anger and contempt towards your father onto me,' this would have made her even more furious and prove how superior I thought I was, etc. Also it would have been nonsense as she is the authority on what she means. She was not projecting anything, nothing was being transferred, but her expressions could be taken as being truthful, just as they stood.

Understanding a person in the grip of a phantasy is rather like finding the humour in a joke (*PI* ¶111). It does not help to explain it or find its cause. Rather it calls for responsive attention. For mastery of the language-games of expression depends on the other's response that supports the sense of our own expressions. Thus to interpret the 'real' meaning of what is said is to unilaterally determine meaning, and so deprive the words of their expressive meaning. The person has to be led away from being captured by a particular picture. We enter into a conversation with them which involves attending to their particular problems and the way they are expressed. Maybe a new aspect of things will strike the patient which will enable her to see the internal relation between the way she is seeing and treating the therapist and her experience of a parental figure as a child. We need to see clearly what is taken to be most convincing, where we are captured by the 'obvious' and the belief that things *must* be a certain way.

8
The Self and Images

In modern society the sense of having a self that is private, or inner, predominates.

Psychological man with his therapeutic culture is obsessed with the self; self-awareness is claimed to be the harbinger of a new era of individual choice, autonomy and self-determination (Rieff 1959). The expression of our inner self and its emotions is the way to become well-rounded people, we are told. This project of a self-determining self gaining enlightenment, through psychological analysis and the exercise of autonomous choice, suggests that our culture is under the influence of a powerful picture of the self. If we are to care for the self, it is important to see what we mean by it.

In psychoanalysis the self and the ego are often confused but roughly speaking the ego is the organised part of the self, while the self covers the whole personality (Klein 1959, pp. 247–63 in Works 3). Freud's account of the development of the self starts with speculations about the infant, who is assumed to be originally wrapped up in the pleasure principle, totally out of touch with 'reality'. Its internal needs are fulfiled in a hallucinatory manner. Freud used the example of a bird's egg, in which the embryo is able to satisfy its nutritional requirements autistically, as a picture of the infant's psychical system (Freud 1911). The problem for him then was to account for the reality principle. How does the infant move from this solipsistic position to be in touch with the real world? He thought that the core of our being is formed by the id, which has no communication with the outside world but detects oscillations in the tensions of its instinctual needs. These 'self-perceptions' govern events in the id with despotic force (Freud 1940, p. 433). This weird mythology has a distinctively solipsistic tone to it.

First of all it is a psychologistic account; there is no recognition that a human being is a living, sensing, *body* which develops the capacity to speak, think and reflect on itself. It assumes that the predicament of the infant is 'how to get out' of the inner world. It begins with private objects, its own experiential data, such as tensions and needs ruled by the pleasure principle. These are 'self-perceptions'; there is no account of what this self is and how it can be orientated 'to get out'.

Wittgenstein showed that this picture of the mind and of human development is incoherent (*PI* ¶¶243–315; Mulhall 2007). The language of sensation, such as that of tensions and needs, owes its meaning to its connections to the physical world; it is essentially shareable and would be meaningless if it were not. The idea of such a language that cannot logically be understood by anyone other than the experiencer is nonsense. The mental world cannot be detached from the physical world and retain meaning.

Freud assumes that when we name a sensation we signify a private mental object. Thus, 'I feel tense' is assumed to be a description of a mental state in the same way as 'I see a robin' is a description of what I see. 'I feel tense,' however, is an expression of feeling, or a report of what I am feeling. It is not a description. 'I sense my big toe' is not the description of an object, whereas 'I see my big toe' or feel it with my hand is. One's own body, as it is experienced by oneself, is not an object, as is the anatomical body. But one could not understand the sentence 'I sense my big toe' unless one had a concept of the anatomical body. The language-game of sensations is different from that of objects, although they are linked.

There is no 'self' in the infant that must find its way to 'reality'. Within and without are not independent variables. They are not spatial phenomena but reflect the scope of action. We may be locked in a room or shut out and we may lock ourselves in to avoid the noisy outside. Inside and outside are ways of altering our relation to the world. The infant is in the world, but it has to go through a long initiation before it can use concepts and speak with ease in our world.

Solipsism

Both Russell and his student Wittgenstein were interested in solipsism. This is the belief that the only thing that can be known for certain to exist is the self, that other people exist is, at best, an inference; we cannot be sure. The solipsist assumes he lives in a private world so that he and the objects of his immediate awareness cannot be connected with other people and common things. Put like this, it is an obscure doctrine which does not make sense. Russell used to say that he once received a letter from an old lady saying that she was glad he was a solipsist like herself, but wondered why there were not more of them!

Wittgenstein's thoughts on solipsism developed over many years and are of great importance in understanding the self–world 'relationship'. As Cavell put it: 'it attempts to undo the psychologizing of psychology, to show the necessity controlling our application of psychological and behavioural categories' (Cavell 1976, p. 91). In other words, our relation to the world and other people is not one of inference but of understanding. He followed a complicated itinerary which has been much discussed (e.g. Hacker 1986, Chapters 4 and 8; Pears 1987 and1988, Vol. 1 and 2; McGuiness 2002, Chapter 13; McGinn 2006, pp. 255–77; McManus 2006, pp. 108–18). I can only give a few hints as to how he is to be understood.

In an enigmatic passage in the *Tractatus* Wittgenstein wrote:

> It is clear, however, that 'A believes that p', 'A has the thought that p', and 'A says p' are of the form ' "p" says p': and this does not involve a correlation of a fact with an object, but rather the correlation of facts by means of the correlation of their objects.
>
> This shows too that there is no such thing as the soul – the subject, etc. – as is conceived in the superficial psychology of the present day.
>
> Indeed a composite soul would no longer be a soul. (*TLP* ¶¶5.542–5.5421)

In actual discourse we do not recognise an object, 'I', standing in a certain relation to what we believe or think. We recognise the belief or thought in the language that is uttered – that 'p' says p. So the subject who represents the world is not part of the world; 'it' is not an object as is assumed by *the superficial psychology of the present day*. If someone says 'I am going for a walk,' it says that he is going for a walk; in other words, it *shows* his human orientation through language and *says* what he intends to do.

There is an internal relation between the thinker and the thought, the believer and what he believes. The thinking subject is not an entity that is apart from what he thinks. This would make the relation between the subject and the world an external, empirical relation. We cannot make sense of a subject that is isolated from its world. A worldless subject is incoherent. It makes sense to imagine a particle floating in space that is worldless, but not a subject. It is in language that subject and world meet. It makes no sense to have the notion of a thinking subject or of a world that are independent of the practice of using words to represent thoughts and beliefs. The thinking subject cannot be represented.

We need to distinguish between the empirical subject – the whole person who is part of the world, who we can pick out and identify – and the subject who represents things in the world, who believes, thinks, makes theories and doubts, but who is not separately identifiable. To recognise another as a subject is to recognise that he expresses thoughts and beliefs without employing a name that identifies the subject of the belief or thought. Thus when he says 'I believe ...', he uses the personal pronoun 'I' which is a shifter, that is, a term whose meaning is only grasped with reference to the event of discourse in which it occurs, and which indicates the speaker. It has no reality and consistency outside actual discourse. It does not refer to an object anymore than 'It is raining' refers to an object that rains. It is only when we stop conversing and 'introspect' that we become a spectacle to ourselves, speculating on what 'I' represents, and conclude it represents 'a self'.

We recognise others as thinking and feeling subjects because they are *not* an object. They express sounds with sense and so are not constituents of my world which I have to infer, as Freud imagined. Like me, they are orientated to the world. Our relation to them is not one of object relations as is axiomatic in psychoanalysis. We distinguish between the empirical subject, who is part of the world, and the subject who represents the world, that is, thinks, judges and believes. This distinction is crucial to the talking cure for we talk to people not objects. In neurosis, however, the subject sees himself just as an empirical object: 'I am a failure,' 'I am neurotic,' etc. He imagines that he is simply part of the world forgetting that this is how he represents himself and perhaps how others represent him.

> Thus there really is a sense in which philosophy can acknowledge the self in a non-psychological way.
> What brings the self into philosophy is the fact that 'the world is my world'. (*TLP* ¶5.641, trans. slightly modified)

An analogy with sanity may help (McManus 2006, pp. 111–12). It makes sense to ask for a physical check-up even if one feels healthy; it is an empirical matter, and a test may show we have some disease. But does it make sense to check up on our sanity? Sanity involves the capacity to make judgements. A test to show one is sane does not demonstrate that one is sane, for one may carry out the test in a mad manner. One's sanity is not a matter of discovery, whereas a physician or oneself may discover, on investigation, that we have a disease. We cannot prove that we are sane, for in sanity there is an internal relation between ourselves and the world; *the world is my world.* Sanity is a given, not a discovery. Trying to prove it to oneself or others is a mark of a shaky sense of sanity. But others may produce evidence that someone is insane for then his representations of himself and his world do not make sense to them.

A similar analogy is to consider how we learn our first language. In 1914 Wittgenstein wrote in his notebook: 'How can I be *told how* the proposition represents? Or can this not be *said* to me at all? And if this is so can I *know* it? If it was supposed to be said to me, then this would have to be done by means of a proposition; but the proposition could only show it.'

> What can be said can only be said by means of a proposition, and so nothing that is necessary for the understanding of *all* propositions can be said. (*NB* p. 25)

There can be no wordless primary experience of being oneself. To say there is would be to bring it into language. Psychic reality is not independent of the subject to which the subject could refer. This would make no sense. It would be a circle in which infancy is the origin of language and language the origin of infancy. We cannot speak of infancy without language and yet we look for the origins of language in infancy. There is no point when human subjectivity existed, but language did not.

> For what the solipsist *means* is quite correct; only it cannot be *said*, but makes itself manifest.
>
> The world is *my* world: this is manifest in the fact that it is in language alone that I reach understanding. (*TLP* ¶5.62, translation modified)

When he says *my world* he is not meaning that there is an 'I' that possesses the world but is using 'my' in the sense of 'my body'. We do not possess our bodies in the way we may possess money, degrees or an important title. We are animate sensing bodies. We may sell our body to others but we do not then loose it. That I am a living body shows itself; I do not have to point it out, or say that I happen to have one! It is similar with language. The world is my world; there can be no experience that would be one of my finding it. I do not discover I have a body, nor do I discover what meaning is. The subject cannot be given apart from his acknowledgement or denial of what there is.

What is essential to representation does not depend on how the world is, and so has nothing to do with discovery and psychology. Logic is internal to the system of representation: there can be no representation of the world without logic. Logic has no content. Logic and the representation of things in the world are reciprocal notions. We can have no notion of the world independently of what is described in the true propositions of *my* language.

The world is my world in so far as I can represent it. This is not exclusive to me. For I represent the world in propositions that are within the cognitive grasp of anyone who understands my language (McGinn 2006, pp. 255–77).

Solipsism, when expressed, is an attempt to make impossible demands on language. If the person's will is at odds with reality, they cannot acknowledge that the world is independent of their will so have a compulsive relation to it. 'The world is independent of my will' (*TLP* ¶6.373). Wittgenstein wrote that the main difficulty of philosophy was one of feeling, of desire: 'the antithesis between understanding the subject and what most people *want* to see. Because of this the very things that are the most obvious can become the most difficult to understand' (*BT* Section 86, p. 300).

Here is a simple example. A man telephoned me giving his name, say Mr Brown. When he saw me he said he was actually Judas Iscariot; he showed me a letter from his former employer, addressed to Mr Brown, saying he was sorry he had to retire on medical grounds of 'ill-health' and wishing him good luck in his retirement. Mr Brown requested me to write a letter to his former employer saying Judas Iscariot was fit for re-employment. In the course of the conversation I said I did not understand what he meant by Judas Iscariot. The man looked at me as if I was an idiot. Of course he was right, in a sense, for there is no dialogue possible with a solipsist who does not understand that the meaning of a name is its role in a language-game. To him there was complete correspondence between what he called himself, Judas Iscariot, and himself. So no conversation about his name was possible (McGinn 2006, pp. 297–303).

Louis Sass (1994) has argued that the schizophrenic, like a solipsist, is the centre of his universe; he is the object rather than the subject of consciousness. He points out that Judge Schreber, who wrote a famous account of his madness, wrote that to stop thinking was to be reduced to the level of a corpse, but at the same time his compulsive thinking was mental torture (Sass 1994, p. 125). But Sass is mistaken to claim that the schizophrenic is hyper-rational or thinks too much. Rather he has lost his reason and is unable to think. As both Wittgenstein and Bion have pointed out, true thought is without a thinker; trying to think is not thinking. The psychotic's hyper-rationality and compulsive thinking are futile attempts to find reason and meaning, but these are not empirical objects that can be found. Rather whenever there is a representation of the world, or entity within it, there is a correlate notion of a subject who reads signs as symbols.

The psychotic does not rigorously think through the implications of solipsism.

> Here it can be seen that solipsism, when its implications are followed out strictly, coincides with pure realism. The self of solipsism shrinks to a point without extension, and there remains the reality co-ordinated with it. (*TLP* ¶5.64)

Bion

It may help to clarify this by comparing Wittgenstein's account of the subject with the psychoanalyst Bion's remarks on thought without a thinker (Bion 1970, pp. 97–105). Bion suggested that Descartes' tacit assumption that thoughts presuppose a thinker is valid only for the lie. True thought is without a thinker. The lie and its thinker are inseparable for the thinker is logically necessary for the lie but not for the true thought. Bion, however, followed Frege and Freud in their notion of the Cartesian ego. All three believed that there is an inner world and an outer world, Frege and Bion claimed there was also a third world where true thoughts belong (Frege 1984, p. 363; Bion 1970, p. 26).

It is difficult to make sense of a true thought existing in itself. Are there objective rail tracks that lead to them? On what do these rail tracks rest? An unthought thought is not a thought. When I say 'I think...', the pronoun 'I' does not refer to an entity, 'thinker', unless I pronounce it with emphasis 'I', meaning 'I the great thinker'.

Frege treated the first-person pronoun 'I' as a proper name and so considered that when 'I' have thoughts they must belong to me. These 'thoughts' he called ideas which are imperceptible things I have; they belong to my consciousness and no other. So his problem was similar to Freud's question as to how the baby moves from the pleasure principle to reality – how can I 'move' from my ideas to truth, from subjectivity to objectivity. Thus I understand Pythagoras's theorem but so do others; we all think it is true. But how do we move from our private mental boxes, my personal beliefs on the theorem, to its objective truth?

A true thought seems to be timelessly true and needs no owner. But my ideas are owned, they are in time and I am responsible for them. So it seems a true thought must exist in some timeless third realm, beyond all causality, floating far away from this troublesome and contingent world of ours. Both Frege and Bion wax lyrical about it (Bion 1970, pp. 62–71; Frege 1984, p. 371).

Bion claims that the truths of psychoanalysis lie in this third realm, an ineffable psychic reality that he calls 'O', to be discovered by psychoanalysts. It is the realm of absolute truth, open only to psychoanalysts and perhaps mystics and other 'exceptional individuals' (Bion 1970, p. 64). This realm is the unknown but analysts must seek it by disciplining themselves to reach it by abolishing memory and desire. Wisely, he says that only practicing psychoanalysts will understand this as he is contradicting himself (Ibid., p. 1). If it is unknown how can we know where and how to seek it or how to recognise it? Analysts assume it lies in the unconscious and they know where that is!

The trouble is that there is no way of judging the truth of these claims; they reek of dogmatic metaphysics. We are told to get rid of all our prejudices. But how do we judge that we are prejudiced? Isn't it a prejudice to try to get rid of all prejudices? A racist, for example, will not agree he is prejudiced; he will say that he speaks a truth and that we are prejudiced! How do psychoanalysts know that they are unprejudiced? They are told to discipline themselves to get rid of memory and desire but how can we or they be sure that they have got rid of them? Surely, they would have to remember that they have got rid of their memory; in the course of disciplining themselves to get rid of desire, they would be desiring to get rid of desire.

> A question is an invitation to look for something …. To understand a question means to know what kind of proposition the answer will be. Without an answer our thoughts do not point in any direction; there is no question. We cannot look for something if we do not look for it in a certain direction. (*WVC* p. 227)

If a thinker imagines himself to have an ego, then he may well concern himself with questions of profit to himself and injury to another; his thoughts contain a lie as Bion rightly says (Bion 1970, p. 97). Wittgenstein wrote much the same in 1916: 'What is good and evil is essentially the "I", not the world' (*NB* p. 80).

The word 'thought' has many shades of meaning but there is no object such as an ego or self that is present when we think truthfully. When children first use the word 'think', it indicates uncertainty and can be replaced by 'maybe'; there is no evidence that they are referring to an entity 'I' as a separate thinker (Tomasello 2003, pp. 250–1). Children are not narcissists as psychoanalysis would have it but they have not learned the language-game of objectivity.

In a discussion with some of his students Wittgenstein said: 'If you think of your brother in America, how do you know that what you think is, that the thought inside you is, of your brother being in America? Is this an experiential business? . . . .'

> The first idea you have is that you are looking at your own thought, and are absolutely sure that it is a thought that so and so. You are looking at some mental phenomenon, and you say to yourself 'obviously that is a thought of my brother in America'. (*LC* p. 66)

We cannot 'read off' from a thought that it is a thought of a brother in America anymore that we can find the meaning of sentences by inspecting what goes on inside one's mind when we utter them. Thoughts or facts cannot be specifiable independently of language use; thoughts are not processes going on in the private space of the mind which somehow must make a connection with external reality. There is no such thing as sentences having to latch onto external reality. We only have sentences, pictures and their uses and misuses.

There is no gap between us and reality; we do not have to get in touch with it as we are in it. Rather we loose touch, as Frege and Bion do, by using words which can be said but cannot mean, words which have a reference beyond the appearances. Language-games and the way we shape them are in an internal relation to the world. We cannot rise above our humanity and our language. As Cavell put it: 'Wittgenstein's motive is to put the human animal back into language . . . . But he never underestimated the power of the motive to reject the human: nothing could be more human' (Cavell 1979, p. 207).

> The reason why the use of the expression 'true or false' has something misleading about it is that it is like saying 'it tallies with the facts or it doesn't', and the very thing that is in question is what 'tallying' is here.
>
> Really 'The proposition is either true or false' only means that it must be possible to decide for or against it. But this does not say what the ground for such a decision is like.

Giving grounds, however, justifying the evidence, comes to an end; – but the end is not certain propositions' striking us as immediately as true, i.e. it is not a kind of *seeing* on our part; it is our *acting*, which lies at the bottom of the language-game.

If the true is what is grounded, then the ground is not *true*, nor yet false. (*OC* ¶¶199, 200, 204, 205)

If we speak outside language-games, trying to rise to a third world, using a decontextualised language in opposition to the natural forms of life which give our expressions power, then we no longer know what we mean. We just chatter.

Es gibt allerdings Unaussprechliches. Dies zeigt sich, es ist das Mystische. (There is indeed the inexpressible in speech. This *shows* itself; it is the mystical.) (*TLP* ¶6.522)

The crucial words here are *es gibt*. The inexpressible is given; it does not depend on a technique or theoretical trappings.

Identity

The concept of identification is of central importance in psychoanalysis as it is supposed to be the operation whereby the human subject is constituted. It *is known to psychoanalysis as the earliest expression of an emotional attachment to another person* (Freud 1921). In identification an object has perceived similarities with the ego. Thus in the Oedipus complex the subject is structured in terms of identification. The small boy wants to become like his father and so have his mother as a sexual object and is jealous of the father for baring the way, whereas the girl wants to have her father and is jealous of the mother; there are many variations of this story. 'The attachment fixes on the subject or the object of the "I" ' (Ibid. p. 58). In the boy on being the father and having the mother and vice versa in the girl.

These identifications 'shape a person's own "I"; the "I" takes on the qualities of the object; the "I" will on one occasion copy the unloved person, on another the loved one' (Ibid., pp. 58–9). Freud understands the 'I' to be some sort of entity in the mind for it can do all these things, split itself into two parts and see that some other objects have similarities to it. The ego commands voluntary movement and with other 'objects' controls the demands of the instincts, striving after pleasure and avoiding unpleasure. The ego is connected to consciousness which is imagined to be in the brain or the inner world.

We cannot both *be* and *have* a self, as we cannot be something that we have. If the self is a something in our minds or in the inner world, then we cannot be identical with one of our constituent parts. But psychoanalysts talk of 'the I' or 'the self' as if they are something we possess. We possess ourselves, they imagine. This delusion is shown when Freud tells us that consciousness is a fact of individual experience that is undefinable and is linked to the ego that seeks mastery of the instincts (Freud 1923). He assumes 'The Law of Identity' that 'A = A' thus 'I am that' inwardly pointing at 'the I'. Consciousness, however, is a word that is perfectly well-defined in dictionaries; saying it is *a fact of individual experience* is not a definition, as it is senseless. The law of identity is an example of an empty proposition which appears to say something of importance. The result is a house in the air; Wittgenstein's word was *Luftgebaeude*. It says little more than ending a business letter with 'I remain, Sir, your most humble and obedient servant' (Baker 2004, pp. 215–17).

'A thing is identical with itself' There is no finer example of a useless proposition, which yet is connected with a certain play of the imagination. It is as if in imagination we put a thing into its own shape and saw that it fits.

We might also say: 'Every thing fits into itself' – Or again: 'Everything fits into its own shape' At the same time we look at a thing and imagine that there was a blank left for it, and that it now fits it exactly. (*PI* ¶216)

How can the 'I' be my identity, for that would mean a part of me would be identical with the whole? If I say 'I am going for a walk,' would it make sense to say 'I hope your "I" or your ego has a nice walk'? 'I' is a pronoun, not a noun as Freud assumes when he refers to 'the ego'. Psychoanalysis perverts the meaning of subjectivity; according to it, the ego is either in control or is under the control of the unconscious. This would be so if we were identified with how we are being represented. There would then be no understanding that any representation of oneself implies an indexical, such as 'I', which is not in the representation. Only by understanding this can we have the concept of spontaneity.

Identity is a representation of who or what somebody or something is; it involves the individual characteristics by which a person or thing can be recognised. People are identified in all sorts of ways, such as by appearance, voice, name, genetic code, iris structure or passport. Our body can usually be identified when we are dead. So identity is not a possession; we do not *have* it in the sense that we may have money or clothes. An embryo, foetus, infant, child or adult all may be one identity, the same individual at different times.

It is when we develop language and reflect that we may become confused, imagining that we have or possess an identity. An infant, like any animal, has an identity but is unable to reflect; so it cannot think or refer to its identity since it cannot talk. As it grows up it develops language, so can talk of the past, present and future; then it can understand stories, make up stories for itself and eventually have a sense of its own history as against other people's history.

This narrative memory is important but does not constitute identity. A person can suffer a severe brain injury, become amnesic and have little sense of who or what he was, but it does not follow that he is a different person, that he has lost his identity. He is a person who is now an amnesiac. There is no inner subject of experience that has an identity. Identity does not depend on psychological continuity, our memory of our past. Memory is an ability to answer certain questions, correct mistaken assertions; it is not a source of knowledge of a 'self'. If asked who I am, I give different answers according to the circumstances. 'J.H.', 'Your doctor', 'a customer' or 'No. 573874' might each be a correct answer. If I am a spy I might wake in the morning and wonder 'Who am I?' and remember that I am Joe Blogs, an American business man. The question 'Who am I really?' is a nonsense if asked out of a context. An amnesiac may not be able to play any of these language-games as he has lost his memory, but he can usually say 'I'; one might say he has an identity but does not possess one.

We may have a series of experiences but there is nothing that unites these; there is no principle of unity, or need for one. For it makes no sense to talk of experience alone since there are no experiences that are not someone's experience. It is logically impossible for me to have an experience that is not mine but this does not mean that there is 'a self' that possesses them.

Some people are in despair as they feel 'I do not exist' or 'I have not been born.' This is to speak of oneself but have no one to speak of. The person cannot speak of a self as though it were a determinate object. In a sense he is correct, but is confused as there is a general expectation to *have* a self in our society. However, the self is found in the reading of signs as symbols. The self is the paradigm of what is unsayable. There is no self to be found by searching (*TLP* ¶¶5.64–6.41). It is neither in the external world as a body or in the internal world as the psyche. The limits of language shrink to a point where the distinction between the external and internal world breaks down.

People in despair cling to an identity and this can be a problem in therapy: 'I am gay,' 'I am schizophrenic,' 'I am a victim of sexual abuse,' 'I am a failure,' 'I have no real self,' etc. These 'identities' may have important social consequences and so one may have good reason to stand up for them: money, power and status are involved. But this does not mean that one is, meaning the same as, them.

How can we understand individual experience? As nicely put by Wittgenstein, '...the man who cries out with pain, or says that he has pain, doesn't choose the mouth which says it' (*BB* p. 68).

> 'When I say "I am in pain", I do not point to a person who is in pain, since in a certain sense I have no idea *who* is.' And this can be given a justification. For the main point is: I did not say that such-and-such a person was in pain, but 'I am ...'. Now in saying this I don't name any person. Just as I don't name anyone when I *groan* with pain. Though someone else sees who is in pain from the groaning.
>
> What does it mean to know *who* is in pain? It means, for example, to know which man in this room is in pain: for instance, the one who is sitting over there .... – What am I getting at? At the fact that there is a great variety of criteria for personal '*identity*'.
>
> Now which of them determines my saying that 'I' am in pain? None.
>
> 'But at any rate when you say "I am in pain", you want to draw the attention of others to a particular person'. The answer might be: No, I want to draw their attention to *myself*. (*PI* ¶¶404–5)

The utterances that I make about my own pain function differently from those I make about other people's. When pains are felt, criteria of personal identity do not come into play; one feels them and may express them. There is an internal connection between pain and its expression.

That I am is indefinable; it does not depend on me or anyone. But my identity, *what* I am, depends on my genes, my parents, the society where I was born and the many contingencies I meet during my life. I have many identities according to the language-game that is being played. Some of these I may strive to obtain as I value them. Thus success may be of great importance; others put much value on their identity as a failure, as being like their father, etc. There are innumerable variations on this, which are explored in novels, films and psychoanalytic literature.

Identity does not mean the same to all people. Its meaning in Chinese, for example, is a matter of performance, of doing what identity demands. Thus:

> Duke Jingo of I asked Confucius about governing. Confucius replied, 'The ruler *acts as the ruler*, and the minister *acts as a minister*; the father *acts as the father*, and the *son acts as the son*'. The duke replied, 'Wonderful! Truly, if the ruler *does not act as the ruler*, the minister *not act as minister*, father *not act as father*, and son *not act as son*, even though there is grain, will I get to eat it?'

If I ask 'Where am I?' then the sane answer is in a room sitting at my desk, or whatever. It is surely deeply confused to say I am in my mind, or in my head or in my inner world. If asked to identify myself I will answer appropriately, perhaps emphasising what I most value about myself: 'I am the one who won £1000 at poker last night.' When we copy a person, we copy the particular identity in them we admire – the way our father behaves, for example; mimesis is a basic ability for humans. But that does not mean that we must think that we are what we mime; we merely can be described by the characteristics that we have mimed. In psychosis this becomes confused. The man I described above said he was Judas Iscariot; he did not say that he was a Judas, or that he had behaved as one or that his name was that. His being and identity were collapsed into one.

The question as to what is the self can be compared to the question what is time. We all can speak of the past and future, what we have done and what we intend to do; we can speak of the remote past before there were humans and of the remote future when the earth will cease to exist. But if we stop and ask what is time then confusion readily ensues. It is as if we think we can stop time and examine it. It is similar with the self. I am myself. It is senseless to split this self from me. I do not 'have' a self.

'I' is a use, not an entity; it is enacted in speaking or thinking which is why talking is so important in psychotherapy. Subjectivity is not a wordless capacity to be oneself. Rather it is an act, not of self-positing but of giving. It is meaningless to say 'I see a tree but I do not know who sees it.' For my remark, 'I see a tree,' is an enactment; the words come from my mouth. 'I' derives its meaning in the flux of life. If we isolate it and ask what it refers to, we start stammering: 'Who am I?' This positing by the subject, as being identical to itself, a solitary 'I' in a vacuum, creates anxiety and so the possibility of neurosis. As people sometimes exclaim when they are getting an insight into this: 'I don't know whether I have found myself, or lost myself.'

Images

The meaning of 'image' is a slippery one; it has several meanings which are often confused. Much psychoanalytic theory relies on these confusions. There are graven images such as photographs, paintings and sculpture; these are material objects. Then there are images of things such as reflections, shadows and the virtual images produced by lenses in the microscope and telescope; these are not material objects. There are rainbows which are neither material objects nor pictures or representations of something real. All of these are objective in that they can be observed and scrutinised by others.

Enormous confusion has been caused by the retinal image. Isaac Newton asserted that a visible object was 'painted on the back of the eye' by rays of light; these pictures 'propagated by motion along the Fibres of the Optic Nerves into the Brain are the cause of vision' (Newton 1952, p. 15). This belief still flourishes (examples given in Hyman 2006, pp. 227, 231). Now it is possible to see someone else's retinal image with a suitable instrument, that is, an image reflected by the surface of the retina which is caused by light, focused by the lens of the eye and then reflected. But a person cannot see his own retinal image for it has nothing to do with vision which depends on photoreceptors deep *in* the retina.

The eye is not a camera employed by the brain to take images. If this were so, there would have to be a little man in the brain to look at the images; he would have to have an eye to see it, so we are back where we started. We use a camera to create an image but we do not use our eyes to see with. There are no images in the optic nerve or the brain. The proteins in the retina and optic nerve convey the information to the brain obtained from the structure of light which stimulates the photoreceptors (Gibson 1966, Chapter 11; Hyman 2006, Chapter 10).

Perceptions have also been called images. They are not, for to see a red apple is not to see an image of one, but to see a painting of a red apple is to see an image or representation of one.

Mental images, thoughts and memories have also been called images. They differ profoundly from the ones we have been describing as they are not objective; they cannot be seen by other people. Suppose we say we have a mental image of Freud. Other people cannot see it, but do we alone look at it? Can we scrutinise it and compare it with what it is an image of? On the other hand, suppose I have a picture which I think is of Freud. As it is a picture it can be seen by others; so someone may come along and says I am wrong, it is not Freud but Jung! But they cannot do this if I have a mental image of him. They may ask me what it is like. I draw it badly, someone comes along and says it looks more like Jung; I will say it is meant to be Freud.

There is no mapping from a mental image onto what it is an image of, whereas there is from a physical image. What makes a mental image of X into an image of X is not necessarily because it looks like X. It is not a representation of X, nor a private picture of him belonging to the imaginer. A mental image does not look like anything for we can imagine a person wrongly, but it is still him we imagine. Knowledge is not in question. Thus we might imagine Freud had a beard going down to his stomach; and we can imagine Moses stretching out his hands over the Red Sea to drown the Egyptian army but have no idea if this really happened (Bennett and Hacker 2003, pp. 137–47).

Looking gives us information about what is around us; mental images do not. It makes no sense to ask if my mental image is the correct one or not; there is no likeness or representation of an actual form. All I can do is to describe what I imagine. The crucial point is that a mental image is not a species of the genus image: just like a physical image, only mental (*PI* ¶¶363–97).

According to Freud, dreams are mostly composed of visual images. The mental apparatus, he says, is like an instrument resembling a compound microscope or photographic apparatus. The images come into being inside the apparatus, like in a telescope or microscope at ideal points (Freud 1900, p. 536). But the virtual image of a telescope or microscope is an optic array containing information specifying an object that has been altered by a lens before entering the eye. The image does not just come into being from nowhere; it is objective. Freud confuses the physical with the conceptual as do many theorists of vision. A visual image is not a physical image that we can perceive; we do not perceive mental images.

If someone says he has a mental image we look and talk to him and maybe ask him to draw it; we do not look into his head or mind. Neuro-surgeons do not find images in the optic nerve or brain but they may stimulate a part of the brain when the person is conscious and ask them if they see anything. Mental images do not exist in the brain or mind or internal world. They are not happenings which we can point to; they are not things or some sort of inner event. They do not adhere to people or are in them, anymore than the value of money adheres to or is in bank notes. The criterion for what a person imagines is what he says and does. 'I imagine ...' is not a description of any *thing*; rather it determines what I imagine.

How do we learn to talk about our mental images and learn when to say 'I have an image?' Not by having a mental image and being told now you are seeing one! Contrast with showing a child a picture of a lion and telling her 'That is a lion.' Wittgenstein remarks:

> One ought to ask, not what images are or what happens when one imagines anything, but how the word 'imagination' is used. But that does not mean that I want to talk only about words. For the question as to the nature of the imagination is as much about the word 'imagination' as my question is. And I am only saying that this question is not to be decided – neither for the person who does the imagining, nor for anyone else – by pointing; nor yet by a description of any process. The first question also asks for a word to be explained; but it makes us expect a wrong kind of answer. (*PI* ¶370)

When we ask about the nature of the imagination we are asking about the use of a concept not a happening in the world or the mind which requires observation and experiment. We behave and speak differently when we perceive something from when we imagine it. We can point to physical things, inspect them and name them; we cannot point to mental images. We become clear about imagination by attending to how we learn the concept and how imagination is used and misused, as, for example, in literature and art.

> When we learn as children to use the words 'see', 'look', 'image', voluntary actions and orders play a part in this training. But a different one for each of the three words. The language-game 'Look' and 'Form an image of ...' how am I ever to compare them? – If we want to train someone to react to the order 'Form an image of ...' we must obviously teach him quite differently. Reactions which belong to the latter language-game do not belong to the former. There is of course a close tie-up of these language-games; but a resemblance? – Bits of one resemble bits of the other, but the resembling bits are not homologous. (*Z* ¶646)

Seeing something and forming an image of it are not just different activities. That would be as if one were to say that moving and losing in chess were different activities. They are different concepts (*Z* ¶645).

Difference between: 'trying to see something' and 'trying to form an image of something'. In the first case one says: 'Look, just over there', in the second 'Shut your eyes!' (Z ¶626)

Suppose someone says he has a vivid image of a unicorn. There are criteria as to whether he is expressing something that is vivid to him or whether he is saying it 'idly', perhaps because he has nothing else to say. But if he says he saw a unicorn while out walking then there are very different criteria we go by. Is he joking? Is he a reliable observer or just crazy? How near did he get to it? Did he get a photograph? As we know that no reliable observer has ever described a living unicorn we would be very sceptical. But we are quite happy to talk of imaginary beings – banshees, centaurs, griffons, minotaurs, sphinxes, sirens, etc. which have a place in many people's imagination and in their mythology.

Freud had a vivid imagination but was confused as to its concept. His fanciful stories are sometimes extraordinary but riveting to many. Thus he claimed when a little girl first saw a penis: 'She makes her judgement and her decision in a flash. She has seen it and she knows that she is without it and wants to have it' (Freud 1905, p. 336). This is supposed to be a fact that is universally true and explains certain features of female sexuality! He declared that the mental structures least accessible to therapy are: 'in a woman her wish for a penis, in a man his feminine attitude to his own sex, a precondition of which would, of course, be the loss of his penis' (Freud 1940, p. 429). Freud's remarks are a good example of confusions between the empirical and conceptual. They appear to be empirical statements about mental structures but he gives no evidence as to how we can observe these structures independently of what he says. The best that can be said is that he is making a conceptual point. He is laying down a rule or making a convention which is to govern psychoanalytic interpretation. Analysts must see people as essentially concerned with the loss or gain of a penis – an economic view of man.

Lichtenberg's remark is pertinent here:

There are people who believe everything is sane and sensible that is done with a solemn face. (2000, p. 72)

The arts are a traditional source of understanding people as they use more of the resources of language than theorisers who represent 'the mind' and then theorise about it. Works of art affect us in various ways and are judged accordingly. Thus they may be beautiful, awesome, amusing, satirical, erotic and so on. Freud's imaginative analogies, his ability to draw connections and his abilities to tell good stories have been and can continue to be illuminating. Thus his sexual theories probably helped to make some people feel easier about their sexuality. But this does not mean that his images of the mind are true anymore than a poet's imagery. When Shakespeare wrote:

> Yea, from the table of my memory
> I'll wipe away all trivial fond records,
> All saws of books, all forms, all pressures past
> That youth and observation copied there,
> (*Hamlet* Act 1, Scene 5, lines 98–101)

He was using vivid analogies about memory and not a literal description or theoretical account of it. It would be beside the point to argue that memory involved a table and then map memory onto it!

Narcissus

If I look in a mirror I can see my reflection, I see *myself* reflected in the mirror. Someone else can also see it and recognise that it is me. In that sense it is like a picture rather than a mental image which no one can see. But a human being is able to recognise that it is his reflection that he sees and not an image. The mirror does not hold anything but reflects what it encounters. What reflects does not have the same form as what is reflected. There is no image that clings to the mirror, whereas in a picture the image does, so to speak, cling to it.

There are deep confusions about the mirror 'image'. A brief look at the myth of Narcissus may help (Ovid 1977, Book 3). Narcissus was a beautiful child and youth. When asked if he would live a long life it was prophesied only *si se non noverit* (If he did not come to know himself). When he grew up, Echo, a nymph who was talkative but could only repeat the last words spoken to her, fell in love with him. He spurned her, refusing to give her power over him, and she died becoming only a voice – echo. Other nymphs fell in love with him but he spurned them all. So one, in revenge, prayed: *sic amet ipse licet, sic non potiatur amato!* (So may he himself love, and not gain the thing he loves). One day he saw his reflection in a pool of water but instead of seeing that it was himself, he fell in love with *the beautiful form he sees. He loves an unsubstantial hope and thinks that substance which is only shadow* (Ibid., Book 3, lines 415–17). He burned with love for this form; he thought he had what he desired, he both kindled the flames of love and suffered them, but of course he could not meet a mere form. He came to wish to be parted from his own body, and so wasted away. He was changed into the Narcissus flower.

Narcissus, instead of seeing a reflection of himself, fell in love with an image of himself; he thought he could know it, grasp it. He confused concepts – beauty, desirability – with an object; concepts are not things one can hold. Likewise Echo could only repeat the last words spoken to her; she could not engage with another person through speech. A concept is not a thing; it can only make sense in a sentence. We ordinarily see *ourselves* in a mirror and recognise ourselves; we do not see an image or form of ourselves as we do when we see a picture of ourselves. Talking to images is a different language-game from being passionate and talking to another. If we talk to an image of someone, he does not feel recognised as it does not make sense. Narcissus is obsessed with an image and tries to grasp it as if his reflection is a picture. He did not care for himself but for his image – he died of anorexia! Echo died becoming only an echo. Neither recognised themselves or another.

The mirror stage and I

In an important paper by Lacan (2006, pp. 75–81), he discussed the psychoanalytic notion of the ego and the way it is determined from the child's response to seeing its image in a mirror. He pointed out that some animals respond to their reflection in a mirror but take it to be another animal. But an infant, he claimed, fixes his image in the mirror, as if the reflection is a picture of him, so that it becomes the root-stock of all further identifications. The captivation of the subject by this image is narcissism. The form or gestalt that she sees in the mirror is the basis of the ego; it symbolises its mental permanence and prefigures its alienating destination.

The ego is derived from an image. But mental images are not objects. A child recognises *himself* in a mirror, not an image of himself as Lacan claims. When we see ourselves in a mirror we see ourselves reversed from left to right; but what we see is our face reversed, not an image. An image, in the sense of a picture, needs to be illuminated in order to see it. But to see an object in a mirror, we need to illuminate it, not the mirror. There is no picture on the surface of the mirror; the mirror simply reflects light. The child may experience *jouissance* from recognising *himself* in the mirror, not his image as Lacan claims, just as he may experience *jouissance* from recognising animals at the zoo.

The illusion of the ego occurs when narcissistic identification takes the place of the recognition of oneself. Thus one may see one's 'beautiful' face in a mirror and think how attractive one is, forgetting one is not one's face or appearance, but that one is attracted to an image. The theory of the ego, reifying the use of 'I', is a confusion between having mental images of oneself, an activity of the imagination, and seeing the reflection of *oneself* in a mirror. It is a confusion of concept and object, of identity. A mirror accepts but does not hold; it reflects but allows the things it reflects to move on without clinging to them. The narcissist, however, clings to images; he has to *have* an identity.

Lacan suffered from the same confusion about identity as Ramsey, a mathematician colleague of Wittgenstein:

> Ransey's theory of identity makes the same mistake that would be made by someone who said that you could use a painting as a mirror as well, even if for a single posture. If we say this we overlook that what is essential to a mirror is precisely that you can infer from it the posture of a body in front of it, whereas in the case of the painting you have to know that the postures tally before you can construe the picture as a mirror image. (*PG* p. 315. An account of Ramsey and Wittgenstein on identity is Potter 2000, pp. 206–22.)

Narcissism raises interesting questions about treatment. To the extent that we are narcissistic, we imagine we can *possess* goodness, beauty, failure or clever theories. But could it make sense for us to say that we are cured of it or that we are an expert in curing it? One can use a proposition to say, with sense, that one has recovered from a physical illness. This is an empirical matter: a physician has examined us finding evidence that we are cured, and we feel fine. But suppose someone is narcissistic, and after treatment we pronounce them cured. What does it mean to express it as 'You are now cured of your narcissism' or 'I am now cured of my narcissism'?

Wittgenstein put it as follows:

> When I say I would like to discard vanity, it is questionable whether my wanting this isn't yet again only a sort of vanity. I *am* vain & in so far as I am vain, my wishes for improvement are vain, too. I would then like to be like such & such person who was not vain & whom I like, & and in my mind I already estimate the benefit which I would have from 'discarding' vanity. As long as one is on stage, one is an actor after all, regardless of what one does. (*PPO* p. 139)

It is only in action and interaction, in the particular *use* of 'I', that we can see narcissism; it is not a *state* that can be judged.

To reveal ourselves we create images; to be loved and desired we must appear in some way for we need to be visible to others. But our appearance does not constitute our being. Our face and gestures are not us: we may like or dislike them and so may others; they are our expressions but not possessions. If we imagine we can find love through our image, we have jealousy and narcissism. But if we imagine we can be loved for ourselves alone without any images, we get banality. The person with a life exhibits in gesture, looks and language the impossibility of being reduced to these.

9
A Non-Foundational Therapy

Understanding desire, wishing and love are central to therapeutic action. Freud tried to explain them. He imagined desire to be based on the initial helplessness of human beings. The hungry baby is in a state of tension, but is incapable of relieving it by itself, so needs outside help. When it gets it, the tension is relieved and it experiences satisfaction. After this, when it experiences tension, the image of the object that produced satisfaction, usually the breast, is hallucinated. So from henceforth, whenever a need arises there will be a psychical impulse that seeks to re-establish the situation of the original satisfaction. An impulse of this kind is a wish and the reappearance of the perception is its fulfilment. 'Thus the aim of this first psychical activity was to produce a "perceptual identity" (i.e. something perceptually identical with the "experience of satisfaction")' (Freud 1900, pp. 565–6).

> There are ... good reasons why a child sucking at his mother's breast has become a prototype of every relation of love. The finding of an object is in fact a refinding of it. (Freud 1905)

This is a story that Freud imagined would explain desire. It is a story of the relationship between wishes and their fulfilment which Freud calls satisfaction. It presumes there is a pre-linguistic self-consciousness, so pleasure is recognised as a desirable sensation and the infant can strive for it. 'Just as the pleasure-ego can do nothing but wish, work for a yield of pleasure, and avoid unpleasure, so the reality-ego need do nothing but strive for what is useful and guard itself against damage' (Freud 1911, p. 223).

According to this story we seek fulfilment of unconscious wishes through the restoration of signs which are bound to the experience of satisfaction. Dreams and neurotic symptoms are all wish fulfilments, in which the basic wish for satisfaction is expressed in a disguised form.

Pleasure is assumed to be a sensation we desire. This is a narrow concept of pleasure; we can take pleasure *in something* which does not mean that this something produced a sensation in us (*Z* ¶502). Most of us know that the pursuit of pleasure is futile while acknowledging that pleasure is pleasant. Wishes are usually distinguished from desires. They are not pursued; we do not usually expect them to be fulfiled. 'I wish you well' or 'I wish I was lying on a beach in the sun' do not express that something particular must happen.

Freud assumes desire is founded on a lack; there is the desire and what fulfils it. He imagines desire is a psychical thing that is in the mind now and that is lacking something. What fulfils it is something else that comes along later and gives the experience of satisfaction. A desire, however, is individuated by the expression of desire, so there is no question of two things having to fit and so produce satisfaction. There is not some kind of identity between two items as Freud imagined where he argued that the subject seeks by hallucination or by action guided by thought an identity with *the perception which was linked with the satisfaction of the need* (Freud 1900, p. 566). The desire that X is the desire that is fulfiled by X. If A desires an apple and is given one, that is the fulfilment of his desire; but it may be rotten and so he would be dissatisfied. The relation of desire to its fulfilment is an internal relation, not an external one.

Wittgenstein discussed the nature of desire in many places. He wrote:

> We meet again and again with this curious superstition, as one might be inclined to call it, that the mental act is capable of crossing a bridge before we've got to it. The trouble crops up whenever we try to think about the ideas of thinking, wishing, expecting, believing, knowing, trying to solve a mathematical problem, mathematical induction, and so forth. (*BB* p. 143)

A mental act such as a desire cannot cross a bridge before it gets to it. There is nothing that makes us fulfil a desire; there is no memory of satisfaction that lies in the unconscious that causes us to produce a perceptual identity with the experience of satisfaction. That is to confuse cause and reason. If someone is confused about reason, then they may feel they *must* cross a bridge before they get to it, so they imagine they are under the influence of a cause. This is characteristic of neurotic thought and much theorising in psychotherapy.

Wishes and desires are not just descriptive but are expressive. It is significant that Tomasello noted that his child learned the word 'need' before 'want' and that she expressed her needs at first only by intonation. Later she learned to request things, while the object of the request was apparent from the context (Tomasello 1992, p. 140). 'I want....' is expressive, so it is bound up with characteristic behaviour, tone of voice; it is dependent for its meaning on the circumstances of its use. Contrast 'I want an apple' with 'I want to marry you' (said seriously). It is difficult to believe that they share equally a set of necessary and sufficient conditions the satisfaction of which entails their instantiation. When we express a desire or a wish, they do not hide behind the behaviour that manifests them anymore than what is expressed in music is hidden behind what we hear and respond to. We make sense of desire by sharing a form of life not by interpreting an unconscious process.

> In what sense can one call wishes, expectations, beliefs, etc. 'unsatisfied'? What is our prototype of nonsatisfaction? Is it a hollow space? And would one call that unsatisfied? Wouldn't that be a metaphor too? – Isn't what we call nonsatisfaction a feeling – say hunger?
>
> Saying 'I should like an apple' does not mean: I believe an apple will quell my feeling of nonsatisfaction. *This* proposition is not an expression of a wish but of no satisfaction. (*PI* ¶¶439–40)

> *As he puts it elsewhere*, but it isn't as if I said: 'I have a craving for an apple, so whatever will satisfy this craving I will call an apple'. (Say, a sleeping pill as well) (*BT* p. 266)

The relation between a desire and its fulfilment is an internal one. Freud's account of desire, however, is an account of craving. He subsumes the many faces of desire under one theory. When we crave we are seeking the experience of satisfaction and so an external relation will do – a bit of pleasure, a drug, an interpretation or a theory. We may become satisfied, perhaps self-satisfied – another name for which is smug. But we are not fulfiled! A person who craves has an instrumental relation to pleasure but is unable to express their desires. Both Freud's and Klein's accounts of desire fails to differentiate between cravings, which are mental states – they have genuine duration and are experiences – from desires and wishes which are not.

This can be seen by considering the rule of abstinence which is a basic rule according to which psychoanalytic treatment is organised. Its justification is that gratification of the patient's demands is not the aim, whereas interpretation is. Surrogate satisfaction must be driven away to be replaced by interpretations which reveal unconscious wishes, the latent meaning of the material that is being produced (Freud 1911, p. 165).

This is confused. Certainly, gratification of demands is unhelpful as a demand involves an external relation between the therapist and the patient, mere manipulation. But the psychoanalyst is following a demand if he follows the rule of abstinence; for what is the rule that tells him when the rule is correctly applied? And what is the rule that tells him that? Understanding desire is intimately connected with timing and mindfulness of the other person, sharing a form of life. It is not a mental state, an empirical process to which rules can be applied; rather it is an expression of freedom, an internal relation between people that is not justified by a particular set of rules or interpretations.

If A says he desires B but B says she does not feel desired then it is questionable if A does desire B, that he is really in touch with her, although he may well make demands on B and perhaps make rules as to how she should respond. How we respond to what others say and do can be a part of the concepts we employ when we are within a form of life which we share with one another. Obedience to rules merely requires subservience to a particular system.

Freud wrote: 'The great question has never been answered – what does a woman want' (Strachey 1936). If a woman is asked out of context: 'What do you really want?' She may answer: 'To be happy, or famous, or rich, or appear on T.V.' If psychoanalytically sophisticated, 'To have a penis'! But these answers are empty and not founded in her actual living in which there is a rich vocabulary to express the play of desires, needs, demands, wishes, likes or hopes. The question 'What do you really desire?' can always be given a vacuous answer if asked out of context.

Many people in a consumer society have the primitive belief that language must always represent something in order to be meaningful. So they are led to confuse satisfaction, which can be represented, with enjoyment which cannot. They feel they are constantly lacking something and so driven to seek an object to fulfil it. When they get it they are satisfied but then must search for another one as satisfaction is a temporary state of mind. Meaning and reality are reduced to 'I have got it' – consumerism. If 'reality' is what is mainly useful, as Freud believed (1911), then this is a reduction of human possibilities to one.

Kraus remarked, 'Psychoanalysis is that spiritual disease of which it considers itself the cure' (quoted in Janik and Toulmin 1973, p. 75).

Joy and delight are not sensations and so measured by pleasure, but are immanent to desire. There is an internal relation between their expression and what they express because they are not a relation between objects. Pleasure and satisfaction, on the other hand, have a causal, external relation to their object. We can roughly measure how long pleasure lasts and what particular object or action causes it.

> Love is not a feeling. Love is put to the test, pain not. One does not say: 'That was not true pain, or it would not have gone so quickly'. (*Z* ¶504)

Falling in love is not necessarily a phantasy, a narcissistic infatuation, in which we overestimate the value of the beloved, getting the reference of the word wrong. Being *in* love may reveal that language is not just a calculus to refer to objects or states of affairs. It can help us change our perspective, understand the non-instrumental use of language and see the point of things that we did not see before, for example, the point of having children and the point of being truthful to one another.

Wittgenstein wrote:

> Just think of the words exchanged by lovers! They're loaded with feeling. And surely you can't just agree to substitute for them any other sounds you please, as you can with technical terms. Isn't this because they are *gestures*? And a gesture doesn't have to be innate; it is instilled, and yet *assimilated*. – But isn't this a myth?! – No. For the signs of assimilation are that I want to use *this* word, that I prefer to use none at all to using one that is forced on me, and similar reactions. (*LW1* ¶712)

In love there is no logical room for a distinction between the words and what they designate. Lovers express themselves, may talk nonsense to each other and, as in poetry, the right words and gestures are vital. In its expressive use, the concept of love is expressive of what it is a concept of. 'I love you' and other sentences and gestures of lovers are instances of love. Of course, 'I love you' can be used as a formula to get what we want. Actors can express love but in their case the question of sincerity to the other does not arise. They are not following descriptions of what goes on in a lover's mind, nor are they externalising libidinal impulses as psychoanalysis would have it. Human lovers are mammals and have the instincts of mammals and were once babies at the breast. Love cannot be understood as the mere externalisation of inner processes or as the causal effect of early experience.

Humans express love in words, actions and gestures, which move us and give joy and delight. In love, desire, imagination, thought and instinct work together. For to express our desires alone is crude while to communicate our images without desire is boring. We are not loved because we deserve it; it would be boring if love and joy was the reward of work well done. To express our desires with imagination is difficult. It is hard to separate what we imagine from what we desire. A fulfiled want is mere satisfaction and an unfulfilable image is empty.

'I feel great joy' – Where? – that sounds like nonsense. And yet one does say 'I feel a joyful agitation in my breast' – But why is joy not localised? Is it because it is distributed over the whole body? Even where the feeling that arouses joy is localised, joy is not: if for example we rejoice in the smell of a flower. – Joy is manifested in facial expression, in behaviour. (But we do not say we are joyful in our faces).

'But I do have a real *feeling* of joy!' Yes, when you are glad you really are glad. But of course joy is not joyful behaviour, nor yet a feeling round the corners of the mouth and the eyes.

'But "joy" surely designates an inward thing.' No. 'Joy' designates nothing at all. Neither any inward nor any outward thing. (*Z* ¶486–7)

Happiness

Happiness as a goal pervades the history of Western thought. Philosophers, religious teachers and now psychologists all have a say in what it is and how to obtain it. Aristotle's *Nicomachean Ethics* begins and ends in it, claiming that every art, investigation and choice tends towards an end, and more generally, that end is its good. The ultimate end for man is 'happiness'. Freud agreed that this is the purpose of life. 'The answer can hardly be in doubt men strive after happiness' (Freud 1930b, p. 25). Both Aristotle and Freud were pessimistic about its attainment. Aristotle thought that only gods are happy. Freud, in a more 'advanced' civilisation, claimed that civilisation, by repressing instincts, thwarts the satisfaction from which happiness derives. He inverted Aristotle's opinion, as he had no use for gods, happiness is pleasure, especially orgasmic pleasure; but that unfortunately requires discontinuity. 'Any persistence of a situation desired by the pleasure principle yields only a tepid feeling of comfort' (Ibid.). So at best we can only have intermittent happiness, but this may be increased by drugs – Freud took cocaine when he was young and now there are many drugs that claim to produce or prolong happiness.

We can have all sorts of aims in the context in which we live – to buy bread, to pass an exam or to find a cure for a disease, but can we talk in the same way of the aim of our life? Even a busy goal-seeker striving after pleasure may go for a stroll occasionally. Is there not a sense in which *life itself* just goes on with various events happening in it? Why must it be turned into a fixed finality? Why must it be any-one's possession? The original sense of the Greek *eudemonia* (happy) was 'good share' or 'good daimon'. The word 'happiness' derives from the old English *hap* meaning to come about by chance, absence of design or intent. In other words, happiness is not something that can be gained by our own efforts. It is not a something that we can get hold of and become attached to; it is not a something that we can have a relation to. 'It seems we cannot say anything more than: Live happily' (*NB*, p. 78). This, of course, is nonsense in that it does not tell us what to do.

How are we to understand happiness? The various ethical traditions are concerned with it, the good life. The basic notions of these traditions are polysemic. They are open-ended and cannot be reduced to a set of rules. Thus the ancient Egyptian 'maat', the Chinese 'tao', the Confu-cian 'jen', the Hindu 'rta' or 'dhama', the Platonic 'Good', the Buddhist 'nirvana', the absolute unity of God in Islam, Christian 'agape' cannot be defined in a detailed rule-bound manner telling us exactly what to do, and what not, to be good and happy. They are best understood as neither stating facts about what is in the world nor undertaking the impossible task of trying to describe or point to anything outside the world, beyond language. They are points of orientation and reference for a diversity of actions. They are on the liminal zone of the 'betwixt and between'.

Fixed rules and doctrines can be useful to capture important fea-tures of ethics if used as a comparison with features that people have overlooked, but that does not mean the good life can be defined by fixed rules, such as we must maximise pleasure. This is illustrated by Wittgenstein in considering colour patches. We can have a colour patch with fixed contours.

> But if the colours in the original merge without a hint of any outline won't it become a hopeless task to draw a sharp picture corresponding to the blurred one? Won't you have to say: 'Here I might as well draw a circle or heart as a rectangle, for all the colours merge. Anything – and nothing – is right.' – And this is the position you are in if you look for definitions corresponding to our concepts in aesthetics or ethics. (Quoted and translated in Kuusela 2008, p. 143)

We can compare the use of words with games and calculi which have fixed rules but this has limits. For meaning and understanding do not require our words to be fully regulated in the sense of being everywhere circumscribed by rules. Thus whenever a new rule is introduced to remove a doubt another crack may appear as to how the new rule is to be applied. 'A rule stands there like a sign-post' (*PI* ¶85). It can always be interpreted in more than one way. Mostly we do not interpret sign-posts but obey or disobey them. In practice we do not have rules for every eventuality and the mere possibility of misunderstanding does not detract from the usefulness of rules. In fact, disobeying some rules can, up to a point, be part of the game, as in football.

The vastness of England swallows you up, and you loose for a while your feeling that that the whole nation has a single identifiable character. Are there really such things as nations? Are we not forty-six million, all different? And the diversity of it, the chaos! The clatter of clogs in the Lancashire mill towns, the to-and-fro of the lorries on the Great North Road, the queues outside the Labour Exchanges, the rattle of pintables in the Soho pubs, the old maids biking to Holy Communion through the mists of the autumn morning – all these are not only fragments, but characteristic fragments, of the English scene. How can one make a pattern out of this muddle? (Orwell 2004, p. 12; Thanks to Mike Harding for the reference)

What is most significant in human life cannot be expressed solely in propositions that have fixed rules as to what is true or false. 'The sense of the world must lie outside the world. In the world everything is as it is, and everything happens as it does happen:*in* it no value exists – and if it did exist, it would have no value' (*TLP* ¶6.41). *This is how things are* only applies to things in the world; it is within the context of a practice that the question of the truth or falsity of particular propositions arises. But we cannot think or draw the limit to the world as this would involve standing outside it, looking down on it and representing what we saw. A complete theory of everything is impossible.

Philosophy should limit the thinkable and thereby the unthinkable.
    It should limit the unthinkable from within through the thinkable.
    It will mean the unspeakable by clearly displaying the speakable.
(*TLP* ¶4, ¶¶114–15, Trans. Ogden)

The question of the status of the propositions of arithmetic may help to understand the limits of rules because it is a restricted and familiar field of knowledge and so is easier to understand. Arithmetic is supremely reasonable. Frege wrote: 'in arithmetic we are not concerned with objects which we come to know as something alien from without through the medium of the senses, but with objects given directly to our reason and, as its next of kin, utterly transparent to it' (Frege 1950, ¶105).

Arithmetic is not just a rule-governed activity which is mechanically decidable, because it involves the concept of infinity. The universal and existential quantifier stops it from being mechanically decidable. For example, if the biggest number was 100 then we could not freely add and multiply. Thus, $40 + 40$ would be fine but what about $70 + 40$? It is because it has quantifiers that we can freely reflect on it, using our reason, rather than just mechanically doing it. Thus we can prove that there are an infinite number of prime numbers although no computer could calculate infinitely. In 'higher arithmetic' difficult problems such as Goldbach's conjecture – that every even number > 2 is the sum of two primes – can be reflected on but has not been solved up to now. Problems are solved in 'higher arithmetic' by recognising patterns, conceptualising rules and rule following, in addition to being able to act in accordance with them. In other words, a mathematician must be capable of reflective judgement concerning his own rule following. This is potentially infinite because reflection on rules is not itself rule-governed. It affirms the possibility of creativity and freedom (Potter 2000).

An interesting example of this is Ramanujan, an eminent Indian mathematician, who was largely self-taught. He had an uncanny 'feel' for numbers. For example, Hardy, a distinguished mathematician, visited him in a taxi, remarking that it had the undistinguished number 1729. Ramanujan promptly replied that it was not a dull number but is the smallest number which can be represented as the sum of two cubes in two essentially different ways! An interesting point about him is that he had little ability to create proofs for his theorems, which shocked the Cambridge mathematicians. Much of his ability to 'read' numbers and their relationship to each other, he said, was given him by the Indian Goddess of Mathematics, to whom he often prayed.

> The proof changes the grammar of our language, changes our concepts. It makes new connections, and it creates the concept of these connections. (It does not establish that they are there; they do not exist until it makes them.) (*RFM* Part 3, ¶31)

Perhaps praying to a Goddess can do this too! What is important is that proof in mathematics is not just a matter of creating and following rules. 'Elegance', 'beauty', 'deep' and 'trivial' are also used in evaluating and describing proofs. Precision is one of the hallmarks of mathematics but subtle value judgements enter it too; thus elegant proofs usually involve other natural elegant statements and these are memorable. As I have pointed out, neurosis and psychosis are disorders of reason, but most writing on psychotherapy has little place for precision or elegance.

In neurosis and psychosis the person acts as if part or the whole of language is a calculus which pre-determines instructions as to how things are, irrespective of the range of situations in which the person may find themselves. Hence the inappropriate and mechanical behaviour, thought and feeling. It is a closed system with no concept of infinity, rather like quantifier-free arithmetic. A computer can go on producing calculations in this arithmetic for ever but it would be mechanical, not creative. Similarly, closed theories and practices can proliferate indefinitely.

The concept of infinity raises the question of the possibilities of phenomena; it encourages us to focus on the kinds of statement we can make about them rather than on the phenomena themselves. For we cannot reach infinity, not because we are too feeble but because it is senseless. Instead of exploring the nature of a neurosis, trying to analyse and penetrate it from outside with our own theories, as if it were an empirical object; attending to possibilities can clarify the actions and speech of the conflicted person. Rather than applying some rule-bound technique to the person in conflict, we attend to the concrete practice of his life with language, for example, how he uses language to signify what he means and how his confused notions of meaning *surrounds the working of language with a haze which makes clear vision impossible* (PI ¶5).

When we reflect on ourselves or our use of language we are not concerned with an independently existing word, sentence or individual, as reflection shows that such objects are artificial. Even the substantive 'language' is not an entity to which the word 'language' refers. Is a smile part of language? It certainly communicates. 'Language' refers to an essential way of being human. We do not learn to speak, how to make sentences, by first learning rules, but to say something relevant, to make sense to someone to express ourselves. The form of expression, the rules of grammar, becomes a paradigm when it is interwoven in the fabric of our life. The relevance, necessity, of something is more significant than its truth. It is not a substitute for truth but is the measure of it.

There is no such thing as a sentence or an individual that exists in itself, isolated. A sentence is a part of language and an individual that can speak is a part of a community. When we learn the use of the first person pronoun we do not have to identify an object, either inner or outer. To know one's own name, to realise one's self, involves understanding that our name, our self and words like 'I', 'me' or 'we' are integrated into a pattern of relationship as speakers and hearers, self and other, that is different from everyone else's. We are not just bearers of a certain name, referents of a system of representation – selves – but people engaging with language and other people.

Reasoning is natural to us and freedom is part of our nature; we are not happy when we act mechanically, which is not the same as following a custom. An aim of the talking 'cure' is the creation of reflective judgements concerning mechanical rule following; this will result in seeing the internal relations between different areas of life. Therapeutic action must be spontaneous and not the application of a theory or technique; for this would merely create external relations between the theory or technique and the one to whom it is applied. Spontaneous action allows the subject to unfold out of itself the richness of meaning. For what is specific to the subject is precisely its ability to elude its own grasp, which is why reflection is called for rather than theory.

We learn and teach words in certain contexts and then we are expected, and expect others, to be able to project them into further contexts. Nothing insures that this projection will take place (in particular, not the grasping of universals nor the grasping of books of rules), just as nothing insures that we will make, and understand, the same projections. That on the whole that we do is a matter of our sharing routes of interest and feeling, modes of response, sense of humour and of significance and of fulfilment, of what is outrageous, of what is similar to what else, what a rebuke, what forgiveness, of what an utterance is an assertion, when an appeal, when an explanation – all the whirl of organism Wittgenstein calls 'forms of life'. Human speech and activity, sanity and community, rest upon nothing more, but nothing less, than this. It is a vision as simple as it is difficult, and as difficult as it is (and because it is) terrifying. (Cavell 1976, p. 52)

Wittgenstein remarks:

> Philosophy may in no way interfere with the use of language; it can in the end only describe it.
>
> For it cannot give it any foundation either.
>
> It leaves everything as it is. (*PI* ¶124)

Neither philosophy, in Wittgenstein's view, nor the talking 'cure' is in the business of finding new information, constructing new rules, making theories and adding to language. It aims at clarity and orientation 'by looking into the workings of our language, and that in such a way as to make us recognise those workings: *in despite of* an urge to misunderstand them.... Philosophy is a battle against the bewitchment of our intelligence by means of our language' (*PI* ¶109). This way of understanding philosophy and therapy is similar to the traditional concerns of ethics.

It is understanding, not knowledge, that is needed to live our lives fruitfully. Kant wrote:

> Enlightenment is man's emergence from his self-incurred immaturity. Immaturity is the inability to use one's own understanding without the guidance of another. This immaturity is self-incurred if its cause is not lack of understanding, but lack of resolution and courage to use it without the guidance of another....
>
> Laziness and cowardice are the reasons why such a large proportion of men, even when nature has long emancipated them from alien guidance, nevertheless gladly remain immature for life.... It is so convenient to be immature! If I have a book to have understanding in place of me, a spiritual adviser to have a conscience for me, a doctor to judge my diet for me, and so on, I need not make any efforts at all. I need not think as long as I pay. (Kant 1970, p. 54)

'Philosophy is not a theory but an activity' (*TLP* ¶4.112). As are ethics and the talking cure which require courage and resolution. The talking 'cure' is a practice in which language in the widest sense – free association, stories, theories, drama, gestures, painting and drawing, music and dance – may be used to enable the person to find their way to think, speak and act, clearly for themselves and others.

Practices are open-ended and require reflection and judgement. Von Moltke the Elder who, as Chief of the Prussian General Staff, summed up at the end of a staff ride with 'Gentlemen, as you can see, the enemy has two options open to him, and of these he will choose a third.'

> Since everything lies open to view there is nothing to explain. For what is hidden, for example, is of no interest to us.
>
> The work of the philosopher consists in assembling reminders for a particular purpose.

> If one tried to advance *theses* in philosophy, it would never be possible to debate them, because everyone would agree to them. (*PI* ¶¶126–8)

The enormous difficulty in therapy is enabling the person to see their situation truthfully rather than thinking up explanations of their difficulty by using empty signs. We may see jokes and be moved by tragedies but it is difficult to see the tragedy and comedy in our own life. The absurdity of many of our cherished beliefs, especially beliefs about ourselves. The sadness of having a desperate and confused childhood, of lost opportunities, of isolation and despair, of no one to love, of loss and disappointment about life.

Laughter and seeing the absurd do not break anything but allow us to move on. 'One does not discover the absurd without being tempted to write a manual of happiness... the feeling of the absurd springs from happiness' (Camus 2000, p. 110). Wittgenstein's writing from start to finish can be seen as an exploration of nonsense and the absurd; he greatly admired Lewis Carroll who wrote on the absurd and whose books are surely happy. As Malcolm noted, Wittgenstein would often grin, during his lectures, at the absurdity of what he imagined. But if someone chuckled, his expression would change to severity and he would exclaim, 'No, no; I am serious.' He said that a serious and good philosophical work could be written that would consist entirely of jokes (Malcolm 1984, pp. 27–8). A great and hugely influential work of philosophy that does consist mostly of jokes and absurd stories is the Chinese Classic: *The Book of Chuang Tzu* written about 200 B.C. (2006).

A favourite quotation of Wittgenstein runs: 'And joking apart, my friends, only a man who has a heart can feel and say truly, indeed from the heart, that he is good for nothing. That done, things will sort themselves out' (quoted in Engelman 1967, p. 116).

As has been emphasised by Baker and Morris (Baker 2004; Morris 2007; and Pichler in 'Wittgenstein and His Interpreters', 2007. Also see Kuusela 2008), Wittgenstein was concerned to help us become free of dogma that is free of the tyranny of pictures and analogies that lead us to think that we or things *must* be a certain way. For example, to live a good life we must have knowledge and theories from experts rather than clarity and taking responsibility for our lives. So he makes central use of appropriate questions and alternative ways of seeing things. 'No fact (even about our grammar) is stated, no thesis advanced. There is nothing to attack, hence nothing to defend against criticism. Wittgenstein advocated nothing more (and nothing less) than different possible ways of looking at things which he offered in particular argumentative contexts for certain particular purposes' (Baker 2004, p. 45).

Concepts and meaning get their lives from practice. These develop and evolve so there is no way of fixing them by rules once and for all. We can fix some of them for some of the time, as is done in mathematics and the natural sciences, but mostly they depend on the various customs and contexts of living (McDowell 1998). Any theory which tells us what *we* really mean is nonsense as it would involve an external relation to what is said. Sets of rules and basic assumptions can be misleading unless taken in the right spirit. Thus the most rigorous of logicians, Frege, asked his reader *not begrudge a pinch of salt* when discussing basic logical concepts (Frege 1984, p. 193). In the talking cure truthfulness is of great importance as it acts as a mirror in which a reorientation can take place. Mystifications play no part such as the therapist claiming to have special knowledge to impart.

When we are disorientated we do not need to learn truths, but we need to make sense. This involves seeing connections which we are blind to and learning to express ourselves in a meaningful way. For example, contrast mourning with depression; in the latter we are disorientated, it does not make sense, it leads nowhere, it is not expressive but symptomatic.

The norms that are found in the course of the talking cure are not dogmatic; they are not fixed aims such as the resolution of the Oedipus complex, attainment of the depressive position, resolution of the transference, correct cognitive processes and happiness. In the talking cure we rigorously avoid maps and plans of therapy, setting goals to achieve requiring techniques invented by the therapist. Instead, by concentrating on the particular conflicts and despair revealed by the patient, we allow ourselves to become susceptible to the flow of therapy.

Any norms are groundless in that there is no external evidence on which they can be judged. Their groundlessness belongs to their logical nature as they play a formative role in shaping thought. They have a regulative role but no independently assessable content. They are not objective empirical facts but guide judgements. They have intrinsic value for the person. Instead of exerting pressure on her, making her feel she must act in a certain way, they carry a sense of genuineness; they enable her to resist the empty babblings and fetishised formulae that easily take the place of the real reasons for why she talks and acts as she does (McManus 2006, pp. 188–234).

In the course of therapy a phrase that is striking and helpful, a perspicuous representation (*übersichliche Darstellung*), may be created. This shows new aspects of what is familiar, another way of seeing things. It reveals connections that we did not see before, which has the power to transform a way of seeing things. For example, Freud's noting the connection between slips of the tongue, dreams and neurosis, or between sexuality and hysterical symptoms. The writings of psychotherapists contain many such connections.

A perspicuous representation is an overview of the assumptions and tangle which are internal to the problem. It may occur in a dialogue between people, much as human language and meaning is created in the dialogue between caretakers and child. Without language there is no understanding. Our world and our understanding of it are logically inseparable from the language we use to speak of that world.

Wittgenstein wrote: 'What is your aim in philosophy? – To shew the fly the way out of the fly-bottle' (*PI* ¶309).

His purpose is liberation, as is that of psychotherapy. But liberation requires we understand the limits of the various theories about us, that any theory involves indexicality, the user of it is necessarily outside it; only by understanding this can we take responsibility for seeing the world and others for ourselves. The reader of a book that aims to show the fly the way out of the fly-bottle misses what he aims to do if he yokes himself to a book or theory on how to get out of fly-bottles.

References

Ammereller, E. and Fischer, E. Eds. (2004) *Wittgenstein at Work*. Routledge, London.

Anzieu, D. (1986) *Freud's Self-Analysis*. Hogarth Press, London.

Aristotle (1926) *Nicomachean Ethics*. H. Rackham, Trans. W. Heinemann, London.

Armstrong, D.F., Stokoe, W.C. and Wilcox, S.E. (1995) *Gesture and the Nature of Language*. Cambridge University Press, Cambridge.

Bacon, F. (2002) 'The Advancement of Learning (1605)' in *The Major Works*, B. Vickers, Ed. Oxford University Press, Oxford.

Baker, G. (1988) *Wittgenstein, Frege & the Vienna Circle*. Blackwell, Oxford.

Baker, G. (2004) *Wittgenstein's Method*. Blackwell, Oxford.

Baker, G. and Hacker, P.M.S. (2005) *Wittgenstein Understanding and Meaning. Part 1 Essays*, 2nd ed. B. Blackwell, Oxford.

Beck, A.T. (1976) *Cognitive Therapy and the Emotional Disorders*. International Universities Press, New York.

Beller, M. (1999) *Quantum Dialogue*. University of Chicago Press, Chicago.

Bennett, M.R. and Hacker, P.M.S. (2003) *Philosophical Foundations of Neuroscience*. Blackwell, Oxford.

Bennett, M., Dennett, D., Hacker, P. and Searle, J. (2007) *Neuroscience and Philosophy*. Columbia University Press, New York.

Bion, W.R. (1970) *Attention and Interpretation*. Tavistock, London.

Boss, M. (1977) *'I Dreamt Last Night....'* S. Conway, Trans. Gardner Press, New York.

Bouveresse, J. (1995) *Wittgenstein Reads Freud: The Myth of the Unconscious*. Princeton University Press, Princeton.

Bracken, P. and Thomas, P. (2005) *Postpsychiatry*. Oxford University Press, Oxford.

Breger, L. (2000) *Freud*. John Wiley & Sons, New York.

Camus, A. (2000) *The Myth of Sisyphus*. J. O'Brien, Trans. Penguin Books, London.

Canfield, J.V. (2007) *Becoming Human*. Palgrave Macmillan, Hampshire.

Carroll, L. (1970) *The Annotated Alice*. Penguin Books, London.

Cavell, S. (1976) *Must We Mean What We Say?* Cambridge University Press, Cambridge.

Cavell, S. (1979) *The Claim of Reason: Wittgenstein, Skepticism, Morality and Tragedy*. Oxford University Press, Oxford.

Chaitin, G. (2007) *Meta Maths*. Atlantic Books, London.

Chapman, M. and Dixon, R.A. Eds. (1987) *Meaning and the Growth of Understanding*. Springer-Verlag, Berlin.

Chauvier, S. (2007) 'Wittgensteinian Grammar and Philosophy of Mind' in *Perspicuous Presentations*, D. Moyal-Sharrock, Ed. Palgrave Macmillan, Basingstoke.

Chuang Tzu (2006) *The Book of Chuang Tzu*. M. Palmer, Trans. Penguin Books, London.

Cioffi, F. (1998) *Wittgenstein on Freud and Fraser*. Cambridge University Press, Cambridge.

Cohen, C.I. and Timini, S. (2008) *Liberatory Psychiatry*. Cambridge University Press, Cambridge.

Conant, J. (2002) 'The Method of the Tractatus' in *From Frege to Wittgenstein*, E.H. Reck, Ed. Oxford University Press, Oxford.

Cushman, R.E. (1958) *Therapeia*. University of North Carolina Press, Chapel Hill.

Davies, J. (2009) *The Making of Psychotherapists: An Anthropological Analysis*. Karnac, London.

Deleuze, G. (1997) *Essays Critical and Clinical*. D.W. Smith and M.A. Greco, Trans. University of Minnesota Press, Minneapolis.

Dennett, D.C. (1991) *Consciousness Explained*. Little Brown, Boston.

Detienne, M. (1996) *The Masters of Truth in Archaic Greece*. J. Lloyd, Trans. Zone Books, New York.

Diamond, C. (2000) 'Ethics, Imagination and the Method of Wittgnstein's Tractatus' in *The New Wittgenstein*, A. Crary and R. Read, Eds. Routledge, London.

Diogenes Laertius (1925) *Lives of Eminent Philosophers*, Vol. 2. R.D. Hicks, Trans. Heinemann, London.

Dobson, K.S. (2001) *Handbook of Cognitive-Behavioural Therapies*, 2nd ed. Guilford Press, New York.

Dover, K.J. (1989) *Greek Homosexuality*, 2nd ed. Harvard University Press, Cambridge, Mass.

Dreyfus, G. (2003) *The Sound of Two Hands Clapping*. University California Press, Berkeley.

Drury, M.O'C. (1996) *The Danger of Words and Writing on Wittgenstein*. Thoemmes Press, Bristol.

Elder, C.E. (1994) *The Grammar of the Unconscious*. Pennsylvania State University Press, Pennsylvania.

Eliot, G. (1965) *Middlemarch*. Penguin, London.

Engelmann, P. (1967) *Letters from Ludwig Wittgenstein with a Memoir*. L. Furtmůller, Trans. Blackwell, Oxford.

Ferreiros, J. and Gray, J.J. Eds. (2006) *The Architecture of Modern Mathematics*. Oxford University Press, Oxford.

Finkelstein, D.H. (2003) *Expression and the Inner*. Harvard University Press, Cambridge, Mass.

Fischer, E. (2004) 'A Cognitive Self-Therapy' in *Wittgenstein at Work*, E. Ammereller and E. Fischer, Eds. Routledge, London.

Floyd, J. (2000) 'Wittgenstein, Mathematics and Philosophy' in *The New Wittgenstein*, A. Crary and R. Read, Eds. Routledge, London.

Fodor, J.A. (2003) *Hume Variations*. Clarendon Press, Oxford.

Fogelin, R.J. (1987) *Wittgenstein*, 2nd ed. Routledge, London.

Fonagy, P. and Target, M. (2003) *Psychoanalytic Theories: Perspectives from Developmental Psychopathology*. Whurr Publishers, London.

Foucault, M. (1977) *Language, Counter-Memory, Practice*. D.F. Bouchard and S. Simon, Trans. Cornell University Press, New York.

Foucault, M. (1980) *Power/Knowledge*, C. Gordon, Ed. Pantheon Press, New York.

Foucault, M. (2001) *Fearless Speech*, J. Pearson, Ed. Semiotext, Los Angeles.

Foucault, M. (2006) *Psychiatric Power*. G. Burchell, Trans. Palgrave Macmillan, Hampshire.

Frege, G. (1950) *The Foundations of Arithmetic*. J.L. Austin, Trans. B. Blackwell, Oxford.

Frege, G. (1979) *Posthumous Writings*. H. Hermes, F. Kambartel and F. Kaulbach, Eds. B. Blackwell, Oxford.

Frege, G. (1984) *Collected Papers on Mathematics, Logic and Philosophy*. B. McGuinness, Ed. B. Blackwell, Oxford.

Frede, M. (1997) 'The Sceptic's Beliefs' in *The Original Sceptics*, M. Burnyeat and M. Frede, Eds. Hackett Publishing, Indiana.

Freud, S. (1891) *On Aphasia*. E. Stengel, Trans. London and New York 1953.

Freud, S. (1895) *Studies in Hysteria*. S.E. 2, 48, 450.

Freud, S. (1896) *Further Remarks on the Neuro-Psychoses of Defence*. S.E. 3, 159.

Freud, S. (1900) *The Interpretation of Dreams*. S.E. 4–5.

Freud, S. (1901) *The Psychopathology of Everyday Life*. S.E. 6.

Freud, S. (1905) *Three Essays on the Theory of Sexuality*. S.E. 7, 123–245.

Freud, S. (1910) *A Special Type of Object Choice Made by Men*. S.E. 11, 170.

Freud, S. (1911a) *Formulations on the Two Principles of Mental Functioning*. S.E. 12, 215.

Freud, S. (1911b) *Psycho-analytic Notes on an Autobiographical Account of a Case of Paranoia*. S.E. 12, 3.

Freud, S. (1912–13) *Totem and Taboo*. S.E. 13, 1.

Freud, S. (1915a) *The Unconscious*. S.E. 14, 161.

Freud, S. (1915b) *Instincts and their Vicissitudes*. S.E. 14, 109.

Freud, S. (1916–17) *Introductory Lectures on Psycho-Analysis*. S.E. 15–16.

Freud, S. (1921) *Group Psychology and the Analysis of the Ego*. S.E. 18, 69.

Freud, S. (1926) *The Question of Lay Analysis*. S.E. 20, 177–250.

Freud, S. (1929) *Psycho-Analysis: Freudian School*. Encyclopedia Britannica, 14, 673.

Freud, S. (1930a) *Address in the Goethe House*. S.E. 21.

Freud, S. (1930b) *Civilization and Its Discontents*. S.E. 21.

Freud, S. (1932) *Why War?* S.E. 22.

Freud, S. (1933) *New Introductory Lectures on Psychoanalysis*. S.E. 22.

Freud, S. (1937) *Constructions in Analysis*. S.E. 23.

Freud, S. (1940) *An Outline of Psycho-Analysis*. S.E. 23.

Geir, A. (2002) *Plato's Erotic Thought: The Tree of the Unknown*. University of Rochester Press, Rochester.

Galen (1963) 'The Diagnosis and Cure of the Soul's Passions' in *On the Passions and Errors of the Soul*, P.W. Harkin, Trans. Ohio State University Press, Columbus.

Galen (2008) *The Cambridge Companion to Galen*. R.J. Hankinson, Ed. Cambridge University Press, Cambridge.

Gibson, J.J. (1966) *The Senses Considered as Perceptual Systems*. Allen and Unwin, London.

Glassner, J-J. (2003) *The Invention of Cuneiform*. John Hopkins University Press, Baltimore.

Goody, J. (1987) *The Interface Between the Written and the Oral*. Cambridge University Press, Cambridge.

Grosskurth, P. (1985) *Melanie Klein*. Hodder & Stoughton, London.

Hacker, P.M.S. (1986) *Insight and Illusion*, 2nd ed. Oxford University Press, Oxford.

Hacker, P.M.S. (1996) *Wittgenstein Mind and Will*. B. Blackwell, Oxford.

Hankinson, R.J. (1994) 'Usage and Abusage: Galen on Language' in *Language*, S. Everson, Ed. Cambridge University Press, Cambridge.

Hankinson, R.J. (1995) *The Sceptics*. Routledge, London.

Harré, R. and Tissaw, M. (2005) *Wittgenstein and Psychology: A Practical Guide*. Ashgate, Hants.

Harris, R. (1986) *The Origin of Writing*. Duckworth, London.

Harris, R. (1988) *Language, Saussure and Wittgenstein*. Routledge, London.

Harris, R. (1996) *The Language Connection*. Thoemmes Press, Bristol.

Harris, R. (1998) 'Writing and Proto-Writing: From Sign to Metasign' in *Integrational Linguistics: A First Reader*, R. Harris and G. Wolf, Eds. Pergamon, Oxford.

Harris, R. (2000) *Rethinking Writing*. Continuum, London.

Harris, R. (2003) 'On Redefining Linguistics' in *Rethinking Linguistics*, H.G. Davis and T.J. Taylor, Eds. RoutledgeCurzon, London.

Harris, R. (2009) *Rationality and the Literate Mind*. Routledge, London.

Heal, J. (2008) 'Back to the Rough Ground! Wittgensteinian Reflections on Rationality and Reason' in *Wittgenstein and Reason*, J. Preston, Ed. Blackwell, Oxford.

Heaton, J.M. (1993) 'The Sceptical Tradition in Psychotherapy' in *From the Words of my Mouth: Tradition in Psychotherapy*, L. Spurling, Ed. Routledge, London.

Heaton, J.M. (1999) 'Scepticism and Psychotherapy' in *Heart and Soul: The Therapeutic Face of Philosophy*, C. Mace, Ed. Routledge, London.

Heraclitus (1979) *The Art and Thought of Heraclitus*, C.H. Kahn, Trans. Cambridge University Press, Cambridge.

Hertz, H. (1956) *The Principles of Mechanics*. Dover Publications, New York.

Hinshelwood, R.D. (1991) *A Dictionary of Kleinian Thought*, 2nd ed. Free Association Books, London.

Hippocrates (1923–31) *Loeb Edition*, W.H.S. Jones, Trans. Harvard University Press, Cambridge, Mass.

Hobbes, T. (1996) *Leviathan*, R. Tuck, Ed. Cambridge University Press, Cambridge.

Hopkins, L. (2008) *False Self: The Life of Masud Khan*. Karnac Books, London.

Houston, S.D. (2004) *The First Writing*. Cambridge University Press, Cambridge.

Husserl, E. (1900) *Logical Investigations*, Vol. 1, J.N. Findlay, Trans. 1970. Routledge and Kegan Paul, London.

Hutto, D.D. (2008) *Folk Psychological Narratives*. MIT Press, Cambridge, Mass.

Hyman, J. (2006) *The Objective Eye*. University of Chicago Press, London.

Janik, A. and Toulmin, S. (1973) *Wittgenstein's Vienna*. Simon & Schuster, New York.

Jones, E. (1953–57) *Sigmund Freud: Life and Work*. Hogarth Press, London.

Jonson, B. (1947) *Timber*. C.H. Hereford and P. and E. Simpson, Eds. Vol. 8, Collected Works. Clarendon Press, Oxford.

Jopling, D.A. (2008) *Talking Cures and Placebo Effects*. Oxford University Press, Oxford.

Jung, C. (1938–54) *Collected Works*, Vol. 9, Part 1. Routledge and Kegan Paul, London.

Kafka, F. (2006) *The Zürau Aphorisms*, M. Hofman, Trans. Harvill Secker, London.

Kahane, A. (2005) *Diachronic Dialogues*. Lexington Books, Lanham.

Kant, I. (1970) 'An Answer to the Question: "What is Enlightenment?"' in *Kant's Political Writings*, H.B. Nisbet, Trans. Cambridge University Press, Cambridge.

Keller, E.F. (2002). *Making Sense of Life*. Harvard University Press, Cambridge, Mass.

Kenny, A. (1973 1st ed. and 2006 2nd ed.) *Wittgenstein*. Blackwell, Oxford.

Kierkegaard, S. (1989) *The Concept of Irony*. H.V. Hong and E.H. Hong, Trans. Princeton University Press, Princeton.

Klein, M. (1959) *The Writings of Melanie Klein Vol. 3*. Hogarth Press, London.

Kripke, S.A. (1982) *Wittgenstein on Rules and Private Language*. Blackwell, Oxford.

Kusch, M. (2006) *A Sceptical Guide to Meaning and Rules*. Acumen, Bucks.

Kuusela, O. (2008) *The Struggle against Dogmatism*. Harvard University Press, Cambridge, Mass.

Lacan, J. (2006) *Ecrits*. B. Fink, Trans. W.W. Norton, New York.

Laing, R.D. (1967) *The Politics of Experience*. Penguin Books, London.

Landini, G. (2007) *Wittgenstein's Apprenticeship with Russell*. Cambridge University Press, Cambridge.

La Rochefoucauld (2007) *Collected Maxims*. E.H. Blackmore, A.M. Blackmore and F. Giguère, Trans. Oxford University Press, Oxford.

Lear, J. (2003) *Therapeutic Action*. Karnac, London.

Lévi-Strauss, C. (1968) 'The Sorcerer and His Magic' in *Structural Anthropology*, C. Jacobson and B.G. Schoepf, Trans. The Penguin Press, London.

Lichtenberg, G.C. (2000) *The Waste Books*. R.J. Hollingdale, Trans. New York Review of Books, New York.

Locke, J. (1706) *An Essay Concerning Human Understanding*. J.W. Yolton, Ed. J.M. Dent and Sons, London.

Malcolm, N. (1984) *Ludwig Wittgenstein: A Memoir*. Oxford University Press, Oxford.

Marcus Aurelius (2006) *Meditations*. M. Hammond, Trans. Penguin Books, London.

Masson, J.M. Ed. (1985) *The Complete Letters of Sigmund Freud to Wilhelm Fliess*, J.M. Masson, Trans. Harvard University Press, Cambridge, Mass.

Mates, B. (1996) *The Sceptic Way*. Oxford University Press, Oxford.

McDowell, J. (1998) 'Wittgenstein on Following a Rule' in *Mind, Value, Reality*. Harvard University Press, Cambridge, Mass.

McGinn, M. (2006) *Elucidating the Tractatus*. Clarendon Press, Oxford.

McGuiness, B. (2002) *Approaches to Wittgenstein*. Routledge, London.

McGuiness, B. (2006) 'Wittgenstein: Philosophy and Literature' in *Wittgenstein: The Philosopher and His Works*, A. Pichler and S. Säätelä, Eds. Gazelle Books, Lancaster.

McGuire, W. Ed. (1974) *The Freud-Jung Letters*. Hogarth and Routledge and Kegan Paul, London.

McLuhen, M. (1962) *The Gutenberg Galaxy*. Routledge and Kegan Paul, London.

McManus, D. (2006) *The Enchantment of Words*. Clarendon Press, Oxford.

Moncrieff, J. (2008) *The Myth of the Chemical Cure*. Palgrave Macmillan, Hampshire.

Money-Kyrle, R. (1956) *Normal Counter-Transference and Some of Its Deviations. The International Journal of Psychoanalysis* 37, 360–6.

Monk, R. (2007) 'Bourgeois, Bolshevist or Anarchist? The Reception of Wittgenstein's Philosophy of Mathematics' in *Wittgenstein and His Interpreters*, G. Kahane, E. Kanterian and O. Kuusela, Eds. Blackwell, Oxford.

Montaigne, M de (1991) *The Complete Essays*. M.A. Screech, Trans. The Penguin Press, London.

Moore, G.E. (1993) *G.E.Moore; Selected Writings*, T. Baldwin, Ed. Routledge, London.

Morris, K. (2007) 'Wittgenstein's Method: Ridding People of Philosophical Prejudices' in *Wittgenstein and his Interpreters*, G. Kahane, E. Kanterian and O. Kuusela, Eds. Blackwell, Oxford.

Moyal-Sharrock, D. (2007) 'Wittgenstein on Psychological Certainty' in *Perspicuous Presentations*. Palgrave Macmillan, Hampshire.

Mulhall, S. (2007) *Wittgenstein's Private Language*. Clarendon Press, Oxford.

Newton, I. (1952) *Optics*. Dover, New York.

Nisha, D., Cavendish, S., Anderson, J. and Edwards, R. (2009) *Service User Perspectives on the Content of the Undergraduate Curriculum in Psychiatry. Psychiatric Bulletin* 33, 260–4.

Nordmann, A. (2005) *Wittgenstein's Tractatus: An Introduction*. Cambridge University Press, Cambridge.

Orwell, G. (1984) *Nineteen Eighty-Four*. Penguin Books, London.

Orwell, G. (2004) *Why I Write*. Penguin Books, London.

Ostrow, M.B. (2002) *Wittgenstein's Tractatus: A Dialectical Interpretation*. Cambridge University Press, Cambridge.

Ovid (1977) *Metamorphoses*. F.J. Miller, Trans. Revised G.P. Goold. Harvard University Press, Cambridge, Mass.

Palmer, A. (2004) 'Scepticism and Tragedy' in *Wittgenstein and Scepticism*. D. McManus, Ed. Routledge, London.

Parry, A. Ed. (1971) *The Making of Homeric Verse*. Oxford University Press, Oxford.

Pascal, B. (1995) *Pensée*. J. Krailsheimer, Trans. Penguin Books.

Pears, D. (1987 and 1988) *The False Prison*, Vol. 1 and 2. Oxford University Press, Oxford.

Plato (1986) *Phaedrus*. C.J. Rowe, Trans. Aris & Phillips,Warminster.

Plato (1987) 'Charmides' in *Early Socratic Dialogues*, D. Watt, Trans. Penguin, London.

Plutarch (1992) 'How to Distinguish a Flatterer from a Friend' in *Essays*. R. Waterfield, Trans. Penguin Books, London.

Potter, M. (2000) *Reason's Nearest Kin*. Oxford University Press, Oxford.

Potter, M. (2009) *Wittgenstein's Notes on Logic*. Oxford University Press, Oxford.

Proust, M. (1983) *Remembrance of Things Past*. Penguin, London.

Putnam, H. (1995) 'Philosophy of Mathematics: Why Nothing Works' in *Words and Life*, J. Conant, Ed., Harvard University Press, Cambridge, Mass.

Quintilian (2002) *Institutio Oratorica*. D.A. Russell, Trans. Harvard University Press, Cambridge, Mass.

Rappaport, R.A. (1999) *Ritual and Religion in the Making of Humanity*. Cambridge University Press, Cambridge.

Redpath, T. (1990) *Ludwig Wittgenstein: A Student's Memoir*. Duckworth, London.

Rieff, P. (1959) *Freud: The Mind of a Moralist*. Gollancz, London.

Russell, B. (1971) *Mysticism and Logic*. Barnes and Noble, New York.

Sass, L.A. (1994) *The Paradoxes of Delusion*. Cornell University Press, Ithaca.

Schreber, D.P. (2000) M*emoirs of My Nervous Illness*. I. Macalpine and R.A. Hunter, Trans. Review Books, New York.

Schroeder, S. (2006) *Wittgenstein: The Way out of the Fly-Bottle*. Polity Press, Cambridge.

Schulte, J. (1993) *Experience and Expression*. Clarendon Press, Oxford.

Schulte, J. (2006) 'What Is a Work by Wittgenstein?' In *Wittgenstein and His Works*. A. Pichler and S. Säätelä, Eds. Ontos Verlag, Frankfurt.

Seneca (1932) 'On Tranquillity of Mind' in *Moral Essays*, Vol. 2. J.W. Basore, Trans. Harvard University Press, Cambridge, Mass.

Seneca (1969) *Letters from a Stoic*. R. Cambell, Trans. Penguin Books, London.

Sextus Empiricus (1994) *Outlines of Scepticism*. J. Annas and J. Barnes, Trans. Cambridge University Press, Cambridge.

Shamdasani, S. (2003) *Jung and the Making of Modern Psychology*. Cambridge University Press, Cambridge.

Stern, D.G. (2004) *Wittgenstein's Philosophical Investigations: An Introduction*. Cambridge University Press, Cambridge.

Strachey, J. (1936) *Introduction to Freud: Inhibitions, Symptoms, and Anxiety*. Hogarth Press, London.

Sulloway, F.J. (1992) *Freud, Biologist of the Mind: Beyond the Psychoanalytic Legend*, 2nd ed. Harvard University Press, Cambridge, Mass.

Svenbro, J. (1993) *Phrasikleia: An Anthropology of Reading in Ancient Greece*. J. Lloyd, Trans. Cornell University Press, Ithaca.

Szlezak, T.A. (1999) *Reading Plato*. Routledge, London.

Taylor, T.J. and Shanker, S. (2003) 'Rethinking Language Acquisition: What the Child Learns' in *Rethinking Linguistics*, H.G. Davis and T.J. Taylor, Eds., pp. 151–70. RoutledgeCurzon, London.

Tomasello, M. (1992) *First Verbs*. Cambridge University Press, Cambridge.

Tomasello, M. (1999) *The Cultural Origins of Human Cognition*. Harvard University Press, Cambridge, Mass.

Tomasello, M. (2003) *Constructing a Language*. Harvard University Press, Cambridge, Mass.

Travis, C. (2008) *Occasion-Sensitivity*. Oxford University Press, Oxford.

Van Fraassen, B.C. (2008) *Scientific Representation*. Oxford University Press, Oxford.

Virgil (1918) *Aeneid Vol. 1 & 2*. W. Heinemann, London.

Whitehead, A.N. and Russell, B. (1910). *Principia Mathematica*. Cambridge University Press, Cambridge.

Winnicott, D.W. (1964) *Review of Jung's Memories, Dreams, Reflections*. The *International Journal of Psychoanalysis* 45, 450–5.

Winnicott, D.W. (1971a) *Therapeutic Consultations in Child Psychiatry*. Hogarth Press, London.

Winnicott, D.W. (1971b) *Playing and Reality*. Tavistock Publications, London.

Whyte, L.L. (1960) *The Unconscious before Freud*. Basic Books, New York.

Wortis, J. (1940) *Fragments of a Freudian Analysis*. The *American Journal of Orthopsychiatry* 10, 843–9.

Index

Note: Wittgenstein books are indexed by abbreviation (see complete list on p. xi)

absurd, 212
action, *see* therapeutic action
Ammereller, E., 37
Anzieu, D., 26
aphorism, 59–61
a priori, 80, 96, 101, 118, 121
arbitrariness of grammar, *see* grammar, autonomy of
archetypes, 126, 136–7
Aristotle, 15, 46–7, 72, 205
Armstrong, D. F., 46
aspects, 7, 14, 30, 52, 68, 94, 117–18, 128, 134, 139, 141–2, 145–6, 155, 164, 177, 214
authority, 2, 3, 6, 14, 29–30, 40, 47, 62, 64, 74, 82, 104, 156–61, 163, 177
autonomy, *see* grammar, autonomy of
AWL, 154

Bacon, F., 19
Baker, G., 30, 49, 53, 56, 98, 100, 117, 144, 161, 174, 188, 212–13
BB, 7, 84, 109, 125, 190, 201
Beck, A. T., 2, 11
behaviour therapy, *see* CBT (Cognitive Behaviour Therapy)
beliefs, 8, 10, 20–1, 23–4, 28–31, 42–3, 54, 66, 76–80, 91, 93, 112–16, 127–9, 133, 135–6, 140–3, 155, 163, 168, 202
Beller, M., 94
Bennett, M., 157
Bion, W. R., 48, 52, 183–7
Boss, M., 151
Bouveresse, J., 64
Bracken, P., 139
Breger, L., 26, 136
BT, 14, 59, 115, 128, 130, 141, 143, 149, 183, 202

calculus, conception of language, 96–7, 204
Camus, A., 212
Canfield, J. V., 31, 165
capacity, 83–5, 92
Carroll, L., 146, 212
causes, 1, 3, 21–3, 26, 54, 64–9, 122–3, 127, 138–9, 142, 164
Cavell, S., 49, 80, 180, 186, 210
CBT (Cognitive Behaviour Therapy), 2, 9–10, 76, 92–5, 116, 129, 140, 143
certainty, 158–61
Chaitlin, G., 73
Chapman, M., 89
Chauvier, S., 168
Chuang Tzu, 212
Cioffi, F., 26, 64
Cohen, C. I., 139
communication, 88
Conant, J., 148, 164
concepts, 7, 20–1, 26, 29, 31, 41–2, 48–9, 60, 108, 111, 116, 123–7, 143, 164, 213
  formal, 123–4
  formation of, 81
confession, 21–3, 31–2
consciousness, 188–9, 14, 18, 21–2, 24, 47, 60, 70, 85, 89, 101, 130, 132–3, 155–8, 183–4
consumer society, 203
context, 4, 7, 14, 19, 31, 35–6, 38–9, 42–4, 49, 82, 87–91, 93, 98, 104, 121, 123, 127, 130, 136, 144–5, 147, 151, 160, 163–4, 177, 187, 189, 202, 206–7, 210, 213
conversation, 90, 94
criteria, 3, 9, 31, 42, 81, 84, 89, 112, 136, 151–2, 164, 167, 169, 171, 174–5, 190, 195

culture, 9–10, 12, 26, 28–9, 33, 35, 41, 44, 46, 64, 77, 80, 87, 99, 137, 141, 143, 153, 172, 174
Cushman, R. E., 40
custom and institution, 79–80
CV, 11, 13, 17, 32, 50, 56, 59, 105, 120, 146, 162, 164

Davies, J., 48, 136, 142, 173
death instinct, 164, 170
Deleuze, G., 59
delusions, 112–15
Dennett, D. C., 92, 157
desire, 200–3
determinism, 12, 57, 67–72, 84, 122, 141
  see also necessity
Detienne, M., 38
diagnosis, 138–9
Diamond, C., 162
Diogenes Laertius, 22
disposition, 67–71
dogmatism, 59, 99, 122, 175
Dover, K. J., 36
dreams, 150–3, 193, 201
Dreyfus, G., 41
Drury, M. O'C., 18

ego, 8–9, 27–8, 185, 187–8, 197–8
einfall, *see* free-association
Elder, C. E., 26, 97, 116
Eliot, G., 12
elucidation, 97–100, 165
empirical science, 56, 76, 162
Engelmann, P., 50
envy, 170–1
enthusiasm, 136
ethics, 205–6, 211
expression, 73, 111, 163, 168–70, 172, 202
external relations, 27, 79, 83–4, 92, 102, 108, 113, 129, 164, 180, 202–3

face, 170–2
fear, 31
Ferreiros, J., 52
Finkelstein, D. H., 163, 168, 174
first–person, authority, 165–70

Fischer, E., 37
Floyd, J., 154
Fodor, J. A., 92–3
Fogelin, R. J., 25
Fonagy, P., 2
Foucault, M., 16–17, 22–3, 27, 38, 75
Frede, M., 24
free-association, 1–2, 12, 57, 141, 149, 152
freedom, 10, 14, 17, 30, 78, 82–3, 214
free speech, *see* parrhesia
Frege, G., 113, 135, 150–1, 184–6, 208, 213
Freud, S., 1–3, 9, 12, 18, 20–1, 25–9, 33, 41–4, 47–8, 53–4, 57–8, 61, 64, 67, 69–73, 76, 82, 85–6, 88, 91, 95, 99, 101–2, 108, 116, 122, 125–6, 128–9, 132–3, 135–8, 141–2, 146–7, 149–52, 155, 157–8, 160, 163, 173, 176, 178–9, 181, 184, 187–8, 192–3, 195–6, 200–3, 205, 214
  his self-analysis, 25–7, 174
  see also psychoanalysis
Freudian slip, *see* slips of the tongue

game, *see* language, game; play
Geir, A., 41
gesture, 41, 44, 46–9, 56, 105, 128–9, 204
Galen, 16–18
Gibson, J. J., 192
Glassner, J.-J., 34
Goethe, J. W. von., 160–1
good, 10, 24, 39, 73, 93, 185, 198, 205–6
  object, 72, 127
Goody, J., 37
grammar, 34, 39, 46, 98–100, 103–5, 149, 171–2, 208–9, 212
  autonomy of, 99, 115–16
Grosskurth, P., 58

Hacker, P. M. S., 30, 49, 53, 56, 86–7, 98, 100, 117, 144, 157, 161, 174, 180, 188, 212–13
Hankinson, R. J., 18, 23
happiness, *see* world
Harré, R., 37

Harris, R., 34, 36, 39, 44–5, 88–9, 176
head, being in, *see* thought, in head
Heal, J., 76
Heaton, J. M., 23
Heraclitus, 125
Hertz, H., 5
hinge propositions, 159–60
Hinshelwood, R. D., 91, 125, 170
Hippocrates, 61, 174
Hobbes, T., 18
Homer, 110
Hopkins, L., 43
Houston, S. D., 34, 36
humour, 13, 52, 55, 94, 177, 210
Husserl, E., 135
Hutto, D. D., 89–90, 92
Hyman, J., 192

'I', 180–2, 184–5, 191, 198–9, 210
    see also ego
ideal, 27, 43, 71–3, 116, 136–7
identification, 5, 7
identity, 187–92
illness, concept of, 137–9
insight, 172–5
illusion, 153–5
image, 192–6
    mental, 193–5
imagination, 194–5
indexicality, 4, 7, 38, 214
intentional attitude, 89
internal objects, 125–6, 166, 169–72
internal relations, 68, 78–9, 83–4,
    102, 108–9, 120, 123, 129, 132,
    155, 164, 177, 180, 182, 186,
    201–4, 210
interpretation, 6, 10, 20, 39, 53, 61,
    78–9, 89, 141, 143–4, 152, 157,
    167, 173, 176
irony, 35, 53, 55, 61–2

Janik, A., 203
jokes, 212
Jones, E., 26–7, 72
Jonson, B., 32
Jopling, D. A., 6, 173
joy, *see* world
Jung, C., 42, 135–6

Kafka, F., 73
Kahane, A., 38
kairos, 7, 61
Kant, I., 66, 116, 211
Keller, E. F., 66, 90
Kenny, A., 58
Khan, M., 43
Kierkegaard, S., 62
Klein, M., 1, 54, 58, 72, 91, 125, 170,
    173, 178, 202
Kripke, S. A., 45, 80
Kusch, M., 80
Kuusela, O., 99, 115, 206, 212

Lacan, J., 88, 97–8
Laing, R. D., 130–2
Landini, G., 67
language
    development, 29, 46–8, 101–7,
        127, 182
    games, 29, 109–12, 134, 166
    use, 79, 109–12, 152, 155, 166, 194
La Rochefoucauld, 22, 61
LC, 121, 186
Lear, J., 61
Lévi-Strauss, C., 54
liberation, *see* freedom
Lichtenberg, G. C., 13, 56, 195
life, form of, 10, 80, 107, 159, 187,
    202–3, 210
Locke, J., 88, 136
logic, 2, 3, 18, 24, 48, 51, 57, 67–8,
    72–6, 97–101, 113, 116–24, 130–2,
    135, 148–9, 151–3, 158, 160, 162,
    166, 172, 183–4, 189, 213–14
    logical necessity, 69–71
love, 128, 200, 204–5
    self–love, 16, 21–2
    transference, 175–7
LPP, 104
Luria, 39
LW1, 160, 168, 204
LW2, 158, 169–70

Malcolm, N., 212
Marcus Aurelius, 16
Masson, J. M., 54, 58, 151
Mates, B., 24

mathematics, 34, 37, 78, 116–17
  arithmetic, 74–5, 144–5, 208
  chaos, 141
  geometry, 4, 55, 153
  infinity, 208–9
  proof, 51–2, 55, 153–4, 208–9
McDowell, J., 213
McGinn, M., 117, 123–4, 180, 183
McGuiness, B., 14, 55, 180
McGuire, W., 135
McLuhen, M., 44
McManus, D., 97, 118, 180–1, 213
meaning, 45, 144–8
  determinism, 5
  of dreams, *see* dreams
  experience, 145
memory, 20, 41, 85–8, 150–2, 189, 196
mental apparatus, 68, 70–1
metaphysics, 57, 123, 185
mirror, 13, 196–8
Moncrieff, J., 139
Money–Kyrle, R., 176
Monk, R., 52
Montaigne, M. de, 25, 56–7, 59
Moore, G. E., 163
Moore's paradox, 163
Morris, K., 77, 212
Moyal–Sharrock, D., 158, 160
Mulhall, S., 12, 80, 179
music, 145–6, 202
must, *see* necessity
mythology, 72, 126

narcissism, 196–9, 204
NB, 182, 206
necessity, 7, 66, 115, 117, 120, 177, 212
  see also determinism
negation, 152, 154
Newton, I., 192
Nisha, D., 14
nonsense, 24, 73, 101, 113, 126, 131, 146, 152–3, 155–6, 158, 161, 164, 177, 179, 189, 204–6, 212–13
  see also senseless
Nordmann, A., 4
normative, 15, 80–2, 84, 115, 166, 213

OC, 28–9, 66, 77, 99, 105, 110, 112, 124, 134, 144–5, 159–60, 186–7
oral, 38–40
Orwell, G., 28, 82, 207
Ostrow, M. B., 165
overview, *see* representation, perspicuous
Ovid, 196

pain, 3, 10, 15, 24, 42, 52, 65, 79–81, 89, 104–5, 158, 165–9, 171–2, 174, 190, 204
Palmer, A., 25
paranoia, 132–4
parapraxis, *see* slips of the tongue
parrhesia, 16–19
Parry, A., 110
Pascal, B., 165
Pears, D., 180
persuasion, 6, 136
PG, 52, 88, 198
phantasy, 72, 82, 95, 104, 130, 177
philosophy, 10–13, 51–2, 59, 63, 67, 91, 100, 210–12, 214
phobia, 161–5
PI, 8, 10–12, 19, 31, 42, 51, 53, 56–7, 59, 63, 71, 73, 79, 89, 91, 94, 101, 108–10, 114–16, 122–3, 128, 131, 133–4, 137, 141, 143–5, 147, 149, 154, 156–7, 160–1, 163, 166, 168–9, 171–2, 174, 177, 179, 188, 190, 194, 202, 209–12, 214
pictures, 53, 60, 71
placebo, 6, 55, 173
Plato, 14, 22, 40–2, 173–4
Plutarch, 17
play, 107–9
pleasure, 201, 203–6
PO, 10, 64, 129, 139
poetry, 55–6, 63, 172, 204
Potter, M., 117, 198, 208
power, 75, 82
PPO, 17, 41, 73, 198
PR, 55
practice, 1–2, 14, 52, 62, 98, 110, 207, 211, 213
pride, 17, 32, 54
progress, 11, 205, 211
propositional attitude, 89–90

Proust, M., 60, 87
psychoanalysis, 1–2, 5, 8–11, 25–9,
       41–5, 47–8, 53–4, 72–3, 85–6, 91,
       113–14, 116, 121–2, 125–6, 129,
       135–6, 140, 142–3, 157, 163,
       172–3, 175–6, 178, 185, 187,
       192, 203
    as confession, 143
Putnam, H., 52
Pyrrhonian scepticism, *see* scepticism

questioning, 58
Quintilian, 62

Ramanujan, 208–9
Rappaport, R. A., 47–8
reading, 36–8
reality, 95–6, 106, 125–6, 203
    principle, 91, 178–9, 200
reason, 64, 74–7, 84, 183–4, 210
    causes confused with, 70, 201, 210
recognition, 87
Redpath, T., 55
relativism
representation, 3–8, 12–13, 49, 72,
       92–3, 96, 98, 122, 128, 136, 147,
       183–4, 188
    perspicuous, 149, 174, 213–14
responsibility, 150
RFM, 72, 79, 118, 208
rhetoric, 58
riddle, 149–50
Rieff, P., 178
ritual, 47–8
RPP1, 86, 109
RPP2, 29, 59
rules, 19–20, 34, 37, 39, 45, 47, 68, 71,
       74–5, 95, 105, 110, 114–16, 124,
       127, 206–9
    rule following, 78–83, 98–9, 110,
       114, 206–8
Russell, B., 14, 67, 116–17, 179

Sass, L. A., 183
sanity, 181–2
saying vs. showing, 187, 207
scepticism, 65
    Pyrrhonian, 23–5, 55–6, 107
Schreber, D. P., 75, 82, 183

Schroeder, 64
Schulte, J., 49, 88
scientism, 121, 140
self, 178–81
    self-analysis, 25–7, 174
    self-deception, 9–10, 174
    self-knowledge, 16, 22, 26, 28,
       54, 63
Seneca, 22–3
sensation, language of, 179
senseless, 24, 102–3, 108, 118–19,
       130, 162
    see also nonsense
Sextus Empiricus, 23–4, 107
shamanism, 54–5
Shamdasani, S., 135, 153
sign/symbol confusion, 25, 112, 148,
       150, 162, 189
slips of the tongue, 146–50
smile, 42, 209
solipsism, 178–84
speaking, 38–9, 43–6, 94
spontaneity, 109
Squiggle Game, 39
Stern, D. G., 11, 25
Strachey, J., 203
style, 50, 55, 58, 60
subjectivity, 135–6
Sulloway, F. J., 67
Svenbro, J., 36–7
symptoms, *see* criteria
Szlezak, T. A., 40

talking cure, 10, 19–20, 30–3, 60,
       62–3, 77, 97, 135–7, 139–40, 164,
       181, 210–11, 213
tautology, 118–20
Taylor, T. J., 106
telemental communication, 88–9, 176
theory, 2–3, 6, 8–9, 26–7, 52–3, 92,
       95–9, 122, 161
therapeutic action, 53, 210
thought, 60, 96–7, 143
    in head, 40–1, 84, 93, 123, 127–8
    without thinker, 184–5
TLP, 25, 66, 69, 111, 118–19, 121–3,
       126, 135, 148–9, 170, 180–4, 187,
       189, 207, 211

Tomasello, M., 46, 89, 105–6, 109, 186, 202
transference, 79, 175–7
  thought transference, 88–9
transitional object, 107–8
Travis, C., 45, 144, 158
Tristan Shandy, 55
truth, truthfulness, 9–10, 19, 30–2, 40, 43, 45, 75, 97, 111–14, 136, 144, 148, 167, 169, 174–5, 177, 213
typology, 142

unconscious, 2, 8–9, 18–22, 26, 28, 39, 42–4, 48, 54, 57–8, 73, 85–6, 89, 95, 97–8, 116, 125, 136, 138–9, 141–4, 146–7, 149–51, 155, 157–8, 163, 167, 171, 173, 176, 185, 188, 200–3
understanding, misunderstanding, 5–6, 8, 18, 20, 28, 32, 55–6, 64–5, 71, 82–5, 88, 90, 105–6, 143, 145, 147, 149, 175, 180, 207, 211
use, of words, 1–11, 13–14, 16, 32, 42, 45–6, 52–3, 57, 59, 62–3, 77, 79–81, 90–1, 93, 96–7, 99, 103–4, 107, 110–11, 113–15, 119–20, 122, 136, 140, 143–4, 146, 154, 164, 166, 168–9, 172, 177, 186, 191, 194–5, 198–9, 202, 204

Van Fraassen, B. C., 4, 6
Virgil, 21
visual room, 130–3
voice, 104–5
VW, 98

Whitehead, A. N., 117
Winnicott, D. W., 39, 42, 58, 107–8
wishes, 200, 202–3
Wittgenstein, L.,
  on contingency and necessity, 7, 115, 120, 180
  on craving for generality, 7, 66–7
  on not being dogmatic, *see* dogmatism
  on 'I', *see* 'I'
  on the inner as delusion, 102, 108, 125, 130–1, 135, 137, 157, 172, 179, 186
  on mentalism, 11, 29, 89
  on method, 10, 12, 25, 49–52, 55–8, 62, 174, 211–12, 214
  on pictures, 5, 10, 71, 152, 179, 206, 212
  on self-deception, 9–10, 174
  on writing, 49–50
Whyte, L. L., 44
world
  of the happy and unhappy, 23, 203, 205–7
  internal, 158; *see also* Wittgenstein, L.,
Wortis, J., 20
writing, 33–8, 58
  development of, 33–6
  and meaning, 40–1
  and psychoanalysis, 41–5
  and speaking, 38–9
WVC, 100, 185

Z, 13, 40, 79, 85, 99, 114–15, 123, 124, 145, 156–8, 165, 170, 194–5, 204–5